OPPORTUNITY

OPPORTUNITY

Eben Pagan

GO META PUBLISHING

Printed in the United States of America

First Printing, 2018

ISBN13: 978-1-7321246-0-8

Cover art by Android Jones
Interior book design by Glen M. Edelstein, Hudson Valley Book Design
Cover design by Joe Muscatello

To my wife, Annie.
Thank you for my greatest opportunity...
to be together with you, in Love.

Contents

Special Note for The First Edition

Dear Friend,

I have invested more than twenty years studying entrepreneurship, success, and opportunity. This book condenses many of the important lessons I've learned, for you to use. These ideas have made a huge difference in my life, and I hope that they will make a positive difference for you as well.

You're reading the first edition of this book. You're the first to see it, outside of a handful of friends and family. As much as I tried to say things in just the right way, and get everything right, there will inevitably be things that are unclear… little mistakes… and typos included.

If you see something that could have been said in a better way, or you find an error or a typo, will you do me a favor and send me a note? You email here:

help@ebenpagan.com

…and I'll send you a little gift for finding things that can improve this book.

Also, I've created an "Opportunity Companion Guide" to go along with what you're learning here. It includes summaries, checklists written exercises, and other bonus materials to help you discover and develop opportunity in your life. Go here to download it now as a free gift:

OpportunityBonus.com

Finally, please email me with your stories of how you've used what you learned to find and take advantage of opportunities in your life.

I look forward to hearing from you!

—Eben

Why It's So Important to Learn About Opportunity

A LUMBERJACK, A BOTANIST, and a monk walk into a forest.

What do they see? The botanist sees plants to study, the lumberjack sees trees to chop down, and the monk sees the miracle of existence. Three people, three different perspectives on reality.

Each of us moves through the world perceiving things through our own unique prisms of personality and experience. We are born with similar senses, but we each live in our own version of reality, and the way we see reality impacts the way we perceive opportunity.

Now imagine three people walking into a grocery store. One might see an opportunity to buy tomatoes on sale, another sees an opportunity to socialize, and the third sees an opportunity to start a better grocery store down the street. Each of us is naturally on the lookout for opportunity in our own unique way, but we can train ourselves to see the world - and opportunity - in new ways.

That's what this book is about. Inside, I aim to convince you of three simple, powerful truths:

1. Understanding opportunity is a key to success in life.
2. You can increase the quantity and quality of opportunities in your life.
3. There is a reliable, systematic way to do it.

With this mindset, you'll be better able to navigate a world where change is accelerating and uncertainty is increasing... a world that demands new models for thinking about how things work.

Creating opportunity is about more than just thriving in an unstable, sometimes scary world. It's about becoming the best version of yourself, and creating a life where you have all the opportunities you need to reach your full potential.

To increase the quality and quantity of opportunity available, it's important to take on a series of mindsets that will positively change how you see yourself, how you see others, and how you see opportunity.

That's where this book comes in. Inside, you'll learn:

- What opportunity is, how it works, and where to find it
- How to overcome "opportunity shock" and avoid the paralysis that can come with having too many options
- How your emotional state influences your ability to take advantage of opportunity and how to optimize your state to attract and capitalize on opportunity across different domains of your life
- How to overcome fear of failure, so you can get more of what you want in your life
- What mental models are, and how to use them for estimating the value of an opportunity, comparing opportunities to each other, and choosing those most likely to bring you success and fulfillment
- How to find more opportunities in business, money, investing, health, happiness, relationships, and personal development
- Why collaborating with others multiplies your power to find and develop opportunities
- How to become an innovator and a thought leader in order to help others discover their own biggest opportunities
- The way to discover your greatest personal opportunity in life

I think of this book as a surfboard designed to help you ride the tsunami of opportunity coming in the future. It will teach you to understand and profit from the changes happening around us all. If you use what you learn in this book, it will help you uncover a huge amount of opportunity that currently exists in your life, that was previously hidden. By discovering these opportunities, you will accelerate your growth to the next level in your life and business.

Have You Ever Been Here?

- You are doing a project in your life, and are interrupted by someone who wants you to do something completely different. Both seem important. How do you figure out which is the bigger opportunity for you?

- You have a great opportunity in front of you, and you're about to act on it, but doubt creeps in. You feel afraid, because you might make a mistake either way. What do you do?

- You have a new business or investment opportunity, but you don't know how to estimate its value, or its probability of success. Different people are telling you different things, and you're getting confused. How do you make a decision, and choose the right path?

- You feel stuck in your current work, and don't feel like you have enough opportunities coming to you. How do you set up your life, relationships and career so that more and more high-quality opportunities show up on your doorstep?

- You get a good business idea, and want to find the fastest way to know if it's going to be a winner. You ask a few experts in the domain to see what they think, but get conflicting advice. How can you do a quick test to see if your idea is viable and likely to make money?

- You have saved up enough to make a big investment. As you start considering your options, you realize that there are far too many ways to invest than you could ever understand. Where should you start, and how should you choose an investment that's safest, and most likely to make you money in the long-run?

- You have a new opportunity in your personal or family life, but it will take your attention away from your business and work. How do you choose between very different types of opportunities, that don't seem to be comparable?

- Your new business idea is starting to work, and you're ready to scale it up into something big. What's the best and fastest way to grow your company, so that it brings you sustainable profits?

- You get a great opportunity in business, but realize that taking it might make you unhappy in the long-run. How do you balance your desire for success with your need for happiness in life?

- You find a unique opportunity to work on a project that would teach you important skills that you need to learn - but it's risky, and might not work. Your friends and family are telling you to do something safer. If the project fails, you might look bad to people you care about. What do you do?

- You act on an opportunity and it's showing signs of being a blockbuster success. Should you start taking profits, or should you reinvest the profits for a much bigger future payoff? Oh, and then you notice that someone else with a similar business idea just raised millions in venture capital...

You have probably been in several situations like these. And you're likely to be facing more of them than ever. When you encounter these dilemmas, they can be immobilizing. It can be frustrating to have an opportunity right in front of you, but not know what to do with it. Inside this book, you will learn a set of mindsets and tools that will help you know what to do when opportunity appears. You'll learn how to navigate through situations like these, so you can get the maximum benefit from the wave of opportunity that's coming toward us all.

The Motivational Power of an Opportunity

Many of us struggle to motivate ourselves to do the things we know we need to do in life. Entrepreneur and motivational speaker Jim Rohn used to challenge his audiences by saying "get leverage on yourself." In order to realize our greatest potentials we need to get leverage on ourselves. In order to get leverage, we must must go to work on the deeper levels of our psychology.

And opportunity does just that.

Can you remember a time when you were single and you met someone you found incredibly attractive? Think about the power this person had to capture and hold your attention, to fascinate you completely. Think about how it changed your way of seeing the world. No matter what you did, all you could think about was them.

Can you remember a time when you saw a great opportunity that could create big success for your career, or make you a lot of money in business? Do you remember how it focused your attention completely on the opportunity?

Can you remember a time when you were hungry, and you walked into a restaurant. You ordered food, and then saw the waiter or waitress walking toward you with a plate that looked like it could be yours. Your stomach felt the opportunity, and hoped that this was its big chance!

Opportunity takes hold, not only of your body, emotions, and thoughts, but also of your imagination. It grabs you by your dreams.

The right opportunity gives you instantaneous focus. It brings you into the moment, and you become fully engaged in the activity, where the reward merges with the journey.

It makes sense that we should respond this way to an opportunity. We evolved from a long line of successful opportunists. Those individuals that were the best at discovering and taking advantage of opportunity, across all dimensions of life, are the ones that survived to adulthood and reproduced. For countless generations, these people became your direct ancestors. Every one of them was able to find important opportunities, and then act on them. The occupation with opportunity is woven into our genetic code.

Nature documentaries show us what happens when a peacock spots a potential mate. Out comes this huge display of tail feathers, showcasing his health and genetic fitness. Watch a cheetah as it locks onto the animal that is going to become its next meal. The opportunity is absolutely riveting, taking all of its attention.

Animals see opportunities that are right in front of them, literally staring them in the face (like a tasty-looking gazelle or a fertile peahen). But humans can see opportunity in our imaginations. We can conceptualize opportunities on longer time horizons. We "see" opportunities in the future. We can learn to create those imaginary opportunities, often in places where others see only risk and danger.

And when we can imagine opportunity in our minds, and grasp the potential that a particular situation has for us, something magical happens. Just like an animal seeing a mate, or a predator spotting prey, our brains light up, flooding our system with chemicals and emotions.

Research has shown that the "reward centers" in the human brain are not initially triggered by a reward. Instead, they are triggered by a potential reward, also known as an opportunity. Consider video games, and how they constantly show you opportunities - the next quest, another level, a hidden treasure - to trigger your reward systems. Game designers and marketers know that if we are given an "emotional taste" of a potential reward, it's enough to focus our entire being on the opportunity.

Think of the spinning of the wheels in a slot machine. Each one stopping long enough to give you a taste of pattern recognition - a possibility of winning the jackpot. These aren't just daydreams or goals, these are fleeting glances of real possibilities… of potential value… that ignite our imagination.

In his book "Think & Grow Rich," Napoleon Hill recommends that we imagine the results that we want to achieve and create in our lives, write them down along with definite plans to achieve them, and then say them out loud to ourselves daily. He said that this would have a particular effect: it would create a burning desire within us.

But there's something in my experience that activates desire far more powerfully than an imagined goal. And that's an opportunity.

Opportunity ignites desire. Instantly. On a primal level. It co-opts our biological machinery and focuses it on one aim, while also activating potent forces of motivation.

Opportunity, therefore, is the way to "get leverage on yourself." It's the the way to motivate yourself to take action and achicvc your goals. But it can do far more. Opportunity isn't just about shallow opportunism and animal needs, or about acquiring things you want. It's also about a unique aspect of being human - the need to become the best possible version of yourself.

On a higher level, what happens when you encounter not just an opportunity to sate your hunger or pad your bank account but to live out your life purpose, to have a huge impact on the world?

What happens deep inside when you have a momentary realization of your purpose - the reason you are here on this planet, in this body, in this lifetime, to fulfill your destiny?

Or the moment when you realize that you've met someone who you would spend the rest of your life with?

These are the big opportunities in life, and they don't come along often. Because they are opportunities, they activate all the normal opportunity mechanisms - they focus the attention and create motivation. But they also do something more: they inspire you to become your highest self. They call to your soul.

When you discover an opportunity to live your purpose, to do what you alone can do in this world… to be something more than you thought was possible… everything changes. My wife Annie says that, "opportunity is how God courts you." Something spiritual is happening when you come into contact with your higher potential.

If you want to inspire yourself, push yourself, energize yourself, and call on your highest motivation, then put yourself in a constant stream of high-quality opportunities, across the key domains of your life. If you want to call forth the highest version of yourself, build a life of increasingly better opportunity.

Life in the Creativerse

Opportunity has been energizing us since our ancestors first walked the savannah, but the time we're living in right now is a special time in the history of opportunity.

Look around yourself for a moment. What do you see? For most of us reading this, you'd see a place that was designed and built by humans. Whether it's your home, office, a hotel, or the local park, the environments we live in are created and optimized for our safety, comfort, and convenience.

In the developed world, we have gone from living out in the wild, to living in spruced up caves, to simple homes, to living within multiple layers of purpose-built environments. From the layout of the roads, to the engineering of the buildings, to the design of the objects that fill them, everything around us has been shaped in some way by human minds and hands.

And that's not just true of our physical world, it's true of our cultural, intellectual, and emotional realities as well. I see human life as a process of designing and creating not only the physical structures that we live in, but also creating our experiences, relationships, thoughts, and even social groups.

We now live "designer lives." And if you look closely, you'll see that this process of creating self-designed environments is only accelerating. We are designing more aspects of our lives, and this is happening at a faster and faster pace. The gap between imagining something in our mind and then creating it in the "real world" is shrinking every day.

Until recently it might have taken many months - or even years - to build a house. In Oregon, where I grew up, I knew someone who had an innovative idea about how to speed up this process. He started building the walls of homes in a warehouse, and then shipping them out to the home site for quick assembly. His company was able to build the wall panels of houses quickly, in a more ideal working environment, and then put them together at the building site to construct the main structure of the home in a few days. Fast-forward to now, and we have invented massive 3D printers that can literally print out an entire building in one day.

In the past if I wanted custom furniture, it might take a year to find the right person to design and build it by hand. Now I can go online, use templates for custom furniture design, have it built to my specifications with the help of machines this week, then have it in my house the following week. The same is true for custom clothing. You can upload your measurements, and have custom-tailored clothing delivered to your home in a matter of days.

When I designed my first website in 2001, I needed a computer with the right (expensive) software installed and many hours to get the website to do something simple, like ask for an email address and add someone to my mailing list. Today, automated tools and templates accessible online from any device allow anyone to build a highly functional, beautiful, and integrated website with advanced database and automation functions… for next to nothing.

Ray Kurzweil, the brilliant futurist, believes that within a few decades, we will have extended our minds into the computer cloud and be able to use this "extended neocortex" to design and make anything we want instantly. We'll be able to imagine something, activate nano-scale additive manufacturing technology (think 3D printing, but at the atomic level), and literally construct what we want to create in real-time.

This might sound far-fetched for you, but you don't need to believe in Kurzweil's timeline or specific predictions to see the underlying trend. We have all been moving more and more quickly towards an "imagine and create it" reality. A place where we envision what we want in our minds, and then use knowledge, technology and other resources to manifest what we are thinking. More and more, we are selecting, shaping, designing, or outright creating the environments, tools and other resources around us.

I believe that this pattern points to something fundamental about the nature of the reality we live in. We were born into a world that seems to want us to create what we first imagine in our minds. It is a reality that is spectacularly friendly to creative design and manifestation.

I call this reality the **Creativerse** - combining the words **creative** and **universe**. In the Creativerse, we participate in **the creative design of reality itself.**

And because more of us are getting access to the ideas, tools, technologies, and resources to do this, I believe this idea of the Creativerse is a defining mindset to take on in order to generate the success we want for ourselves. It will be a fundamental frame that underlies the ideas in this book.

In order for you to create opportunity and change your life, you must believe that opportunity can be created. You must be convinced that you have the power to shape and create the various aspects of your life.

You must also understand that the better the design of the spaces in which you live, work, collaborate, and love, the more creative you become; it's a virtuous cycle. That's why it is so important to practice and develop your ability to create.

If you aren't imagining, designing, and creating the environment you want to live in, then someone else is going to be doing it for you. Too many people sit in front of screens watching realities that other people have dreamed up, rather than taking over and crafting their own futures.

Those of us who don't know how to imagine and create our own environments, relationships, thoughts, feelings, and communities will be less able to cope and thrive, while those that have developed this mindset and skill will be at a huge advantage.

The Great Acceleration

We are entering a time that I call "The Great Acceleration." In this time, we are crossing over into a key threshold: Reality is changing faster than we have the ability to predict, in ways that most of us don't have the ability to model.

Ray Kurzweil studied the increasing speed of computers and the decreasing cost of processing power over the last hundred years, and found a pattern: Double exponential growth and change. When he looked deeper, it turned out that this pattern actually went way back. Intelligence and processing power has been accelerating, essentially since life began.

Exponential change is hard to imagine, so let's use a simple metaphor. Imagine a pond where lotus flowers grow. Start with one lotus plant. If the number of plants doubles every day, and it takes 30 days for the pond to be completely covered, then what does the pond look like as this process is happening?

On Day 25, only about 3% of the pond is covered. On day 27, only 12% of the pond is covered. But then on Day 28, it's a quarter of the pond. Then on Day 29, it's half of the pond. Then on Day 30, it's the entire pond.

For most of the time, it didn't really look like anything was happening. And then BAM, the pond is covered. And it's only in those last few days that you even notice that anything is happening.

Now imagine that no one told you that the pond was filling with lotus plants, and that it would take 30 days to be completely covered. What if you walked by each day, and only looked in once in awhile? One day, you might say to yourself: "Hm, I don't remember all those plants in the pond... maybe I never noticed them."

What's interesting to me about the rate of technological change is that it is finally becoming **visible**. For the first time, we can actually see it happening in real-time. It's like walking to the top of a hill and looking down, and seeing the lotuses increasing each day in many ponds at once.

When I get a new mobile device, it is noticeably faster. All of a sudden, I can talk to it, and it knows what I'm saying. I can get someone to build me an app of my own. Delivery goes from a week to same day. Search gets smarter. I can see it happening.

This is the product of the convergence of technological advances in computing hardware, artificial intelligence, user interface design, programming languages and models, and much more.

But again, the key is that now you can actually **see it happening in real-time**. This is the Great Acceleration becoming visible.

We Get to Practice in Slow Motion to Prepare

The wonderful thing about living right now is that we get to practice in "slow motion" - to prepare for the time in the future where our creative power will accelerate to the point of becoming almost real-time.

Today, it might take me weeks or months to go from an idea for a website to a completed project, because I have to work with several people, look at a bunch of versions, make changes, etc. In twenty years, I might be able to start speaking and have artificial intelligence start building a site design in real-time, as soon as I ask, making changes as I say them. And eventually, we will able to design things just by thinking about them.

This acceleration will continue all the way to the point where we reach the "technological singularity" - the theoretical point where self-enhancing machine intelligence surpasses human intelligence - a point where this ability to imagine, create and manifest could possibly be faster than thought is right now.

In the past, our biggest obstacles were physical things, people, time, or maybe money. If you wanted to publish a book, for example, you needed to find and convince a publisher to work with you so that they could print your book and get it stocked in physical retail bookstores. Now, anyone can publish a book quickly and easily, and offer it directly or through Amazon (as I have). There is no printing or shipping cost for an eBook. The biggest obstacles for authors now is imagination and time.

As we move into the future, time will be less of a bottleneck, since we'll be moving so much faster. Then the biggest bottleneck will be our imaginations. That's why we need to start strengthening our imagination and design skills now while things are still happening at a more human pace... so that we're ready when they start happening at the speed of thought.

We can practice by simply imagining a change in our lives, then make it happen. Imagine moving your furniture around, and then actually move it. See it in a new place in your mind, and then move it there in reality. Or imagine creating a home office that is purposefully designed to inspire you and make your more productive. Then go create it!

Imagine what an ideal day would look like in your life. Then plan all of the pieces in order to create it for yourself. Then go and live it, and feel what it's like to have a great day that was designed and set up in advance.

My wife likes to go and find fascinating intricately-shaped objects online, and then have them 3D printed in plastic. We have a table near the front door of our home that has probably fifteen or twenty of them on it. She offers them as gifts to guests who come to visit. We just had someone over, and we all had fun looking at complex pretzel-like tubes that would be impossible to make through fabrication. It's fun to find shapes like these, then have them made by a machine that didn't exist until recently.

Find ways to imagine and then create the reality that you want to live in. Practice it as a skill, and collaborate with others to do it. I invite you to move into the Creativerse with me!

What is an Opportunity?

As humans, we have an astonishing ability that it seems other animals have not developed yet. We can use mental symbols called words, and we can modify those symbols and change their relationships to other symbols and concepts in our minds.

When you define a word, you are doing something mysterious and powerful: you are modifying the relationship between things in your mind. You are making and modifying meaning.

As we grow, most of us learn the definitions of words "intuitively" - meaning that we infer the meaning of the words through their use in conversation with others. As I watch my 4-year old daughter learning language, I can see this process in action.

She has recently started asking "Do you love me 100%?" Of course, my wife and I answer "Yes, I love you 100%." I know that she can't yet understand what a percentage "really" means, but I also know that she has somehow gotten the message that 100% means yes.

Later, when she reaches a developmental stage where she can understand percentages, the meaning of a phrase like "I love you 100%" will change for her. It will become more subtle and metaphorical.

Because most of us establish the meaning of most of the words we use unconsciously, you might say that we carry around general definitions, rather than precise definitions. And this represents a big opportunity, to me.

In life, if the way that you think is better matched to what actually happens and the way the world actually works, it allows you to better imagine what could happen or what will happen. More precise thinking creates more precise analysis, estimation, prediction, explanation, decision making, and much more. It also helps with communication.

We humans often use one word to describe something, when we actually mean another. If your friend says "I'm going to Hawaii on vacation" you might respond by saying "I'm jealous!" But in reality, you're probably not jealous… rather you feel envy. When you wish you had what another person has, that's envy. It's when we covet an experience.

Jealousy however, is the emotion you feel when someone you care about pays attention to someone else instead of you. Generally, jealousy involves three people where envy only involves two. So it's possible for you to feel jealous of your friend going to Hawaii, but only if they are going with your spouse!

Why does this matter? Because most of us don't take the time to actually check our own definitions, and I believe that this winds up costing us a lot.

Because most people use the word jealous to describe the emotion of envy, this leaves them without a word to use when they are actually feeling jealousy. A consequence is that when they do feel jealous, they are not aware that they are feeling it. Instead, they might believe that they are feeling angry, or just generally upset. Their unconsciousness leads them to behave in ways that are insecure, controlling, and possessive, and often drives their partner away. If they actually knew the correct word for what they were feeling emotionally, I believe that it could allow them to communicate better with their partner about it, and possibly even save their relationship.

Quite a consequence for confusing one word with another. But once you start paying closer attention, you realize that this is almost the rule, rather than the exception.

The point I'm making here is that **most** words are fuzzy like this for **most** people. We have a word that has an approximate meaning, that's something like what we're trying to convey. But we haven't fine-tuned our definitions to make sure they're precise and accurate. Most people have not "gone back" and updated their definitions of the words they use in everyday thinking and communication.

You might say "Yes, but most of the words I use are not like that. I know what they mean."

And I invite you to test that theory out a bit. Start looking up the definitions of more words, and I think you'll find that there is a much more precise definition for the word that you're using. And by understanding that definition, you can sharpen your thinking and increase your ability to understand, communicate, consider and predict what happens.

Do you know what the word "opportunity" means? Take a minute, and write down your definition of the word, before reading further. Use this as an opportunity to see what I'm talking about. If you take a minute and articulate your definition for opportunity, you'll get a lot more from the next section.

Once you've clarified your own definition of opportunity, come back and start reading again.

Write your definition here:

```
┌─────────────────────────────────────────────────────────┐
│                                                         │
│                                                         │
│                                                         │
│                                                         │
│                                                         │
│                                                         │
│                                                         │
│                                                         │
└─────────────────────────────────────────────────────────┘
```

OK, so what did you come up with?

When I find an interesting word, I like to look up the etymology or evolutionary history of the word, along with as many definitions as I can find. If you look at the evolution of the word opportunity, you discover something interesting. It comes from the Latin word "opportunus", which it seems means to move toward a port or harbor (ob = toward +

portus = harbor). When a ship is coming into a harbor, and it can see the port that is its destination, this is opportunus.

It's interesting to discover the metaphorical meaning of words, as they give you access to aspects of meaning that you can't get to conceptually. It feels very different to think of being on a ship in a harbor, and seeing the port that you are sailing towards.

I also mentioned multiple definitions. We tend to think of words as having "a definition" when most words have several definitions. Just like letters are reused and recombined in multiple senses to form words, words themselves are reused - often having many different definitions. For important words, I think you need at least three distinct definitions, and ideally five to seven. Counter-intuitively, each one, like a facet on a diamond, allows the word to sparkle with more precision & clarity.

Because I believe that opportunity is an important concept to understand, I want to share several definitions with you. Notice how the concept becomes richer and more dimensional as you consider these definitions. I personally like to collect as many definitions of a word as I can, as I feel that this offers a much richer understanding.

Go back and look at your own definition for opportunity, and then compare to these...

The simplest definition I have for opportunity is: **Potential value.** An opportunity is when you can see possibility to produce or capture value. Value is the thing you want, and potential is the possibility that you can get it. This definition depends upon you knowing what value means to the individual or group who would like to achieve it.

Some values are affirmative or positive values, and some are negative values. One person may value getting a new home. Another might value avoiding losing the home they already have. One is a positive value (to get something) and one is a negative value (to avoid losing something). If your are looking to buy a home, and you find a one that meets your needs, you might see that as an opportunity. If however, you've been informed that your home is going to be taken from you because the mortgage wasn't paid, but you find someone willing to lend you the money to pay it, you might see that as an opportunity. In both cases, when the potential for realizing your value arises, it is felt as an opportunity.

The metaphorical phrase "window of opportunity" is often used when describing situations like this one. A person trying to sell you a home, or someone lending you money to keep your home may say "the window of opportunity is going to close" - meaning that the way for you to realize your value, get what you want, or avoid what you don't want is available now, but not forever.

It is this interesting quality of opportunity, that it usually comes with a time limit or a shelf-life. This gives each opportunity an emotional and psychological charge. The potential value is here, but not forever. And somehow our motivation and reward systems seem to come highly attuned to this dynamic. When an opportunity arises in our awareness, it is often accompanied by a sense of anxiety. We don't want to miss out on the value, or lose it because we didn't pay attention. I believe that explaining that opportunity is increasing right now for all of us, and that this increase is very counterintuitive and potentially overwhelming. as it increases this anxiety. It is this interesting quality of opportunity, that it usually comes with a time limit or a shelf-life, which gives each opportunity an emotional and psychological charge. The potential value is here, but not forever. And somehow our motivation and reward systems seem to come highly attuned to this dynamic. When an opportunity arises in our awareness, it is often accompanied by a sense of anxiety. We don't want to miss out on the value, or lose it because we didn't pay attention. I believe that opportunity is increasing right now for all of us, and that this increase is very counterintuitive - and potentially overwhelming - because it increases this anxiety.

Let's consider more definitions of opportunity.

Merriam-Webster first defines opportunity as **"a favorable juncture of circumstances."** Google says that opportunity is **"a set of circumstances that makes it possible to do something."**

A bear standing next to a mountain stream catching migrating salmon is taking advantage of a favorable juncture of circumstances. It's a set of circumstances that make it possible to do something: eat. I'm guessing that this type of predator-prey interaction is likely the source of the term "opportunistic" - which has a connotation of being or acting in a way that is all about finding places to "snatch and grab" or get instant gratification.

Taken to an extreme, people who approach life opportunistically are often thought of as having predatory natures. There's something to this.

It's important to always be watching your environment and the dynamics of the situations that you move through. Reality often presents coincidences, intersections, synchronicities, convergences and collisions that create possibilities and potentials that weren't there before. If you're alert, and you understand the potential implications of the emergence of new forms and dimensions of opportunity, it can lead to a game-changer in your life.

Shakespeare writes in Julius Caesar:

There is a tide in the affairs of men.
Which, taken at the flood, leads on to fortune;
Omitted, all the voyage of their life
Is bound in shallows and in miseries.
On such a full sea are we now afloat,
And we must take the current when it serves,
Or lose our ventures.

Robert Frost writes in his poem The Road Not Taken:

Two roads diverged in a wood, and I—
I took the one less traveled by,
And that has made all the difference.

These are sentiments spoken in metaphor which convey the importance of seizing an opportunity created by favorable circumstances. If you notice, each of these not only includes the importance of circumstances, they also imply the importance of seeing and seizing the moment.

In definitions based on a juncture of circumstances it is often forgotten just how important judgment and action are to the equation. The more academic definitions make the circumstances the star of the show. They imply that the opportunity is the result of the circumstances. But buried in this type of language is the assumption that the opportunity is created "out there" in the world rather than the opportunity being created or generated internally, from within your own mind and imagination.

Always remember that opportunity isn't just "out there", it's also "in here."
I actually believe that it's a lot more in here than out there. More on that later.

Another definition of opportunity is **arbitrage**. This is a term
that stock market traders use to describe a situation where a stock or
commodity is for sale in one place at one price, and in another place for
a different price - a situation where you can capture risk-free profits by
buying low and selling high at the same time.

In life, if we see an opportunity, we most ideally want it to be an
arbitrage situation, so we can get what we want quickly and without risk.
Whether we want money, attention, power, fame, security, or relief from
pain or worry, the part of us that likes instant gratification wants it right
now, and without having to risk or give anything to get it.

More generally speaking, arbitrage is where you can buy low and sell
high with a high degree of certainty, even if the transaction involves multiple
steps and happens over time. The spirit of arbitrage is that it happens relatively quickly, with relatively high certainty, and without much risk of loss.

If you work on Wall Street, a good portion of your attention is likely
dedicated to discovering potential arbitrage situations. And when you
find one, you bet on it appropriately. Billions of dollars are invested in
complex computer systems to monitor world markets, searching for arbitrage opportunities, then to quickly make trades that offer instant profits.
In many cases, these systems actually manipulate the markets in order to
create arbitrage opportunities.

Many hedge funds try to create models and algorithms to find arbitrage opportunities over time. If you know what's going to happen in the
future with a degree of certainty, you can place appropriate bets, and
have a higher probability of winning.

Arbitrage situations come up in "real life" as well. When I was in my
late teens, I would visit second-hand stores and look through the books
for good deals. I would search for books that I believed that bookstores
would pay high prices for, often buying books for fifty cents or a dollar
and then selling them for eight or ten dollars at a bookstore a few miles
away - and paying for my food and gas for the day in the process.

I know friends who have found pieces of real estate that they recognized as being priced well, and then submitted offers contingent upon raising the financing for the purchase. This allowed them to "lock up" the property for a month or two, while they then went out and found someone else to buy it for more money. In a case like this, the risk was very low, because they hadn't actually purchased anything. They just created an opportunity for themselves to earn a profit that was relatively risk-free. This is essentially creating an arbitrage opportunity with real estate.

In business, advertising and marketing can create opportunities that are very close to arbitrage. If you have an ad or marketing piece that generates more in profit than it costs to run, then you can earn increasing profit by running the ad over and over again. This is one of the reasons why it is important to continually experiment with new advertising and marketing channels, especially in the current environment of rapid online innovation. I have watched million dollar (and billion dollar) businesses emerge out of the discovery of one new marketing or distribution channel that was discovered at just the right time.

I started my online business in 2001, just as "pay per click" advertising was emerging on the scene. This represented a massive opportunity, as very few marketers were using these systems, and traffic could be purchased at incredibly low prices (in some cases, for a penny per click). This was a big help in building my business in the early days. I thought of it as arbitrage when it was happening.

Another definition of opportunity that I'll suggest is that it is **"the heart of entrepreneurship."** This definition steps a bit outside the box of our others, as it defines opportunity as being a key part of something larger: being an entrepreneur.

In the modern day, an entrepreneur is someone who builds a successful, profitable business. People like Mark Zuckerberg, Oprah Winfrey, and Jeff Bezos are considered icons of entrepreneurship. And if you look carefully at their histories, you'll see a common denominator: They were great at seeing and seizing opportunity.

Dan Sullivan, founder of The Strategic Coach, has paraphrased Jean Baptiste Saye in defining an entrepreneur as someone who takes resources from a lower level of productivity to a higher level of productivity. This is a wonderful way of thinking about entrepreneurship in the bigger picture.

I have had the good fortune to know and watch many successful entrepreneurs up close in my life. They tend to be good at watching for opportunity across all of the areas that their business touches or involves.

They look for opportunity by finding out what their customers want. They look for opportunity by negotiating better prices when buying things. They look for opportunity by hiring the best team members possible. They look for opportunity by studying the latest knowledge and news. They look for opportunity by analyzing their business processes to make them more efficient.

Some of the most successful entrepreneurs I know are actually what you might call "opportunity agnostic." They are always scanning the horizon of the business and financial environment, and watching for the types of changes that signal the emergence of new opportunities. I have watched people who have worked in one domain of business stop what they are doing and shift to a completely new thing because they sense a big opportunity. These types tend to be on the more extreme end of being opportunistic, but the example is important because it offers an insight into a way of thinking that most people never even consider.

Steve Jobs was almost psychic at changing course when the timing was right, and when the opportunities presented themselves. He started out building computers, but later purchased the company that became Pixar, and built it into the first major computer animated film company. Not only did Pixar create one blockbuster success after another, but it later sold to Disney for over $7 Billion. Steve also famously made a daring business move by launching the iPod, which was the first big mainstream portable music and media player. Again, he started out building computers, so this was not something that was expected of a company like Apple.

Steve Jobs saw opportunity where others didn't, and this led to many business success stories, and him making himself a billionaire with two different companies. He was an iconic entrepreneur, and he was an artist when it came to opportunity.

In this book, we will invest a lot of our time and attention focused on the business side of opportunity, so for now we will move on to other definitions.

To me, the most important aspect of opportunity isn't the circumstances that are given to you, or the situations that you find yourself in.

Instead, it's what we might call the domain of **"creative opportunity."**

Creative opportunity is when you use your mind to envision things in a new way, creating novel possibilities of value in the process. This is different from the "juncture of circumstances" model in that it puts the primary emphasis on how you see things, rather than on how they happen to be in the moment. It takes you from being passively at the mercy of circumstances and puts you in the pilot's seat of creating new ones.

Imagination is one of the most miraculous things we can experience in life. Albert Einstein said:

"Imagination is more important than knowledge. For knowledge is limited, whereas imagination embraces the entire world, stimulating progress, giving birth to evolution."

In your imagination, you can create entire worlds of possibility, try out an infinite variety of experiences, and look at things from every possible perspective. When you marry this ability to the skill of creating opportunity, the sky, or rather the universe, is the limit.

Realizing the power of your creative imagination is the starting point for new worlds of opportunity. It is the pathway to solving everything from problems in your life to problems in the world.

I like to believe that the spirit of opportunity is essentially creative. I want to live in a world where we use our minds to their highest capacities, and to contribute to reducing suffering and the evolution of all life.

Creative imagination is also how we transform scarce resources into abundant opportunities. Paul Zane Pilzer, the economist and thought leader, wrote an inspiring book titled "Unlimited Wealth." It sounds like a self-help title, but within its pages Pilzer conveys an inspiring model of the world.

He says that traditionally, economics is defined as "the study of the distribution of scarce resources." But as he was looking at history, he saw a clear pattern: Whenever a resource becomes scarce, we humans use our ingenuity and creative imagination to find new ways of doing things, effectively transforming the scarcity into abundance.

He uses the example of oil, pointing out that in the 1970s there was talk of us reaching "peak oil" and running out very soon. Immediately, people went to work to figure out new ways to do things, inventing technology to help cars get more miles per gallon of gasoline, and generating more electricity per barrel of oil. This quickly extended the horizon of how much oil we "had left" and took us from peak oil to thinking about how to create new sources of energy that were far more sustainable.

The key is that once humans recognize that a resource is scarce, we either extend the resource or invent something new to replace it… again, essentially creating abundance where scarcity once was. This is the "Unlimited Wealth" that Pilzer is speaking of in his title, it's really related to unlimited **ingenuity**.

Entrepreneurs love to discover gaps to fill… places where desirable resources are considered scarce… or where an inefficient system is creating a bottleneck… so they can innovate new ways to produce and capture value. This always involves some form of creative imagination, and some form of generating opportunity.

If you go back through the history of great inventions, you'll see a clear pattern: People who creatively imagined, discovered, combined, and integrated things together that had never been invented before. From the printing press, to the telescope, to the airplane, to the space shuttle, each was a feat of creative imagination. Each represented potential value, and each was a huge opportunity.

REMINDER: Download the "Opportunity Companion Guide" to Get Your Summaries, Checklists & Exercises

This book has an **Opportunity Companion Guide** that goes along with it, which you can download for free. It includes key chapter summaries, implementation checklists, and written exercises - plus extra chapters and other bonus material. Go here to get it now, so you can review the summaries and start implementing what you're learning:

OpportunityBonus.com

The Nature of Opportunity

HAVE YOU EVER HAD the experience of looking for something at a grocery market, but not seeing it, then realizing that the packaging or location of the item has changed? Once you see what's changed, it's easy to find what you're after. It jumps right out at you. But before that, the change acts as a kind of camouflage. You couldn't find what you were searching for because you were looking for a particular color, design, or location, and it just wasn't there.

Opportunity is like this. It's changing right now, and that is making it harder to see in many domains. It's important to update our ideas of what it looks like and where it is. Once we have that update, opportunity pops into view. It becomes abundant. You start to see it everywhere.

Another reason that it's important to update your ideas about the nature of opportunity is that the mind often misses seeing things that it doesn't have patterns or models for. Something can be right in front of you, but if you don't know how to recognize it, then you can't see it.

In this section we're going to take a deep dive into the nature of opportunity and how it is going to change and evolve. In order to better understand the nature of opportunity, we'll to review a series of predictions and models that I believe will become more true as we move into the future. Some of these ideas are grounded in patterns I've observed in the past, and some are my creative calculations of what I believe will happen in the future. As you think through each of these concepts, the nature of opportunity will become clearer and make more sense to you. These patterns will give you the lenses you need to recognize more opportunity in your life.

In the future, opportunity will increase exponentially.

We can all feel our options increasing rapidly. We have more opportunities to try new foods, travel to new locations, learn new ideas, experiment with new exercise methods, have novel experiences, meet diverse people from different places and domains, start different types of businesses, engage in new hobbies and artistic interests, and contribute to others in general.

As we've learned, the Law of Accelerating Returns states that there is a double exponential increase in the rate of change. As knowledge and technology grow more sophisticated, building upon previous achievements, this curve continues to go parabolic.

When new technology "enters" a domain, researchers, entrepreneurs, and artists start applying the technology to the area and things often change rapidly. And technology is reaching into many domains of opportunity right now.

Galileo learning how to combine two glass lenses inside of one tube to make a telescope is an example of how powerful the force of technological change can be. One convex lens to gather and magnify light and one concave lens to focus it allowed him to see 30x further than the naked eye alone. This revealed not only that the moon has mountains and the sun has spots, but that Jupiter has moons that go around it, just like the moon that goes around Earth. I've read that Galileo even made and sold telescopes as a business. He recognized the opportunity on multiple levels - and became a scientific entrepreneur!

But look at what happened next. Galileo started asking others to look through his telescope to see the things that he was seeing. There was one group of people who had no interest at all: the Roman Catholic Church.

Why would they be opposed to a new technology some guy was using to look up at the night sky? Because for at least 1,500 years, the "religious story" in the West was that the Earth was the center of the universe, with hell below us and heaven above. Everything revolved around the Earth and this proved that God put us here to be the rulers of this realm.

Galileo showed up with a piece of "heretical technology" which proved that something else was going on. If another planet had something orbiting around it, then maybe everything wasn't orbiting the Earth. Maybe we humans weren't at the center of the universe.

The pope definitely didn't want to look into the telescope because it would call into question the entire foundation and legitimacy of his power structure. And they were pretty serious about this stuff back then. Galileo was called in by the Inquisition in 1616 and threatened for his activities (to put it mildly). But nothing could stop the new current of ideas and models that flowed from Galileo's telescope. A revolution in ideas and culture was sparked, and the fire could never be extinguished. The technology of the telescope changed everything.

The point I'm making here is that when scientific and technological innovation enters a particular domain, it often triggers a series of cascading explosions of change. These changes echo through neighboring domains, and through seemingly unrelated domains. The changes are predictable in some ways, and completely unpredictable in others.

Consider what happened after the gasoline-powered motor was united with the horse-drawn carriage. Now you could get from one place to another faster, and you didn't have to feed and take care of a horse in order to do it. But this was just the beginning. Automobiles contributed to the massive increase in demand for gasoline, which drove the demand for oil. This led to the discovery of oil all around the world. In the Middle East, the discovery of oil under the sand led to a massive, sustained financial infusion into a culture that was not a major global influence previously. Again, we see how technological innovation had widespread and unpredictable effects.

Because this type of radical innovation is happening in more places than ever before simultaneously, and because there are more people combining knowledge, methods, designs, and innovations from diverse domains, we are experiencing a spectacular explosion of possibility and opportunity. Old models are being disrupted more and more rapidly, as we tear down the old to build with the new.

If you were interested in becoming a writer before the rise of the internet, you were limited to a few main narrow options. You would almost certainly have needed to write for some type of news, marketing, or publishing company, and this meant that you would have to conform to the rules of that organization.

Now, you can go online and start a blog, write articles for any number of websites, be a micro-blogger and tweet all day, write an eBook and publish it yourself, or become a copywriter... and you can do these things as an employee, as a contractor, or as an entrepreneur working for yourself (or any combination of the above).

If you are a writer, you have so many options right now, and I believe that we're still early in the process of transformation that is being fueled by technology in this domain.

Now think about other industries and how technology is changing them...

If you're a musician, you have dozens of ways to perform, share, and publish your music (although overall music revenue is down, so you also have to get creative if you want to monetize your music into the future). If you're an artist, you can find a community of other artists around the world who share your style and interests, and explore ways of expressing your vision. If you're an entrepreneur, you are looking at an explosion of new types of products, new ways of marketing them, new ways of reaching customers, and new ways of growing your business.

Each of these new options represents a new form of opportunity. And because you can combine them, you are looking at something that has never existed before: so much opportunity that you could never begin to explore even a tiny fraction of it in your lifetime.

Technological innovation and the spread of knowledge has been dramatically accelerated by the rise of the internet. Change is now reaching into every domain and it will transform our lives as radically as the telescope and the automobile. Your domain, whatever it is, will be transformed. This is creating the biggest explosion in opportunity that humans have ever seen. And it's going to increase exponentially over the coming years.

In the future, windows of opportunity will open faster and close faster.

"Potential Has a Shelf Life" -Margaret Atwood

The two founders of Uber were trying to find a cab one snowy night in 2008 while attending a conference in Paris. As they were standing in the cold, they had an insight: you should be able to push a button and have a car pull up and take you wherever you want to go. This spark of an idea was essential to the funding of Uber, but it wasn't enough.

Other forces were at play as well. A year earlier, the iPhone had been released. For the first time, your mobile device knew where it was, and it could give you directions to anywhere you wanted to go. 4G wireless networks were also about to take over. The window of opportunity for ride-hailing apps opened up right as they had Uber's founders' had their insight, and the rest is history.

This intersection of idea and multiple enabling innovations is what I mean by a window of opportunity. More and more of these windows are opening up as we move towards the future. Why? Because faster change combined with more people and groups innovating creates more and more new innovations and ideas in more domains. This leads to more possible intersections – and more windows of opportunity.

It is a virtuous cycle. More innovation leads to more opportunity which leads to more new innovations. And because of the accelerating rate of change, these windows of opportunities are opening faster and faster.

But because more people are now able to actualize these opportunities using the internet and other technologies-, the "shelf life" of opportunities is also becoming shorter. The windows not only open faster, they also close faster - because people quickly seize available opportunities and run with them.

The increasing competition for ideas and its consequences on relative laggards can be seen in the general trend of how long companies and industries survive. I read a story about a researcher named Richard Foster who calculated that in 1958 a company in the S&P 500 could expect to stay on the list for 61 years. Guess how many years they can expect to stay on the list today? 18.

These days delay is suicide when it comes to seizing an idea. What if the founders of Uber had waited a few years to launch their idea? Garrett Camp and Travis Kalanik are brilliant entrepreneurs, but if they had started three years later, their company would probably have had 1% of the success that Uber enjoys today.

In addition, there's another factor that causes windows of opportunities to close faster: you have increasing opportunities available to you. If you're looking at a good opportunity today, but you decide to sleep on it and come back in a month, it's likely that in that time you will have several other newer opportunities to consider. These new opportunities take your attention from the first potential opportunity, which, in effect, causes that window to close for you. It's a kind of "opportunity noise" that you have to manage.

If you're single and looking for a date, the one you pass today is less likely to be there tomorrow. If you're thinking of starting a business, the idea is less likely to be viable later. If you're thinking of making an investment, the market is going to change.

All this means that in the future, great ideas will have a shorter shelf life. We don't have time to wait around and maybe take action some day. Now you need to test it out in the real world immediately, because the window is not going to stay open for very long.

In the future, we'll have relatively more smaller opportunities, and relatively fewer larger opportunities.

Even though opportunity is increasing exponentially and becoming far more diverse, you'll also notice that most of these opportunities are smaller, and few are larger "blockbuster" opportunities.

With the exponential increase in the rate of change, and the multiplication of opportunity, I like to imagine that the opportunity distribution curve compresses more and more into a "power law" curve, yielding mostly smaller opportunities, and fewer large opportunities.

If I have a room with 100 people in it, and I measure how tall they are and put it on a chart, you'll see a normal "bell curve" - with most of the heights bunched around the average height, and a few distributed out at the edges.

If I have a room with 100 internet companies in it, things are very different. Leaders in each area tend to win a huge share of the market, leaving a few to compete for what's left over. In a power law dynamic, the leader will be 10x as big as the next biggest competitor, with #3 typically trailing the leader by a big margin as well.

Google has 80% of the search market and Microsoft (Bing) has 8%. Facebook is 10x the size of Twitter. Amazon is so much bigger than its competitors that it's hard to even decide who to consider for #2.

This is one of the paradoxes of opportunity. Once an innovation emerges, an entrepreneur or business typically steps in and works to popularize the innovation by offering a product or service for sale. If successful, a product or brand can take over the market and become the avatar for an entire category. Google is now a verb synonymous with search. Facebook and the idea of social media are often used interchangeably.

This dynamic can lead to massive success for the leader, who comes up with the blockbuster. But for the rest of the pack, the opportunity - while sometimes still good - is relatively smaller. If you owned the 10th most valuable social network or search engine, you'd still be doing just fine. But becoming #1 is getting harder.

This reality of there being more small opportunities and fewer large opportunities is wonderful if you're satisfied with having lots of small wins, but it's also potentially distracting and confusing if you're interested in finding the biggest opportunities for yourself. The seemingly endless supply of smaller opportunities can become noise through which the signal of a blockbuster can be lost.

This is another reason why "opportunity literacy" becomes more and more important in the future. If you know how to discover and create bigger opportunities, you can leverage your time, attention and other resources to create much bigger success.

As you move into the future, it's very important that you recognize those opportunities most likely to have bigger payoffs in your life and business, and not get distracted by "shiny objects" that grab your attention, but that aren't as valuable.

Pay attention and watch for those rare, unique, big opportunities that are a perfect match for your personality, passions, knowledge, and purpose in life. When you discover one that is a real potential blockbuster, bet more heavily, and invest more attention. These are where the big payoffs are for each of us.

I have used examples like Google and Facebook in order to bring this concept into relief, and to make it easier to see in the real world. But each of us has our own chance to carve out a niche or category in our lives or businesses where we can be a leader. We'll cover this more in depth later, but for now it's important to remember to think big, and to find a place where the opportunities are right for our unique personalities and gifts.

And again, we're not interested in "opportunism" here. The study of opportunity benefits us most when we take a holistic perspective. We aren't interested in becoming greedy or chasing outward success for its own sake. Instead, we're interested in creating a successful life in all domains, physical, relational, mental, spiritual, all domains. And this means looking for big opportunities to improve our health, our relationships, our self-development, our spiritual lives, and much more.

In the future, the value of things will change faster and faster.

Economists use the term "liquidity" when describing a market where you can buy or sell something without causing a big change to the price. If you are selling stock in a liquid market, that means so many other people are buying and selling the same stock that your order doesn't really have an effect on its price. Liquidity is typically thought of as a good thing, and speculators and traders rationalize their efforts to profit from markets as being beneficial to everyone because their actions are "creating liquidity."

As different kinds of markets connect to each other, this creates a sort of "meta liquidity" where you can exchange one form of value for another through a chain of transactions in different marketplaces.

I can use PayPal to send US dollars to a friend in England, who will receive pounds sterling, who can deposit those pounds in their bank account, then wire them to a cryptocurrency exchange and trade them for bitcoin, and then send those bitcoins to a company who is doing a launch to purchase shares in the business... and this can all happen inside of a few hours.

If you zoom out a bit, you can see how this "cross-domain value exchange" has much wider implications. I can borrow money from a credit card and use it to hire a designer in another country, who can design a digital skin for a particular type of gun in an online video game, which I can then take and upload to a digital asset exchange platform and sell for fiat or cryptocurrency, which I can then transfer to my bank account and send back to my credit card company to pay for the original loan. Again, this can all happen relatively quickly, if I am successful in my little entrepreneurial venture.

Because value is moving at faster and faster velocities through and across more diverse systems, accelerated by impossibly fast computer networks, the value of many things is changing more and more rapidly.

In the past, change in general happened much slower, and so one could rely on the value of something being more or less stable over long periods of time. Yes, there were occasional booms and busts (more on that later), but if you lived a thousand years ago and you had some gold or silver, the local blacksmith would probably charge you the same amount of it to put a new shoe on your horse tomorrow... or a year from now.

Now, if you have gold, it might be worth 10% more or less next month. And if there is a big change in another market, the price of gold could half or double.

The stock market is famous for being unpredictable and having swings of volatility through its various cycles. This reputation was formed back in the day when stock markets were mostly isolated from each other. Now, with stock markets all connected directly and indirectly, a change in one market can trigger a domino effect that quickly spreads through other markets. There are more things that now amplify this effect of changing prices and values. The quickening in rising and falling values is spreading to other domains as well.

I have been fascinated watching how quickly billionaires are created in new markets, and how this process is accelerating. It seems that in the old days, a self-made billionaire like Andrew Carnegie or John Rockefeller would take decades to make their billions. Bill Gates took 12 years to do it. Jeff Bezos did it in under 5 years. Mark Zuckerberg did it by age 23. Founders of cryptocurrencies are sometimes doing it in a year or two. This pattern is going to continue as new forms of value emerge, and new entrepreneurs enter these domains to innovate. I predict that we'll see our first self-made billionaire go from zero to billionaire in under a month within 10 years. At that point, we might have to redefine "billionaire," because there will likely be some new form of currency that we'll be measuring the value of things, and who knows what those individual units will be, and whether the idea of "billionaire" makes sense anymore!

To clarify, when I say that the value of things changes faster and faster, I am saying that, on average, the relative value of various things like currencies, securities, assets, intellectual property will change faster and faster over time. You may not notice it day-to-day in your life, but if you pay attention over time, you'll see that this is happening.

And the time will come (relatively soon, I predict) where the value of something that you thought was stable changes dramatically in a short period of time.

The changes in value that we're seeing are, in part, due to "meta liquidity" or "cross-domain value exchange", but another contributing factor is that new forms of property, assets, and value are being created at an increasing rate. We now have digital property and assets, along with intellectual property, securities, bonds, options and other derivatives, cryptocurrencies… with more coming over the horizon. As each new type of asset class emerges, it creates a migration (or stampede) into the new form of value. This activates cycles of boom and bust, and often inflates massive bubbles that then pop along the way.

In the 1600s, the Dutch went crazy for tulip bulbs. At the height of the bubble, some people were paying the equivalent of ten years' worth of income for one bulb. The value of tulip bulbs was fueled by fashion, manipulation, and greed. Smaller versions of this happen across new and exciting markets everywhere when new discoveries are made or trends emerge.

Over the past several years, I have become fascinated with the art market. Individual paintings now regularly sell for over $100 million US. Several have now sold between $250 million and $450 million. I remember watching a documentary about the band Metallica maybe ten years ago. In the movie, the drummer Lars Ulrich was selling a bunch of paintings from his art collection. He had several paintings by the American painter Jean-Michel Basquiat, some of which he was putting up for auction. Back then, nicer examples of Basquiat's work were selling for maybe $5 million to $10 million. I remember looking at the pieces and thinking to myself, "Are you serious?"

In 2012, a Basquiat painting sold for $20 million. Then in 2013, another one sold for close to $50 million. In 2017, someone paid $110 million for one. Each time I've seen these prices, I've thought to myself "I wonder if Lars Ulrich is bummed out that he sold his paintings for only a few million each?"

But that's nothing compared to the cryptocurrency craze. New currencies are launching regularly that hit billion dollar market caps instantly. And the swings in cryptocurrency prices make the art and stock market look like safe havens by comparison.

The emergence of the blockchain also holds a promise for the future: That all forms of value can be "tokenized" then sold and traded freely in always-on global markets. Imagine being able to buy a fractional ownership in a piece of real estate or an art piece, the way we buy fractional ownership in companies by purchasing stock.

This will welcome yet another exponential increase in the speed of value exchange, and also, I predict, in the velocity of overall change in the value and price of things.

Every time value changes, a window of opportunity opens or closes in some way, for someone. And the acceleration of value changes accelerates opportunities and combinations of opportunities.

We're going to need models and tools to deal with the acceleration in the change in values, and the exponential increase in opportunity that's coming. We will come back to this later in much greater detail. But the most important thing to remember is that opportunity is changing, and it's accelerating, so that you won't be surprised as it continues to increase over time.

In the future, opportunity will come from increasingly unexpected places.

If you look across your life, you'll see that many things that happened were just serendipitous. You were accidentally in the right place at the right time. I went to the Burning Man Festival nine years ago for the first time with some friends on a whim. People had been talking about it and I finally said, "Okay, I'm going." So I went and had a amazing time.

The next year I decided to do a talk and share some of my most radical ideas. A woman walked into the middle of that talk, sat down, and watched the rest of it. Then she and her friends came up at the end and started talking to me. She and I followed up via email, and within several months we fell in love. Now we have a daughter and a family.

That opportunity came from a very unexpected place! The last thing I expected was that I would meet my future wife in a dusty tent at Burning Man.

Increasingly, opportunity is going to come from unexpected places. And if we're not expecting the unexpected, we may not recognize huge opportunities when they present themselves.

Maybe someone pops up and says, "Hey, do you want to go to this foreign country and go on this tour?" Normally you might say, "No, it doesn't really sound like my thing." But if you know that opportunity is going to come from unexpected places and it's important to explore novel domains, you might say, "You know, it's been a while since I've done something outside the box. Let's go check it out."

When I say opportunity will increasingly come from unexpected places, I don't just mean in terms of novel geography or life experiences. I also mean that opportunity will come, more and more, from unexpected combinations.

In systems theory, there is a phenomena called an "emergent property." Emergence is what happens when many elements operating on one level create a property on a higher level. A good example is an ant colony. If you take one ant away from its colony, and put it in a field alone it will die. But if you take a million ants, that together weigh a few pounds in total, who have all grown up together as part of one unified family, something interesting happens. The group begins to demonstrate abilities that appear to come from a higher 'mind', a unified planning and decision-making process. The colony can architect a complex nest, placing the eggs where they're warmest. The groupe-mind can find food, fight off enemies, and even make decisions about where to move next. And this all appears to happen with a few simple communication tools and a handful of chemical signals that ants send back and forth. The ant colony demonstrates the qualities of an **emergent property**, because it has order on a higher level. The sum of its parts adds up to something entirely new and unexpected.

A cell is an emergent property relative to the molecules that make it up. A molecule is an emergent property relative to the atoms that compose it. A body is an emergent property relative to the organs that constitute it. A family is an emergent property relative to its members.

To me, the greatest opportunities are **emergent opportunities**. They come from taking what is currently available, and then combining these elements in new ways to create something on a higher order, the way subatomic particles self-organize into stable atoms, bees organize into a hive or the way fish self-organize into giant schools, swimming as one entity.

A mobile phone was an emergent phenomena that combined electronics, plastic, buttons, displays, transmitting and receiving circuits, an antenna, and much more. Individually, none of these components was groundbreaking, but put together they allowed you to do something revolutionary - make a call from anywhere.

The iPhone was an emergent phenomena that combined a mobile phone, a video camera, a music player, an operating system, applications, an internet connection, a touch-screen, and much more. The emergent property was an incredible new device that you could use to take videos, check email, go online, play music, buy things, etc.

Uber was an emergent phenomena that ultimately combined a smartphone, GPS navigation, 4G wireless networks, drivers who owned cars, the internet, and much more.

Note how the iPhone used the mobile phone as one of its components, the way a cell uses molecules as components, and combined it with many other elements to create something on a higher order - an emergent property like being able to shoot, edit, and upload a video to the internet in real-time. And note how Uber used the iPhone as one of its components in a similar fashion, combining it with several other diverse innovations to create something on a higher order. Emergent properties build one on top of the other.

The most unexpected direction to look for opportunity is up! Look up to the higher order innovation or entity that you could create. When you look up at a higher order, or for a possible new emergent property, everything changes.

What's interesting about emergence is that it's always a surprise. The behavior of a cell can never be deduced by looking at a molecule. The behavior of an ant colony can never be deduced by looking at an ant. This is, to me, what makes emergence so mysterious and cool.

Of course, with the acceleration of technological and cultural innovation, there will be many other types of surprises. As the old saying goes: "expect the unexpected." When you have an eye open watching for what you don't expect, it's easier to see when it appears. And when you're watching the horizon for emergent innovations and emergent opportunities, you will be looking where almost no one else is.

In the future, creativity will become more and more important to opportunity.

The study of creativity is the study of using your mind to connect and combine things in new ways, and then to use those insights to create in the world. Creativity is largely a game of training your mind to connect things you learn in one domain to situations that seem unrelated.

The physicist Richard Feynman was famously trying to work out the spin of electrons around atoms when he walked into the cafeteria and saw someone throw a plate up in the air. He saw how the plate wobbled as it spun around, and it fascinated him. This activated his curiosity, so he tried to work out the math of how this worked, and in the process discovered the solution to how electrons went around atoms.

Bill Bowerman, a track and field coach from my home state of Oregon, was looking for ways to make running shoes that worked on different types of surfaces. As the story goes, he was in the kitchen with his wife making breakfast and noticed the pattern that the waffle iron made in the waffles, and connected this up with his search for a better sole for his shoes. He went and got some rubber mix, put it into the waffle iron, and the Nike Waffle Trainer was born (along with one of the biggest companies in the world).

Steve Jobs famously wandered into a calligraphy class when he was in college and learned how to create beautiful, proportionally spaced letters. Later, when he worked with his designers on the Macintosh, they created an all-new system inspired by Job's early exposure to elegant typography.

If the past was about doing things a little better than others in order to succeed, the future is about looking at what everyone else is doing and finding something innovative to do instead. I believe that in the future copying everyone else is not going to lead to health, success, happiness, love, meaning, purpose, and fulfillment. If you want to live an epic life, then it's going to take creativity.

Again, creativity is usually about taking something you learn in one place and using it in other places (or combining several of these things together to create novel innovations that create a lot of value). This isn't a mysterious gift of the universe - some 'Eureka!' moment that comes out of nowhere - this is a skill you can consciously develop.

One way to practice creativity is to take any two things and ask yourself, "How can I connect them?" You can notice what the objects have in common. Or you can imagine a third object that could relate them to each other.

If you're looking at a car and a tree, you can imagine ways that they could be connected. Maybe the car has wood paneling inside. Or you might notice that the wheels on the car are round, just as the tree trunk is round. Or maybe the car is green and the leaves of the tree are green. Or maybe that they are both on Planet Earth. Get as creative as you can.

Or, better yet, practice connecting really diverse things. Look over and say, "Okay now I see my recording device and then I also see a candle. What connects these two things?" Maybe the candle makes light and there are lights on my recording device. When you make connections like this, the more diverse the better, you start connecting up all of the knowledge in your mind and finding new analogies.

These types of exercises train the mind to look at things in new way, so it becomes automatic and habitual. I practice creativity exercises like this one constantly, and I find that they make a big difference and develop my ability to spot new possibilities that others miss. It's very powerful.

My wife Annie and I were discussing this book a couple of nights ago, and she said:

"Opportunity is what you bring to reality, not what reality brings to you. You're responsible for the amount of opportunity in your life."

This really captures the importance of taking a creative approach to life, and to opportunity. It makes all the difference.

REMINDER: Download the "Opportunity Companion Guide" to Get Your Summaries, Checklists & Exercises

This book has an **Opportunity Companion Guide** that goes along with it, which you can download for free. It includes key chapter summaries, implementation checklists, and written exercises - plus extra chapters and other bonus material. Go here to get it now, so you can review the summaries and start implementing what you're learning:

OpportunityBonus.com

The Emotional Game of Opportunity

Opportunity Shock

ALVIN TOFFLER WROTE A book titled *Future Shock* which introduced the idea that too much change happening too quickly can leave people feeling disoriented and in a state of shock. He introduced the term "information overwhelm."

Al Reis and Jack Trout wrote in their book *Positioning* that "we are the world's first over-communicated society. There is too much communication happening for us to be able to take it all in, and understand it."

Future Shock was written in 1970. *Positioning* was written in 1980.

These issues are only going to get more intense. As we transition into the 2020s, we will be entering the era of Opportunity Shock.

Ray Kurzweil and Peter Diamandis, two futurists, point out that we carry more knowledge and potential power in our mobile devices than was available to a king or president 50 years ago. They show how our access to tools and resources is increasing as their cost decreases, and they predict that we will enter an age of unimaginable abundance as machines automate the monotonous drudgery of life, freeing us to express ourselves creatively and enjoy lives of leisure and happiness.

That is likely to be a good thing for many people, and for many societies, but all this opportunity also has a shadow aspect. Access to abundant resources also brings with it an a mathematical puzzle of exponentially increasing difficulty: as your opportunities multiply in quantity and quality, how do you decide which ones are right for you?

We will each have so much opportunity individually with our businesses and in our organizations.... and in social domains of family, friends, and politics... that it will be shocking to our systems. This shock will manifest as moments of dazed confusion, where we find ourselves zoning out in a trance of distraction, overwhelmed by opportunity and choice.

Let's say that you have an opportunity for a business project that you will personally enjoy and learn a lot from, and that has a 50% chance of paying you $100,000 in one year. Alternately, you could do a business project that you will enjoy half as much, learn half as much from, and that has a 25% chance of paying you $1 million in two years. Which one do you select? What other factors do you take into consideration?

Or let's say you have one year's income saved up, and you want to invest it. You can invest it in something that you are knowledgeable about, where you feel confident that the investment will grow over time, or you can invest it in something that you have much less knowledge about, where you feel less confident that it will grow in value, but that will force you to learn about something new and important for your future. Which do you choose?

These aren't just hypotheticals. You probably already face these sorts of complex decisions all the time on a smaller scale. Yesterday, I was writing down a big insight that was coming to me, and I heard the patter of little feet behind me. My daughter walked up and said "I'm hungry, dad." She took my hand and led me away from my computer to the kitchen. These moments when I am writing down an important idea and my daughter needs something or wants to play bring this dilemma of where to put my attention home for me. I always try to smile in these situations, as this type of opportunity dilemma seems to be happening more and more in life.

Lately, I have noticed another pattern: while I am thinking about a new idea, it triggers a different idea about some other part of my life. I know that if I think about the new thing, I might lose the thread of the original idea, and if I try to write the original one down first, I might forget my new inspiration. And if I go back and forth to try to get both of them down, I can't continue either train of thought. I lose good ideas maybe once every week or two this way.

These types of problems are going to increase exponentially in the future. Remember the pond filling with lotuses, and how on Day 25 only 3% of the pond is full but in just five more days, it's going to be completely covered? Right now is Day 25, across many areas of our lives. Many more options and opportunities are coming.

The Emotional Side of Opportunity

As we've learned, an opportunity captures your attention in a way that is almost supernatural. When the right convergence of events, ideas, people, and other resources comes together, it can appear as a miraculous synchronicity.

We've also learned that too much of a good thing, in this case opportunity, can also be overwhelming, and even immobilizing. But as you begin exploring all of the opportunity that is available to you, another thing can start happening: a lot of mixed emotions.

As we've learned, we humans come wired with both a mammal emotional and social system, and also a reptilian survival and sexual system. One of the consequences of these base layers of our and psyches is that the situations we find ourselves in are more and more complex. They require increasingly counterintuitive responses and adaptations in order to cope with and thrive in the face of them.

When we are overtaken by an emotional rush, it changes us into a different version of ourselves, often without us even realizing it. When we are really activated or triggered, it can cause us to do something that actually sabotages our long-term success.

Let's talk about how to manage our emotions as we learn to surf the wave of opportunity that's coming our way.

The Complexity of Emotion

At any particular moment, you will likely be feeling a combination of emotions.

You might experience a mix of happiness, joy, gratitude, sadness, anger, fear, and possibly others. You may have had a great day at work, but gotten a ticket on the way home, then received a surprise call from an old friend that you enjoyed, then saw that one of your investments was down, then heard that your favorite band is coming to town to play soon, then saw that your romantic partner made an affectionate comment on social media to an ex-flame of theirs. Layers of rising and falling emotions course through our bodies continuously.

Feelings are like cocktails. They are combinations of feelings. They are ever-changing and dynamically unpredictable.

Let's check in right now with your emotions. To do this, start by tuning into the physical sensations that you are experiencing inside your body that indicate the presence of emotions.

If you haven't done this before, just start with your "physical senses."

Can you tune in to your senses? Can you feel the surface of your skin? Now, can you feel the interior of your body? Can you feel your hands from the inside? Can you feel your feet from inside? Can you feel your legs and arms, your torso and head? Can you notice the taste in your mouth and the combination of scents around you? Can you notice what you hear? And what you see?

Now, can you now notice your mind, and your thoughts? Can you remember what you did yesterday? And can you imagine what you will do tomorrow?

We have just touched in with the physical body and our senses, and then with the mind and our thoughts.

Now, let's tune in to our emotions. Can you feel your emotional state? For most people, they can feel a sort of ephemeral set of "beyond the body" sensations that are experienced as emotions.

If you're feeling mostly happy, it will have one signature complex of feelings and sensations. If you are feeling mostly sad, it will mean a different set of sensations. If you are feeling joy, it will be another set. If you're angry, it will be yet another.

Some people feel joy as lightness in the chest, or they feel sadness as heavyness or coldness in the body. Some feel anger as heat pulsing over their faces, and some feel love as warmth in the heart area.

Emotions seem to arise in our body systems from outside our conscious awareness. It takes effort to tune in to and label them. This makes sense if you consider the part that emotions play in holding relationships together and pushing relationships apart - keeping them in a state of dynamic tension. In my experience, emotions control minds and bodies a lot more than minds and bodies control emotions. And emotions are so subtle and stealthy when they take over. They often come with an instant cover-story that reframes what's happening as being rational, willful, and chosen.

When you're getting angry or defensive with your romantic partner, it's always for a "good reason" that makes perfect sense to you. But upon reflection later, you may see that the trigger was about something much more primal and animal in nature, and that the "good reason" you had was a made-up rationalization to protect your own ego from having to wake up and take responsibility for your part in the conflict.

If you invest some time noticing and actually feeling your emotions, you can switch on the lights in parts of your experience that are usually almost completely dark. These are your blind spots. This awareness has you observe the process by which the older, more instinctive parts of your psyche assert themselves and influence how you think, communicate, behave, and interact.

It's most powerful to notice the internal physical sensation of emotions because it allows you to process them much better. Once you start learning to feel how your emotions manifest in your body, you can breathe into and help them move through you without getting stuck.

Most people, in my experience, do not allow themselves to have complete emotion cycles. If they become upset something that another person said, they become sad or angry and go into a pattern of complaint or attack, but then never return to feel the sadness and hurt that was activated in the first place. If they feel envy because another person has something they want, or jealousy, this often manifests as aggression - which can trigger a cycle of escalating conflict that distracts from ever going back and feeling the deeper, more relevant feeling that was activated.

As you notice your emotional state, try asking yourself these questions:

1. Where exactly are those sensations in your body?
2. Is it below the skin, deep inside your body, or at the surface?
3. What color are the sensations?
4. Are they warm or cold?
5. Do they have a texture?
6. Are they moving? In which direction?
7. Do they have a form or shape, or even a personality?

As you notice these aspects of your emotional state, you'll also see that your emotions are typically in flux. If you stay with an emotion, especially one that's unpleasant to experience, such as sadness, or anger, or fear, or jealousy or envy, you not only get a much better sense of what the emotion is trying to tell you, but you help the emotion process through your system to completion.

NOTE: If what I am saying right now is particularly resonating with you, and you want to go deeper with this type of work, you may want to look up a somatic therapist who is familiar with multiple therapeutic modalities. I prefer to work with people who know both Western and Eastern methods, who integrate science and intuition to create their own style.

Emotions change our thinking, and our behavior. When we are under the influence of strong emotions, it essentially changes us into a different person. We all have multiple "subpersonalities" - and just like the Pixar movie "Inside Out" shows so brilliantly, when one of these multiple aspects of our personality takes over, it can have powerful consequences.

In a discussion of emotions, it's important to also remember that emotions serve a primarily social function. If you're feeling a strong emotion, it's likely that it is over a relationship with another person or group of people. And because this strong emotion is influencing your perceptions, thinking, decision making, communication, and actions… and because others are also feeling different types of emotions in the situation which are influencing their thinking and behavior… there is a sort of higher dynamic that is controlling the interactions. You can imagine a marionette standing over the group, pulling strings on different people emotionally, and conducting the play from another dimension.

Shakespeare and other great dramatists had a brilliant intuitive understanding of these higher patterns and dynamics of human psychological and social drama. In Romeo & Juliet, the juxtaposition of teenagers from enemy families falling in love, navigating through a tragedy of conflict, then ultimately killing themselves, resulting in the families reconciling… puts one on a rollercoaster of emotions. But it also reveals underlying human social dynamics in a way that no "real" story could. By recognizing these mythological meta-patterns, timeless storylines, and recurring human dramas, we can start to see how each emotion we feel is a puzzle piece in a bigger puzzle… itself just another iteration of an infinite variety of the similar narratives being played out through the history of the world.

Emotions play a big role in how you relate to and interact with the opportunity in your life. And getting in tune with some of the emotional dynamics that you'll encounter as you discover and design opportunities is important to the process of development in this area.

I mentioned that emotions are primarily a social phenomena. They tend to be strongest and most influential when other people and groups are involved. Because other people are also very interested in pursuing opportunity, this creates a very high probability that strong emotions will be triggered as you interact in social dynamics with others around it.

Envy

It's an interesting experience to be in the presence of someone who has already achieved the thing you want in life. For me, it often feels like an interesting cocktail of awe, admiration, excitement, anxiety, and self-consciousness… combined with coveting and wanting what they have… which is envy.

If you are going to master opportunity, it will require you to spend more and more time around people who are increasingly successful. It's an interesting experience to be in the presence of someone who's already achieved the things you want in life, or someone who is a master of a domain that you would like to master yourself.

I can remember the first time I saw Joe Stumpf, a coach and real estate teacher, on stage. I was 22 years old and had just gone into real estate in Eugene, Oregon. He did a free half-day seminar at a local hotel conference room. I was trying to understand sales and marketing at the time, and he was probably the most charismatic person I had ever seen. I can still remember feeling a rush of excitement, because I was learning something that felt like it was going to change my life… while at the same time feeling envy and self-consciousness because I wanted that kind of success and didn't know how to get it.

I can also remember the first time seeing the visual art of Android Jones at Burning Man. I had never seen anything like it. The sophisticated digital style was so alien to me that I was both attracted and somewhat confused by it at the same time. The more I looked at it, the more I realized that I was in the presence of something new and important. I could not believe that someone could layer in so many different ways of looking at reality into one picture. I was seeing everything in new ways, and this created a feeling of excitement, anxiety, and curiosity. I was also overcome by the desire to have a piece of this art on my wall. As I have gotten to know Android over the last several years, I am continually floored by his ability to create visual masterpieces, and I feel envy because no matter how hard I try, I can only accomplish a tiny fraction of what he can visually.

I can remember the night I fell in love with my wife. We were having a conversation about mathematics, philosophy and culture, and she started comparing the personalities of different cultures to each other, while referencing abstract mathematics. and I was in awe of her. She was using terms like, "fractal" and "holographic" and referencing Godel's incompleteness theorem . Very Sexy!

But along with the feelings of awe and appreciation, I also felt other feelings in these situations. Pangs of fear, shame, envy and discouragement.

It has only been through the process of exploring my emotions that I have learned emotions are never "pure." We are always carrying the mixed cocktail of emotions in our systems, some designed to get us to move away from certain things, some designed to get us to move toward certain things, some that trigger certain thoughts, and some that repress other thoughts.

As I become more sensitive to my own emotions, I notice that I experience at least a little bit of envy every time I hear about someone who's more successful in a domain that I am working on. Sometimes I even experience it when I see someone doing something I'll never want to learn how to do!

If you're going to master opportunity in your life, it's important to get real about what's actually happening in your body, emotions, and mind - so you can work with it. I have watched people who became completely immobilized by envy, who were so "green with envy" that they couldn't function in their normal lives.

If you find yourself experiencing envy, try this approach that I learned from author and motivational speaker T. Harv Ecker. In one of his seminars, he recommended a blessing that he learned from the Hawaiian Huna tradition. It goes like this: "Bless that which you want." The idea is that if you see someone who has achieved success in the domain that you are pursuing, say "Bless you." When you bless that which you want, you remember that it's a positive thing that the other person has achieved this success.

Another approach is to remember the power of social influences. When you can see a person with your own eyes who has achieved something that you would like to achieve, it becomes instantly more possible for you. People thought it was impossible to run a mile in under four minutes until Roger Bannister did it in 1954. Then almost immediately, another person ran a four minute mile. Then soon after, three people ran a mile in under four minutes all in one race.

If you were a runner at that time, you likely would have envied Roger Bannister when you saw him finish in under four minutes. But if you then realized that it was **possible** because you knew about a real person who did it, another part of your unconscious mind would have also been saying to itself "Oh, this is possible. Maybe I can do this."

So if you see someone who is highly successful doing something you want to do, or who discovered or created an opportunity before you, bless them. And remember that they have just shown you proof that it's possible. They have saved you a lot of time, and you can use them as a positive role model. Even if they had an advantage that you don't have, bless them, and appreciate them.

As you become more successful in your life, remember that your success will trigger envy in others. One of the reasons why it is important to be grateful for your good fortune, and to remain humble, is to prevent the suffering that goes along with the feeling of envy for others.

Showing off, bragging, and broadcasting your success unnecessarily might feel good to the ego, but it doesn't feel good to others' egos. And in the long-run, it's not the way to build a good reputation and a happy life, or to attract good people to your social and business circles. Even as you learn to integrate your own envy, avoid unconsciously or consciously doing things that trigger it in others.

The Fear Instinct

Opportunity and fear go hand in hand. As you discover and develop more opportunities in life, you will see there are risks and sometimes dangers involved. It's useful to get to know your fear better, so you may dance, rather than fight with it.

All mammals (including humans) are programmed by evolution to feel fear when confronted with certain stimuli. We respond in certain ways to keep ourselves safe, to live another day and reproduce.What's important to know about fear is that it completely changes how you perceive the world. It also changes how you perceive your own thoughts and ideas, and how you perceive yourself.

Fear tends to trigger us to do things that worked in the **past** to help us **avoid loss or death**. Fear does this instinctively, without engaging our rational minds. In fact, it short circuits our rationality, and shuts it down. When we're scared we tend to act first and think later. If we think at all when afraid, it tends to be a particular type: imagining what could go wrong. This catastrophizing tends to amplify the fear and our tendency to act on instinct. Instead of reflective and considered thought, we revert to programmed actions that have worked in the past.

If it's dark and we hear a sudden noise, we might duck and hide, because this was the best way our ancestors knew to avoid hungry predators that prowl at night. This is an automated adaptation we carry inside us, a sequence of perceiving a situation and then an impulse to do something in response, that has little to do with our conscious mind (which knows there's no lions in our bedroom).

What's important to note about this pattern is that it compels you to avoid novelty and experimentation. Fear increases our aversion to risk. It activates a conservative "avoid loss" strategy. And if you want to avoid loss, the safest bet is to do what has worked in the past.

But as we're learning, the future we are rapidly transitioning into is increasingly novel, and requires us to use not only tried-and-true approaches, but also new and innovative ones. Fear can be an impediment to thriving in this future.

If you find yourself in a situation that triggers fear, but that also requires a novel approach, you'll be less likely to discover that approach - or even be aware of it. Fear blinds us to opportunity in this way. When we are fearful, the very meaning of opportunity changes. The understanding of opportunity that we're learning and developing here disappears. It becomes invisible. When we're afraid, the only opportunities we can see are the ones that involve preserving the status-quo, staying safe and avoiding loss.

Fear & Cognitive Biases

Nobel prize-winning psychologist Daniel Kahneman and his research partner Amos Tversky ran a series of experiments, seeking to understand how people behave when faced with choices related to risk and return.

If you say to someone "I'm going to flip a coin, and if it comes up tails, you lose $100. How much would you have to win if it comes up heads in order to take this gamble?" Most people respond that they need to win at least $200 to take the bet. In other words, most people will not take a risk unless their potential gain is double the potential loss.

If you do the math on this one, you realize that you should take the bet at any amount over $100, as you have the odds in your favor. Let's say that someone offers you $120 if it comes up heads, but you have to pay $100 if it comes up tails. Now imagine doing this exercise 100 times in a row, and averaging out the results.

If it comes up 50 times heads, you win $6,000. If it comes up 50 times tails, you lose $5,000. At the end of the day, you win $1,000 in this thought experiment. The odds are 10% in your favor, and when situations like this arise in life, we need to go for them, and experience the cumulative benefit that comes from these incremental wins.

This phenomenon scales up and down, to any amount of value being considered, in any situation in life. If you're saying "I can't afford to lose $100" - that's fine. But we can't afford to lose our lives, either - and most of us go out driving on roads at freeway speeds without a second thought.

Kahneman and Tversky called this insight - that people will do twice as much to avoid losing something as they'll do to get it in the first place - "Prospect Theory." Again, stated simply, it's that people are twice as motivated by loss as they are by gain. This is one of many "cognitive biases," the discovery of which have led to a field called behavioral economics that is worth studying at some point for all of us.

Some key types of fear to notice are:

Fear of loss.
Fear of conflict.
Fear of rejection.
Fear of the unknown.
Fear of ambiguity.
Fear of missing out.
Fear of death, the mother of all fears.

Each has its own subtle character and experience. And each affects us in a particular way, depending on its strength.

In his book *Emotional Intelligence*, Daniel Goleman explains the process of "flooding" - where our systems become flooded with chemicals that activate our primitive emotional systems, and prepare us to run or fight.

If you find yourself flooded with fear, it's important to know you've been pulled into your lower animal mind, and to not make any long-term decisions if at all possible. When in fear, we are in pure "avoid loss" mode, and essentially unable to make good long-term decisions.

This is particularly true when it comes to opportunity. You can't make a good decision about opportunity when you're fearful, so don't even try. If you find yourself afraid, or activated by strong emotions in general, stop and take a few breaths. Even if you can just stay still a few minutes and wait for that flood of chemicals to subside, it can make a huge difference in the long-run.

Making the wrong decision, saying the wrong thing, making the wrong commitment, can be so expensive. When you're flooded with fear, your mind is hijacked, and you are put into a state of impulsive loss avoidance. You are basically thinking the way an animal would be thinking if it was faced with being eaten. Making decisions based on the survival instinct will not get you to your goals, or help you become self-actualized.

Fear is not a good place from which to assess the long-term value of an opportunity. You become "strategically blind" when you are fearful.

If you find yourself in a fearful state, try this NLP technique: Imagine that you're standing behind yourself, looking over your own shoulder at the situation. This is a conscious dissociation exercise, and it can help you step outside of your emotions for a moment - long enough to take a few breaths and get control. Try doing this exercise right now, and notice how it shifts your emotional state instantly.

Breathing is also particularly helpful. If I find myself in fear, I will often start taking slow, deep breaths, keeping attention on the breath. If thoughts come up, I release them and return to attending to my breath. The combination of the oxygen, plus the mindfulness, helps me relax and release spikes of fear.

What else should be done if you are feeling fearful? The first thing to remember is: **Don't think about the future or make decisions that will impact the future when you are in fear.**

If you think about the future when you are fearful, you will enter a pessimistic imaginary dystopia where "success" means "not having your nightmares come true." This state is akin to paranoia. The best you will be able to imagine is hanging on to what you currently have. Fear-based imagination is devastating to growth and progress in life. It causes you to make decisions that reduce opportunity in the future.

Other tips for responding when you feel fear:

- Deactivate imagination, and come into the moment
- Stop looking at the signals that are triggering the fear
- Go on a data fast immediately - stop going online, stop reading news
- Engage in a productive activity with other people

FOMO

An interesting manifestation of fear that comes up for many of us is FOMO, or "fear of missing out."

As I'm writing this book, cryptocurrency has been hitting mainstream consciousness. I have been watching as my friends and family are freaking out over having not invested yet. I am getting contacted by people I haven't heard from in years, asking me if I think that they should invest. What all of them have in common is that they have a powerful case of FOMO. They are afraid that they are going to miss out on a big gain, and then possibly hate themselves for it later.

Fear of missing out is cousin to another psychological-emotional state in humans: Anticipatory Regret. Many of us do not make decisions based on what we want but instead based on avoiding a potential negative consequences of the decision or action, and subsequent regret. Let's say you've been building a business for a year, but then you see others you know successfully launching businesses in other niches.

Some of them have become financial winners. You can see they are achieving success much faster than you, and you start to notice a part of yourself saying, "Maybe you should quit what you're doing, and go start one of those other businesses."

This is FOMO talking.

It's important not to make any rash decisions from this state. When you make a decision based on FOMO, you will definitely not take all of the possible variables into consideration, and your decision ultimately won't be the most strategic, long-term, and beneficial for you. It also looks bad to others. People can sense when you are making a decision out of desperation and FOMO, and they'll respect you less for it.

If you find yourself thinking about doing something other than what you're doing because you don't want to miss out on some benefit that others are enjoying, remind yourself that this is what FOMO feels like.

In order to master FOMO, as with any emotion, it's important to notice when you are feeling it. Can you remember a time where you experienced the fear of missing out on something? Can you remember the feeling you had about it? See if you can get back in touch with the feeling of that physical-emotional-mental state. Once you have it, notice the inner sensations that it brings up. Tune in to the feelings in your body, and notice where they are. Feel their texture, pressure, color, movement. Now say the word "FOMO" to yourself, to anchor the experience to the word. This can help you identify when you're experiencing FOMO in real-time in the future, so you can be proactive with it.

As another exercise, if you are feeling FOMO in the present moment, pause and mentally project yourself to much later in your life. Look back, and consider for a moment how many opportunities you are going to miss or pass up. Realize that you're going to be OK if you miss this one, because there are a lot more opportunities coming.

Discovery in the Light & Darkness

In the history of evolution and innovation, nature often solves the same problem in several different ways. This is called "convergent evolution." The ability to use light to observe surroundings has come in the form of the eye, which evolved independently in humans, beetles and spiders - along with dozens of others. So too the wing for flight has developed in birds, insects and bats.

Human innovation contains examples as well. Calculus was independently invented by Newton and Leibniz at the same time. Evolution was discovered independently by Darwin and Wallace. In science, they call this pattern "multiple discovery." I have personally noticed this phenomenon accelerating dramatically with the rise of the internet.

When I have an insight about a potential opportunity, I now think to myself "someone else is already thinking about this, or will think about this soon. It's going to happen whether I do it or not." I find that this helps me stay closer to a state of equanimity, and be less apt to be pulled into a state of possessiveness or obsession if I see that someone else is executing on the idea that I had. It also helps me be more open with my ideas.

It's intuitive for some people to be secretive about ideas that they think might be valuable. I have people ask me questions like these regularly:

"Should I trademark my name or idea before I tell anyone about it?"

"Will you sign this Non-Disclosure Agreement, so I can tell you about my idea?"

"How do I prevent people from stealing my digital book or teaching product?"

This tells me that we're all thinking about these things more and more.

Something to keep in mind: Each of us has our own unique way of expressing or implementing an idea. I regularly collaborate with my "competitors" - we speak in each other's courses and programs, we promote for each other, and we advise each other.

If you and I work in a similar market or niche and see each other as competitors, we'll feel threatened by each other. We will become overly vigilant, and territorial. We might even become suspicious and obsessed. On the other hand, if we see each other as collaborators, and we have faith that each of us has our own unique way of doing what we do, and that we are better off working together, we can build a relationship and help each other. If I teach you how to write a book, and someone else teaches you how to write a book, we are each going to do it very differently.

This mindset requires you to remember that most of the time, as long as you are dealing with people who have integrity, that everything will work out. There are going to be times where it doesn't work out, and part of the long-term success game is taking those setbacks, losses, and missed expectations in stride.

If you find yourself becoming overly possessive and secretive about ideas you haven't implemented yet, it's probably a signal to relax a little, and remember that someone is going to come up with the same idea (and likely already has), and that what you really need to do is implement it and see if you can get traction and turn your idea into a successful project - rather than worrying about what other people are doing.

Jealousy

Of the emotional experiences that "abduct" us, jealousy is one of the most powerful. Jealousy is typically defined in sexual and romantic terms. It's the experience of becoming emotionally activated by a fear of abandonment, typically combined with humiliation and anger, because you believe that your love interest might leave you for someone else.

When you are under the influence of jealousy, you typically become passively or actively aggressive. This feeling of anger usually masks the underlying fear of abandonment that is the hallmark of jealousy. When someone is jealous, they'll often project their emotions outward, getting upset about something besides the real issue.

"She's trying too hard," a woman might say about a perceived rival.

"He's an idiot," a man might say about a romantic threat.

These statements are typically laced with anger, contempt or moral indignation. As jealousy usually masquerades as aggression, when a jealous statement is made, the person saying it actually believes in the moment that the anger is the "real issue." Jealousy is stealthy. It hides its tracks as it pushes us into becoming a "shadow version" of ourselves. But jealousy has a unique feel to it. Both emotionally as you're experiencing it, and also when you are witnessing someone else feeling it. Once you learn to recognize jealousy, hiding behind the mask of anger, it becomes much more obvious to spot.

CAN YOU REMEMBER A time in your life when you felt jealousy? Maybe you had a partner who left you for someone else, or was cheating on you. Perhaps you were worried they would leave you, and you became suspicious and obsessed about their communication with others. Can you remember the feeling?

Have you ever felt jealousy in a different context? Jealousy extends beyond romantic relationships. You can feel jealous if a good friend of yours becomes better friends with someone else. Or if a business partner you are working with on a idea leaves your project to go to work with someone else. Or if someone "steals" the idea that you have, and uses it to start a business.

It feels very vulnerable to reveal that you're feeling jealous. Even to yourself. I suspect our emotional systems are designed to conceal jealousy from our consciousness, as it's too painful to admit it because it feels shameful and degrading to your status.

Jealousy starts early, and stays with most of us in some form through our lives. My 4-year old daughter often displays signs of jealousy when I'm hugging my wife (and there's evidence that children feel it starting as early as 6 months old). My daughter will often stop what she's doing, come over to us when we are hugging, and push us apart so she can be in the middle.

I can remember when I was maybe 12 or 13 years old going out for a day to a water park with two friends. At the end of the day, one of them was angry at me for playing with the other one most of the day. It didn't make sense to me at the time, but now I recognize that he was feeling jealous.

If it's hard to admit to ourselves when we're jealous, it's even harder to admit to another, especially your partner. It's even worse to be accused of it by them. When a person is in the throes of jealousy, it's essentially impossible to reason with them. They are typically self-deceived into thinking that the issue is something other than jealousy, so you aren't going to be successful trying to talk sense with them.

It's actually an interesting learning experience to try to reason with someone who is feeling jealous. Every time you make a good point about something, they only get more upset, because it's making them feel more suspicious and possessive. Because they are interpreting everything you're saying through a lens of being threatened, every rationale that you provide only serves to heighten their paranoia!

I can remember going out on a date with a girlfriend years ago, and visiting a nightclub where a male friend worked. We walked in together, and I immediately spotted my friend's girlfriend standing nearby. I walked over to give her a hug, but when my date saw this, she immediately became angry and upset. I asked "What's wrong?" and she said "Who's that girl?!" I tried explaining it was my friend's girlfriend, but this seemed to only upset her and make her more suspicious. Have you ever been in a similar situation?

It's easy to see it when you look at other people, but much harder to spot when you're the one feeling jealous. If you're feeling jealous, you are under a spell, possessed by this ancient, dark animal spirit. And you will likely not know consciously that it's jealousy that is animating your fear, aggression, and imaginings.

Remember: We don't tend to think of ourselves as feeling jealous in contexts outside of romantic relationships, but it happens all the time. When you're feeling threatened and possessive, you're typically feeling jealous, even if it's over an idea. If you find yourself fearful and paranoid that you might lose something because someone else will get it first, or take it from you, it's possible that jealousy has possessed you. This also means that if you're feeling jealous, YOU are under a spell, possessed by this ancient, animal spirit. And you will likely not know consciously that it's jealousy that is animating your fear, aggression, and imaginings.

I was recently having a dialog with an artist who has been gaining some popularity, and who has had his style copied by someone else online. He was upset, and he was investing a lot of time, thought, and energy into trying to protect his style from others copying it. I immediately sensed the presence of jealousy.

Competition can activate jealousy. Watch for it when you see a person or business that occurs as a potential rival. Again, the signal you're looking for is anger or aggression. You'll possessed by the thought of possessing something or someone.

If you say "I'm just not a jealous person," that's great. It might also mean that you haven't had something that you really cared about and then were faced with losing it. Keep an open mind, because it just might arise when you have something that you perceive as really important on the line.

When jealousy arises, just notice it. Say, "hello jealousy," and then do some breathing. Reflect on the thing, person, or idea that you might lose if your worst fear comes true. Make peace with that potential outcome, and go to work creating more opportunity in your life. Even treat it as an opportunity in and of itself, to figure out how to make that part of your life even better than you might have expected before.

I also like to notice that if I'm feeling jealousy, that there's often something to admire about the other person or group that I feel threatened by. If you notice what you admire, you can get a free lesson in how to upgrade yourself or your project. Try it!

If jealousy really seems to have you, then you might want to get some professional help. Some people are more sensitive to these types of emotions, and if you're one of them, that's fine. Just know what you're dealing with, and be proactive. There are expert therapists who specialize in helping people who have strong jealousy, and it just might help you to find one.

Don't let this powerful emotion abduct your good sense and prevent you from being successful in the long-term.

The Stress of Increasing Opportunity

Part of the stress that flows from opportunity comes from the sheer choices that we are faced with.

As we mentioned earlier, Dr. Barry Schwartz, in his book *The Paradox of Choice*, explains that we believe that more choices will make us happier. And up to a point, they do. But past a handful of good choices, we start to experience a decreasing level of happiness and more stress, because too many choices overwhelm our judgement systems. The cognitive load is too big when faced with so many choices. There are many ways we could make a choice that we'll regret later, or miss the choice that will make us the happiest. Mapping all those permutations can be harrowing.

I was just shopping online for a headset to use for calls. I wanted something that plugs directly into the headphone jack on my computer. As I was searching through the options, trying to find something that would work for my needs, I was shocked at how many different types of headsets are available. I spent probably an hour just trying to find a simple headset.

In his book, Schwartz explains two strategies for dealing with increasing choice. He calls these "maximizing" and "satisficing." Maximizers look at all their options and then compare them to try to find the very best one. They won't settle for less than the very best. Satisficers use a different approach. They decide what they want, then go look for a solution that will satisfy their needs. If there's something marginally better out there, then so be it. They're not bothered.

For example, a maximizer will buy a car by comparing all of the models to each other, test driving all of them, finding the one with the best features and most options. They will research online and in person to find the very best price. And then after they buy, they will watch the market to see if something better comes along or the price drops, and feel bad if it does because they missed out.

If a satisficer is buying a car, they will consider what they need in a car, and make a list of what they care about. Then they will go looking for something that satisfies their needs, and when they find it, they will buy it. They will move on to other things, and not worry about whether or not they made the right choice. Once a satisficer finds something that meets their needs, they move on to other things.

These are obviously stylized descriptions of idealized types. But you probably recognize yourself in one of the descriptions, and if you're a "maximizer" then it's useful for you to know that maximizing is not only a strategy for finding the very best thing at the very best price, but can also be a recipe for dissatisfaction and unhappiness.

Satisficing is more than just a technique. It can also become a way of approaching life. It turns out that there are a handful of things in life that lead to a feeling of wellness, happiness, meaning, success and fulfillment. These are things like enough sleep, daily exercise, balanced meals, time with people we care about, continual learning, thinking positively, and being present in the moment. None of these is revolutionary or sexy, so we tend to miss their importance in life.

A big part of the fulfillment game is to allow yourself to be satisfied with something that does what you need it to do, and not to become obsessed with getting the best thing at the best price, being a super-parent, looking like you're on the cover of a magazine, or having more money than you need to live a lifestyle that is sufficient for your needs.

Maximizing as an approach can really lead us to be overwhelmed by all of the options and choices in our lives, because each option has slightly different trade-offs, and slightly different potential implications. The opportunity you don't need to consider is the one that will create a big positive result that isn't going to contribute to your overall fulfillment with life. If you pursue an opportunity that also stresses you out, makes you feel anxious or worried, puts you in a situation where you're working with people you don't like, changes your values to a configuration that's not right for you, etc. then it's probably not a good opportunity for you.

Cool, Calm, Collected

Dr. Hans Selye, a Hungarian doctor and scientist, noticed that patients who were sick had a type of common appearance - they all "looked sick" - and he proposed the generalized phenomena that he called "stress."

The idea is that when a person experiences sickness, emotional trauma, or external pressure, that we have an overall response that we experience as a feeling of stress on our systems. I think that it's important to understand this generalized experience of feeling stress, and to develop the ability to recognize when we're feeling it in real time.

The Great Acceleration, while miraculous in its creative power, is also creating more stress in our lives, across more dimensions, than we have experienced before. Witness the rise in depression, suicide, mass shootings, and general anxiety about the security and safety of life - even while we're enjoying the lowest levels of war and violence in recorded history - along with the biggest growth boom, and extension of lifespan.

We're living longer, we're more successful, we have access to more amazing technology and knowledge, and yet we're feeling more fear and anxiety about it all. I believe that this is natural, because the stakes in life just keep going up, and it's appropriate to feel some level of anxiety when a lot is on the line.

One of the reasons why I am fascinated with the study of opportunity is this paradox of having more and more opportunity in our lives, and yet feeling more and more stress as a result. Some of this comes because growth, success, and wealth is not equally distributed in the world, and this triggers much envy, jealousy, and sour grapes. There's a great video of an experiment with capuchin monkeys, that caricatures this phenomenon. An experimenter walks up to a pair of cages, each one with a monkey inside. The monkeys can see each other and they can see what happens next.

The experimenter trades one monkey a grape for a little rock (monkey money), then goes to the other cage, and when the monkey gives her a little rock, she gives the monkey a slice of cucumber (instead of a grape).

Now, normally capuchin monkeys love cucumbers, and will gladly trade one of their little money rocks for a slice. But in this case, the monkey just watched its neighbor trade its rock for a grape - which monkeys like even more than cucumbers. When the experimenter does the same thing again, trading the first monkey a grape, then moving to the second monkey and offering a cucumber, the monkey becomes angry and throws the cucumber out of the cage! Even a great opportunity can be upsetting if we see others getting better ones that we think are unfair.

I like to learn about new domains in life, and build skills in areas that are unknown and challenging to me. I can remember when I went into the real estate business in my early 20s. I often felt a sense of envy when people would call my broker, and ask her to come over and list their property for sale. I would think to myself "She just had someone call out of the blue and invite her to go make thousands of dollars... why didn't they call me?" It felt very unfair.

I can remember when I was in my mid-twenties, and socially awkward. I would see men who could go out anytime and meet women and get dates. It felt so unfair that some men could meet girls anywhere, and I could only meet the feeling of fear and anxiety!

Over time, I have learned that there is a deeper lesson in situations like these. I've seen that by making a commitment to learn for myself, and by overcoming my initial emotional upsets, that I could befriend and learn from people who got great results in life... and I could make the investment of time and effort to go and learn for myself.

I also learned that most people who were successful in a particular domain are good people who like helping others. They aren't living their lives in order to stress other people out or make them feel inferior, and they will gladly help you if you show an honest desire to learn.

I'm always on the lookout for a hidden benefit within an apparent pain, cost, loss, or stress. And in the case of exponentially increasing opportunity, what I've personally tried to do is use this experience to practice staying cool, calm and collected in the middle of an increasing sense of chaos in many simultaneous life domains - and in the face of increasing unfairness.

As you probably know, in the center of a hurricane is the eye, where things are completely calm. Often, after hours of gale-force winds, people going through a storm will hear things suddenly go quiet. They will look outside, and the wind will have stopped, and it might even be sunny and clear. What they don't realize is that the eye of the storm is passing over them, and that the wind is about to return going just as fast, only in the opposite direction. This has led to many great tragedies - just like it does when someone standing on a beach watches the sea recede, not realizing this sign precedes a tsunami. They often walk out INTO the space where the tidal wave is about to hit.

But we can turn this concept around, and transform the eye of the storm from a period of terrible danger to one of recuperation. If we're experiencing dramatic and stressful change or instability, we can remember that somewhere near the most intense part of the dynamic there will be a calm spot where we can catch our breath, relax, and get perspective that allows us to master the challenge.

I like to imagine that every tsunami has a type of surfboard that allows you to ride the big wave, and to move with its power. I live at the beach in Miami, Florida, and when there are storms we will often see kiteboarders out in the wind and waves, cruising at car speeds, leaping dozens of yards at a stretch, and obviously turning the storm into an opportunity for radical enjoyment.

Big wave surfers go even further. They watch the global weather forecasts, specifically looking for huge weather systems that will create huge surf, then they will drop everything in their lives, and fly to that part of the world in order to surf the monster 50-foot waves!

This might sound a bit far-fetched for most people, but inside of each of us is a fearless warrior that can rise to the surface, and take on the challenges that life throws at us. There is also a peaceful monk inside of us, who can take a deep breath and meditate on the gift and miracle of life when necessary.

Receive Your Gifts From the Universe

A Zen monk was walking through the forest, when all of a sudden, a huge tiger appeared and began to chase him. Running away, he came to the edge of a cliff. He saw a vine growing down over the cliff, so he started to climb down. As he got out of reach of the tiger, he looked down, and another tiger appeared below, growling. At that moment, two mice appeared, one white and one black. They began to chew away at the vine that the monk was holding on to. As they got closer and closer to chewing through the vine, the monk looked over, and noticed a small plant growing out of the side of the cliff right next to him, with a single, ripe strawberry hanging from it. He reached out with one hand to pick it, and put it into his mouth. He closed his eyes. "Delicious!"

Android Jones, the artist, has a painting titled "Monarch Dragon." If you look closely, you'll see the outline of a child standing in front of the dragon, looking up to its face. Upon closer examination, we realize the dragon is made up of butterflies.

When I am triggered by my wife, and I've been upset with her over something, there is a moment when I start "coming back" and remembering that I love her and that our relationship is the most important thing in my life. Sometimes it takes a few minutes, sometimes hours, and sometimes days. But that transition always comes. If I can remember to notice my state right as I'm coming back, and then consider how we got into the conflict in the first place, I always have a powerful insight.

Your ability to do this in diverse situations in life determines much of your experience as a human. I recommend that you see and receive the gifts from the universe, even if there is a hurricane raging outside, or a tiger growling at you.

The Ethics & Morals of Opportunity

We are about to cross over into learning powerful mental models for discovering and developing opportunities in our lives. As we leave the emotional conversation, this is a perfect juncture to discuss the ethics and morals of opportunity.

As I have gotten to know "brilliant opportunists" in my life, I have noticed a pattern. Most of them seem to be unconsciously analyzing, estimating, and calculating opportunity in relationship to the benefit or return that they will receive individually. Most strong opportunists are not basing their mental equations primarily on the costs and benefits to others, to groups, to societies, to ecosystems, etc. They are unconsciously externalizing the bigger picture costs of the opportunity, and internalizing the benefits, without realizing that this is happening.

An extreme version of this would be someone who destroys a natural ecosystem and plunders the resources so they can turn them into money and power for themselves. In the world of business and finance, this type might be characterized by the corporate raider doing a "leveraged buyout corporate takeover" - which buys a company and dismantles it to sell in pieces, so they can make a profit. There is typically no consideration of the effect on the people and families that depend on the survival of the corporation for income, or the loss of the benefit that the company provides to the world.

I have come to believe that this pattern of only seeing "benefits-to-self" as having its roots in a deeper level of animal-human nature. Once it is understood better by society, it will serve each of us and all of us to help us achieve our values and purposes in life.

Let's consider the conversation of ethics and morals from the perspective of personality type. In reading Ken Wilber's work, I was introduced to the dual modes of life and expression of "agency and communion" as first described by David Bakan.

Agency is the impulse or instinct to assert or express self, to master the environment and world around you, to achieve and become powerful. Communion is the intuition that the group or collective is the "real" entity, and it's the impulse to synchronize with others to serve the greater good.

Some people seem natively oriented "agentic" - meaning they see the individual self as basic unit of reality and life. They see people as individuals who are separate, autonomous agents who have their own agendas. They tend to orient their lives based on their own survival, expression, and success. This archetype experiences a sense of success and fulfillment through their individual accomplishments and realization of independence. They think that everyone "normal" is this way, and should behave this way.

They say things like "self-preservation is the first law of nature" (Samuel Adams). In my study of this type (of which I am one), the key distinction is a sense of boundaries. They perceive themselves as separate at a fundamental level, and their psychological structure is about putting themselves and their needs first.

On the other hand, people who seem to be oriented "communal" see the group as the basic unit of reality and life. This type experiences a sense of fulfillment through their relationships with others and a sense of belonging. They seek to help the group survive, express itself and succeed. These types also feels that everyone "normal" is like them, and all should behave as they do. They experience the group, the family, the collective as their central concern in life. They tend to look at things from the perspective and others as their main way of orienting in the world.

Some research I've read suggests that these communal archetypes take a more holistic perspective. My experience with this type (of which my wife is one), suggest they are naturally oriented to being a good member of their "group entity," whether that be a couple, family, organization, or culture (e.g. nation, religion, fashion).

Of these two types of agentic and communal, some are extreme. Ayn Rand, an icon of individualism or what we're calling the agentic type, went so far as saying that inferior minds had collective instincts, and that a collective mind or entity doesn't exist. This is not uncommon with the agentic type. Many people are triggered and offended at the idea of a "collective entity" or the idea that there is a group intelligence or entity existing beyond the level of the individual human or animal body.

Gandhi was a powerful icon of collectivism - or what we're calling communion - or the communal type. He said things like: "Where there is love, there is life" and "The best way to find yourself is to lose yourself in the service of others." This goes all the way to equating individual meaning and purpose with complete dedication and service of others.

Science has its own version of we are calling a communal paradigm. It comes from the evolutionary-biological domains. They call it "group selection" - where the basic unit of evolution is the group (or in multi-level selection, a more sophisticated model in my opinion, it considers multiple levels of groups and individuals as co-evolving entities).

At their extremes, agentics tend to feel repulsion, revulsion, or even hatred for the other polarity. Strong individualist types are often willing to die before coming under the influence of a communal group or culture. Individuals sometimes risk going to prison because they don't want to pay taxes and contribute to the nation where they are a citizen.

Magda and Joseph Goebbels killed their own children (and themselves) because they couldn't imagine their kids growing up in a society that wasn't national socialist. Many people kill themselves performing suicide missions for their causes or groups. Again, we're talking about extremes, but I see these anecdotes as making a strong case for underlying agentic and communal types.

Agentic types like to keep their opportunities secret. They use opportunity to benefit themselves. Many highly agentic types will take opportunity from others in order to have more (unconsciously and consciously). Communal types feel compelled to share opportunity. An opportunity for them is an opportunity for all of us - or for the planet. The communal type gives their opportunity away freely to others (unconsciously, and consciously).

As you consider opportunities in your life, I encourage you to look at them from both the perspective of self interest and the perspective of collective interest. A great opportunity should ideally benefit you personally in a very meaningful way, and also be an overall contribution to social and even ecological good.

Avoid the trap of thinking that if something benefits everyone, then it also benefits you. Or that if something benefits you, then everyone benefits. While these can be true, my experience is that they are sentiments that are typically used to camouflage obsessive or maladaptive over-identification with one of these two polarities that we're discussing.

Frederic Bastiat said: "By virtue of exchange one man's prosperity is beneficial to all others." I like to paraphrase sentiments like this one as "The way to eliminate inequality, eradicate poverty, and save the world is to MAKE ME RICH!" These types of quotes are often used by selfish people who are trying to avoid contributing to the systems that supported their existence, life, and growth... so keep an eye out.

As you consider an opportunity, ask yourself if it will contribute to the long-term health and wellness of all of the people that are touched by it. Ask yourself if it will contribute to their growth and evolution. Ask yourself if it will ultimately reduce suffering and help enlighten everyone.

Will this opportunity make the world better? Will it help us become more evolved as a species? Will it put the planetary ecosystem into healthy balance? Will it encourage us to be our best selves, and make a world that works for you, the people you care about, for everyone else, and the people they care about?

Will this opportunity make my life better? Will it help me evolve personally? Will it put my life into balance? Will it encourage me to be my best self, and make my life really work?

As you work more consciously with opportunity across the different domains of your life, remember to be what Jay Abraham calls an "ethical opportunist." It's better to do something that balances the benefit between you and others than it is to do something that benefits you at the cost of others and the environment in the long-term.

I have a wise therapist friend who is often called by very wealthy people that are in their deathbeds. They call him because they need someone who can handle the intensity of what they are going through. When he arrives, they tell him how they are feeling bad because they lived their lives selfishly, neglected their families, were ruthless in business, and only considered themselves in their dealings. He looks at them, and says "Yes, and what would you like me to do about it?" When he told me this story, I was shocked awake from my trance of everyday life. My friend attempts to also offer comfort to these people who are about to die, but he made the clear point that the time to do something about this is in the beginning, not the end.

My wife and I were talking recently, and she said something that I'll never forget. She explained that our moment of death holds the potential to be either the worst experience of your life, or the most exquisite. She said that if you have really lived to your highest potential, loved with all of your being, and went for it, then the adventure of death can be your ultimate triumph.

She uses mortality as the test frame from which to assess all current behaviours. This instantly changed how I saw my life and all my actions. The question that now accompanies me daily is: Would my current behaviour contribute to me having a happy and triumphant death?

Look for opportunities that benefit you, and that also benefit others. And check in with your conscience to feel your way through the complex opportunities that you will encounter in the coming years. How you approach your opportunities will determine a lot of how you ultimately feel about the value of your life.

REMINDER: Download the "Opportunity Companion Guide" to Get Your Summaries, Checklists & Exercises

This book has an **Opportunity Companion Guide** that goes along with it, which you can download for free. It includes key chapter summaries, implementation checklists, and written exercises - plus extra chapters and other bonus material. Go here to get it now, so you can review the summaries and start implementing what you're learning:

OpportunityBonus.com

Mental Models for Creating Opportunity

A MENTAL MODEL IS a miniature map of a particular domain of life that you carry in your mind. It's a simplified version of how things work that you can learn, then use as a reference as you move through life. It's a tool to make thinking more efficient. Mental models can be used make more productive decisions when encounter situations where you would normally do something impulsively.

The word model is often used to describe a miniature version of something that you either put together as a practice, or to learn how something works. Sometimes, we assemble model cars, buildings, or machines as a hobby. When we assemble the model, we get a sense of how the bigger version works in the process.

A model is essentially a mental simulation. We all use models in our minds unconsciously to navigate through life, as we perceive our surroundings, interpret meaning, make decisions, communicate, and take action. The distinction here is that most of the models we use are unconscious. We don't mentally "pull up a map," reference it, then engage in a consideration and decision intentionally when we're using models unconsciously.

In a sense, we have already discussed these unconscious models. They often manifest in things like cognitive biases, impulses, and automatic responses to people, situations, and thoughts. We are using models to navigate in these dynamics, even though we aren't aware of their action in our perception and decision making processes.

But we want to make mental models conscious now. We're interested in learning models we can use intentionally in order to succeed, get to the next level in our lives, and discover opportunities for ourselves and others.

To better understand what a mental model is, let's use the analogy of a recipe. If you are trying to cook a particular dish, you could just guess at the ingredients and cooking process, or you could look up a recipe, and then follow it. The recipe acts as a guide, to tell you what you need in terms of the ingredients, and then how to combine them and cook them in order to create the finished dish.

A mental model, in a simple sense, can be like a recipe for thinking about a particular type of situation, or making a decision, or taking an action. You can think of mental models as recipes for success. What's great about the best mental models is that they are actually "meta recipes" meaning that they can be used as success recipes to make many different dishes, or to create many different types of outcomes. You can also use them in combinations, which multiplies their power.

I think of mental models as corrective lenses for thought. When humans invented glass lenses (eyeglasses) to correct problems with vision, we made a huge leap forward. Just imagine what a miracle it was several hundred years ago to go from being unable to see to having clear vision, by simply putting a piece of glass in front of your eye.

Mental models do this for thinking. They take fuzzy, distorted, impulsive thinking and give you a lens to use to look at a situation, your emotions, and your thinking, and see how to correct it to get better results. A good mental model helps you become more objective about a situation that previously caused you to think and behave in an automatic way that was likely invisible to you.

Another common use of the word model is the "business model." If you make a big spreadsheet, and design it so that it shows how money flows in and out of your business, how much it costs to get customers, what your expenses are, and how your investments and returns work in your business cycle, what you have created is a model of your business. It's a simplified, abstracted version of how the real business works in the real world - but it's been simplified and streamlined for ease of understanding and modeling.

A spreadsheet business model allows you to experiment with possibilities, estimate the effects of changes, and predict how investments will play out. There's something reassuringly logical and mechanical about a spreadsheet business model, because it keeps track of all of the flows from one place to another. (Business models aren't perfect, and neither are mental models, but once you use a spreadsheet to model a business, you see what a huge leap forward it is, similar to corrective lenses for vision.)

Like a spreadsheet business model, a good mental model gives you a guide to use for estimation, prediction and planning. When you use a recipe to cook a dish, you have the advantage of knowing the ingredients and the order of them, so you can plan ahead, prepare your cooking area, and scale up the recipe if you want a bigger amount of the finished dish. Mental models give you this kind of anticipatory, estimation, and predictive power.

Another fascinating thing about mental models is they act as a form of data compression for knowledge. Instead of having to carry around a perfect understanding of a domain, you can learn a mental model instead, and get most of the positive results without having to invest years of your life learning about how to deal with every possible variation of a situation.

As you learn and use mental models, you will run into challenges. This story will illustrate: One day, a farmer wanted to create a map of their property, in order to better utilize it for farming. The farmer took out a piece of paper, drew the rough shape of their land, drew the approximate location of their house, and their barn, and their fields. The farmer then realized that this map was too small and not detailed enough, so they went out to their barn, and used a much bigger piece of paper to draw their property. After working all day on a more detailed map, the farmer realized that it still wasn't detailed enough, as they needed to see how all of the contours of their fields looked, in order to better prepare them for farming. Eventually, their map got so big that it covered their entire property...

This is a silly story, but it points to the problem with maps. You can never have a map that perfectly describes the territory that it refers to, as the map would have to be the same size as the original territory. Alfred Korzybski, a Polish scholar, created a field called General Semantics, where he studied this phenomena. He famously said "the map is not the territory." His work was highly influential in the formation of Neuro-Linguistic Programming (NLP).

The trick is to have a map that is small and compact enough to be easily carried and used, but that points to all of the key features of a terrain, so that you can use it as a reference when navigating or working.

When I refer to models or mental models, this is the type of conceptual map that I'm referring to. I'm talking about an optimized model, that's just the right size.

A good mental model acts as a mental simulation tool, which you can pull up as a reference internally, and use to navigate through various situations more adaptively. It gives you enough relevant details and landmarks that you can relate the map to the experience and the process you're using it to navigate, but it doesn't bog you down with needless detail.

An example that we all know and use of an optimized model is basic math. With the numbers 0 through 9, and four operations (plus, minus, multiply, divide), we can calculate quantities, areas, volumes, costs, balance sheets, behaviors, estimations, and much more. Fourteen individual items, with an infinite set of uses.

With just this simple model, we can not only calculate much faster, but we can also calculate things that were inaccessible to us prior to knowing the model. And after using this model in our lives, we eventually begin looking at reality in a new way. We approach situations with the intuition that they can be understood. This is a huge step up in self esteem.

A great mental map is like an art piece. They can be truly beautiful in their elegant simplicity.

Another miraculous feature of mental models is their combinatorial power. The ability to use them in sequences and combinations. If I'm making a holiday meal, I can use recipes to cook many different dishes at the same time. Some will be cooked before others, and some will be cooked and prepared at the same time. One can bake while I'm making another one by hand. Some recipes make ingredients for others, and must be prepared first. Some need breaks between steps. Some need to be cooled before serving, and some need to be hot.

If I have all the recipes for all of the dishes, all loaded up into my mind, I can make the entire meal preparation process much more effectively by orchestrating all of the different recipes to work in sequences and combinations that optimize the preparation, cooking space, activities, and time.

When you have several great mental models, you can do something like this when organizing your life or business. You can see how different areas and activities all fit together, and you can get so much more done, and create so much better results.

Great mental models are essentially "modular wisdom." They are like modules of condensed knowledge and understanding that you can carry around in your mind, to reference anytime you need them.

If I am doing a marketing project, I can use different models to write my marketing copy, design the site where it will appear, buy traffic to visit the site, and calculate my return on investment. Without models, I am flying blind. But with the right combination of models, I can find opportunities and develop them into profitable campaigns.

I use models when targeting new business niches, designing products, creating marketing to get customers, hiring super-star team members, scaling my business, and building masterminds. I also use models when designing my diet, working out conflicts with my wife, raising my daughter, exercising, framing artwork, writing songs, investing, traveling, studying evolution, and doing spiritual practices.

I have invested a lot of attention and time finding and refining the models that I use to make my life work. Many of the following sections will introduce you to some of the most valuable models that I use, as applied to the discovery and development of opportunity. These models will help you understand, anticipate, predict, prepare, and position yourself for success in the future.

If you learn and use these models in your business and life, you will begin reprogramming yourself to think in a new and more conscious way. You will reshape your instincts and your intuition. You will increase the quality and quantity of opportunities in your life. And you have the potential to dramatically increase your overall success.

The Latticework

One of the early champions of the value of mental models is Charlie Munger, the self-made billionaire partner of Warren Buffett. Charlie believes that each of us should learn about one hundred mental models from diverse fields, and then practice them together in combinations in our lives.

He has spoken extensively about this, and in his book "Poor Charlie's Almanack" he explains many of his favorite models.

Charlie says that you need a "latticework of mental models." This is a beautiful metaphor. The idea is that when you combine mental models and use them in combinations to estimate, predict, analyze, make decisions, take action you get an exponential multiplying effect. Charlie calls it the "lollapalooza effect."

As you start collecting models, you begin to realize not only how valuable they are, but you also start to wonder which one of the models is most valuable. Some models are only useful in a specific situation (like a recipe for rice pudding), and some models are useful in almost every situation (like the Pareto Principle, or the 80/20 rule).

Build a "Mental Dragonfly Eye"

A dragonfly's eye has approximately 30,000 different "facets" which they use to see reality in a completely different way from humans. Instead of thinking of their eyes as being "singular," it's more useful to think of them as being "compound eyes" - each combining all of these different facets into a unique view of the world.

Dragonflies also have approximately 5-10 times as many different types of color receptors as humans, and they also perceive reality at about 4-5 times the speed that we humans experience things. To a dragonfly, we are moving at the speed of a sloth.

As you add models to your conceptual vocabulary, you begin to realize that each new model you learn and begin using in your thinking adds another facet to your mind's eye, and allows you to think more dimensionally. This is something that is difficult to describe with words, like it's difficult to describe riding a bicycle with words - compared to the thrill and experience of doing it in real life.

Mental models can both sharpen thinking and also accelerate it. And when used in combinations, and linked up into a conceptual network in the mind, they can give you a higher perspective on situations that previously had you feeling confused, trapped, or afraid.

When I learn something new, I am now mostly interested in learning the model of the particular domain that I'm experiencing more than I'm interested in learning the particular actions, procedure or skill. When you can model how a process works in your mind, you have a powerful new ability that you can take with you to other situations, and have a big advantage.

The job of an economist is to model an economy in their mind, so that they can imagine how the economy functions, and make predictions about how changes will affect the short and long-term real economy.

The job of an architect is to model a building in their mind, so they can imagine how every part of a building will come together to create a stable, usable structure. They need to be able to hold the bigger model as well as all of the component models in their mind, because they need to be able to predict how making a change in one place will affect the rest of the structure they are designing. If you move a wall, you need to be able to predict whether or not the rest of the structure will fall down!

The job of a doctor is to hold a model of how the human body works in their mind, so they can diagnose an underlying issue by checking on the visible symptoms. If they don't have an accurate model of the body, then their diagnosis is likely to be wrong, in which case the "cure" that they offer you might cause you to get worse, not better.

The job of a mechanic is to hold a model of how a car works in their mind, so they can make any repair necessary to get the car working again after a breakdown.

The job of a chess master is to hold a model of how a chess games works in their mind, how each piece works, how combinations of pieces work, how strategies of attack and defense work.

The job of a parent is to hold a model of how a child develops physically, emotionally, and psychologically, through each age range, so they can offer the appropriate guidance and optimal support as the child actualizes their highest potential in the world.

In order to succeed in a particular domain, you need to hold a model of how that domain works, inside your mind. If you don't have a model of how a domain works, then you're basically feeling around in the dark with a stick. Once you have a model of how the domain works, it's like turning on the light.

Models are interesting in that each of them tends to have a "key" or an insight that illuminates the situation and makes it click for a human mind. This often occurs as a flash of insight, a peek into the critical counter-intuitive nature of the way this particular area of reality works.

After having a child of my own, I became so much more aware of how other parents were interacting with their children. Most adults didn't have parents who were able to regulate their own nervous systems (I know that mine didn't have this skill). This then trickles down into their dynamics with their own children.

I was walking through an airport last week, and saw a small family - a mother, father, and daughter who was approximately three years old - walking off of a plane. The little girl was pulling their wheeled carry-on bag. It was obviously much too big for her, but she was pulling it along, very slowly. The father walked over and said "stop playing with that!" in a harsh, shaming tone. The little girl said "daddy, I'm helping" as he pulled it out of her hands. The mother attempted to soften the blow by saying to the daughter "Daddy needs us to hurry up, honey."

It was obvious to me that this father was not carrying a model of how young children learn and develop, and that he had not experienced a model of self-regulated parents as he was growing up. He was not even consciously aware of the cost of the emotional shaming he was burdening his daughter's psyche with, as he dismissed her attempt to help her family as bad behavior.

I have bad days myself, and often do things that I'm not proud of with my wife and daughter. But it was blindingly obvious to me that this man wasn't interested in the experience of his child. If he was interested, and if he held a model of how his daughter was experiencing the world, he would have assumed a positive intent, and would have been gentler in his taking control of the bag.

This is the power of having a model in your mind of how something works in reality. It can completely change how you think, feel, and behave, as well as how you interact with others and reality itself.

I actually define intelligence as "modeling ability." Your intelligence is your ability to model. Because we can learn mental models relatively quickly, this means that we can increase and even accelerate our intelligence dramatically by learning new, relevant mental models.

Keep the image of the dragonfly eye in your mind as you learn models. Each new diverse model adds another facet to your mind's eye.

Shift Between Models

People tend to orient their lives around a core value or set of values, and they view everything through this lens. We humans don't "naturally" seem to use a variety of lenses for estimating and calculating the value of experiences, events, objects, relationships, outcomes, etc.

As Robert Anton Wilson points out in his book Cosmic Trigger, we humans tend to like "single reality" models, and we often get uncomfortable when faced with the idea of multiple realities, or simulated realities, or realities inside of realities.

Even further, conceptions like the Multiverse (that there are an infinite number of universes, and that we're in just one of them - or moving between them constantly), or the Simulation Hypothesis (that we are inside of a virtual reality, as in the movie The Matrix), the Holographic Universe (that the whole of reality is contained in every part), or the model that Jane Roberts writes about in Seth Speaks (that each of us is a multidimensional spiritual entity of which one aspect - you - is experiencing physical existence, and that mind creates physical reality)... these are typically not considered seriously by those who are conditioned deeply by either religious or scientific cultures.

But more and more, we are opening our minds to play with other conceptions of a "non-singular" universe or reality. Elon Musk says openly that the chances that we are living in a reality that isn't simulated is basically zero. These kinds of models, held by people as creative and influential as Elon, are starting to make headway. I believe that this conversation is important to the evolution of thinking and our understanding of the nature of mind and culture in general.

When you use a mental model, you can leverage your attention, energy and thinking by orders of magnitude. Models can be powerful that way. But models should carry a serious "warning label" on them, that everyone should read before using them. The warning label should say:

This model is potentially powerful technology. You can use it at will to view situations, experiences, feelings, relationships, ideas, challenges, and opportunities. If you find it working for you, and bringing you consistently positive results and value, beware of the mind's tendency to start "believing in" the model, and considering it as "truth." If you become overly identified with any particular model, you are in danger of becoming trapped in a way of looking at reality that will fail you at some important point.

I remember Tony Robbins telling a story of being taught by John Grinder, one of the founders of Neuro-Linguistic Programming: Don't believe anything too much, because there will always be a situation where it isn't true.

The trick with models is being able to switch them out quickly and naturally, and to use them in sequences and combinations. Ultimately, the way you get the most from using models is by learning and practicing the skill of designing and create your own.

Think of models like eyeglasses, or binoculars, or magnifying glasses, or telescopes, or microscopes, or zoom lenses. You use the model as a lens or prism to view something through, in order to observe it, see it more clearly, and study its nature. A model gives you a different quality of perspective when seeking to understand how something works.

Models are conceptual tools. Just like you pick up a screwdriver if you need to turn a screw, or you pick up a hammer if you need to pound in a nail, or you pick up a pair of pliers if you need to grasp something firmly… you mentally pick up and use different models when you are faced with different types of situations.

One of the ways that we'll learn to use models is for estimating opportunities, evaluating them, and for calculating the value an opportunity will produce. As you dig into this material, remember that it's counter-intuitive for most people to use multiple models for evaluating anything in life… including an opportunity.

If someone pushes their way in front of you in line, it's not intuitive to think to yourself: "Let's look at this using multiple models of value. First, I am going to lose two minutes of time, which is worth one dollar of income. Second, the other person is going to save time, which is valuable to them. Third, I am going to get to practice patience, which is something I need more of. Fourth, I can study group dynamics up close by noticing if this person feels guilt or shame…"

Likewise, when we encounter an opportunity in life, we don't tend to pick up multiple valuation lenses in a conscious and systematic way. We don't think through the cost to us in terms of time, effort, money, hassle, attention, and energy. We don't estimate the probability of success based on realistic models. We don't estimate the likely return using intelligent, sane ways of calculation. We don't consider the impact or cost to others of our success or failure.

But part of the message of this book is that using multiple models to evaluate opportunities (and to evaluate situations, relationships, ideas, and decisions in general) is fundamental to building a successful and fulfilled life. Just like learning math requires deliberate, intentional practice, learning to use multiple models to estimate value also requires you to learn something new, and to practice it.

Charlie Munger has taken his favorite mental models and translated them into checklist form, so he can use them to analyze potential investments, to make sure that he is using multiple models to analyze a particular opportunity. Think of these models as prisms or lenses that you pick up and use to see a situation more clearly, or more dimensionally, or more accurately. They are tools for estimation, prediction, calculation, modeling, and valuation.

The more you use them, the easier it becomes to use them in sequences and combinations, in order to discover and develop opportunity in your life. But remember to use at least a few of these models in each situation, so that you can see your opportunity from multiple perspectives - and so that you don't fall into the trap of only looking at things one way in life.

It is only through this process of examining your opportunity from more than one mental viewpoint that you wake up to what the opportunity really represents in terms of potential benefit and cost to you and to the people, groups, systems, and values that you care about.

The more diverse your models, the better. The models I'm going to share here are highly biased towards business, as this is a common interest of many people who are learning about opportunity and entrepreneurship. Continue to learn and use models from other domains of life as well, in order to develop wisdom in your life.

Once you "load up" all of these models into your mind, and you begin using them in your daily life, something mysterious happens mentally. There comes a spontaneous moment of realization when you understand an individual situations in several different ways, when you can finally perceive from many perspectives at once. Instead of feeling trapped in one point of view, you can now take the view of different elements of a system, or of different entities in an ecosystem. This power becomes creatively generative.

When you can start seeing the world through models of different values systems, different incentive models, different time frames, different cultural lenses, you become less black and white, and less attached to any one way of thinking or doing things. You live more from a transcendent position in life, and you help others to understand the underlying dynamics of life so they can develop and evolve on their paths successfully as well.

Opportunifying Your Mind & Preparing Yourself for Opportunity

"Chance favors the prepared mind." —Louis Pasteur

The models that you're about to learn in the next sections are specifically designed to prepare your mind for opportunity. If your mind is properly prepared, opportunity will stand out in situations where you didn't see it before. You will also look for it in places that you have never looked. You'll discover new forms of opportunity that were in plain sight, but camouflaged behind old ways of perceiving and thinking.

The best way to prepare for opportunity, in my opinion, is to be continually engaged in the search for opportunity, and continually in an experimental dance with reality to discover diverse, evolving opportunities to produce value and collaborate with others on producing it.

We'll warm up with a set of models to use to prepare ourselves for opportunity. This is the most "concentrated" part of the book, and it contains the essence of what I believe to be the most powerful models for moving through reality relative to discovering and developing opportunity.

I'm visualizing taking you on an adventure through exciting new territory in your imagination and your life. Before setting off on a tour through new territory, it's valuable to read up about the terrain, learn about the local weather, get a few lessons on the culture, and get a preview of what to look for - so that as you move through the new land, your mind is prepared to recognize the wonderful new things that it's going to see around it.

"Luck is when preparation meets opportunity." —Seneca

By learning and imprinting these models, you give yourself a better chance of noticing and creating the increasing opportunities that will be coming into your life. It's the most potent type of preparation I know of, and it is designed to literally make you more lucky. These models can sculpt and shape your thinking so that it opens you to possibilities that weren't within your frame of awareness.

Let's start with one of the most fundamental considerations and fundamental models - the model of value itself.

The Riddle of Value

I have an important question for you. It might be the most important question I ask you in this book:

What is value?

At the core of opportunity is the concept of value. If you don't know what value is, then you don't really know what an opportunity is.

When we assign value to something, we assign a worth of some type to it. The value can be financial, but it can also be saving hassle, giving us time, making us feel happy, bringing us closer to someone we care about, helping us learn, or assisting us in achieving our purpose.

Because the internal processes that we go through to value things are mostly invisible, it's worthwhile to continually ask yourself "What is value?" This helps you get perspective on the concept, process, and experience of value.

I recommend writing that question on a note, and putting it up somewhere obvious, so that you see it several times a day. This is worth doing right now, so that you ask yourself this question daily for at least a month or two. Keep asking yourself what value means in different parts of your life, and you'll keep coming up with more interesting and insightful answers.

I asked my mentor Wyatt Woodsmall the question 'what is value?' and he responded with something like this: "The word value is a nominalization. It's a process (to value something) or a verb that has been turned into an abstract noun. To understand value and what it is, you must look at how humans assign value to things, and examine this process and experience of valuing. You have to de-nominalize the word value, and change it back into a verb - to value. To do this, start noticing how you assign value to things, and what it feels like when you are in the process of receiving value from something. We more toward some values, and away from others, and both are valid."

If you explore this further, and you discuss it with others, you'll quickly discover that, while we share common values, each of also values different things, and we value them in different ways.

You might value time alone, and I might value social time with others. You might value novel experiences and I might value consistency. When we drill down into why we value these things, we might discover that you value time alone because you are able to relax better by yourself, and I value time with others because it helps me get new ideas. You might like novel experiences because they distract you from pain in your life, while I like consistent experiences because I avoid anxiety by doing things that are predictable.

If we go further, and get down to the level of how we each have a felt experience the value that we get, we might discover that you experience the felt value of being alone as a calming of the emotions and a relaxation in the body which feels pleasurable to you, and I experience the felt value of being with others in social situations as increased energy and emotional joy.

Because these types of experiential rewards and pleasures (or discomforts and pains) are so primal and visceral, they typically happen outside of awareness. We're not conscious of them happening, and we typically don't link them up to more central causes in our lives.

All too often, we walk through life out of touch with why we are doing what we're doing, and the felt benefits and experiential costs of those things.

When the process of valuing turns into a "thing" called value, we make another leap with the term. It becomes something that we are trying to quantify.

What is the value of this thing or this experience? We can start comparing the value of one thing to another. We can ask "what is it worth?" and "what would I pay to get it?" and "what would I give to avoid it?" This starts objectifying value a bit more, and allows us to wrap our heads around value by considering it in relationship to several other things.

One way to begin developing a more sophisticated relationship to valuing and value is to measure it in multiple denominations. What is a day of free time to you worth? Let's this question a different way: How much would you pay, in money, for an extra full day off to do with as you wish next week?

Let's turn the question around, and ask it a different way: How much would someone have to pay you, in order to get you to use a day off that you have coming, and get you to work doing whatever it is that you do for typical professional work?

You will likely get two different answers, and at this point you would want to ask why you have two different amounts of money as answers. If you stop to really consider it, this will give you some insight about how you value your time.

Let's try another example. How much do you spend each month to pay all of your expenses, approximately? How many days of full-time work do you have to put in to make enough money to cover these expenses? In this one, we are totaling monthly expenses, then calculating in terms days of work. Days of work is the currency that we are measuring in. We can then ask ourselves if we feel like it's worth it to be spending that many days per month to earn our expenses (rather than asking ourselves if we're getting paid enough for our time, which is thinking in the "other direction").

The exercise of measuring using something other than money as our basic unit is useful, as it helps us think about the value of other things in our lives more easily.

If you track the price of gold, you might start using gold as the denominator for this exercise. How many ounces of gold would you have to pay per month to support your current lifestyle? How many ounces of gold would you receive if you got paid in gold? Start doing the mental exercise each month to calculate this, and maybe even write it down or track in a spreadsheet.

Pain, or hassle, or discomfort, or stress is a different form of value. For most people, they would consider it a sort of "negative value" that they'd like to avoid. But what if you could spend one day doing things that you really don't enjoy, and earn as much as doing two days of work that you would enjoy? If that's not enough, then how about if you earned as much as three days of enjoyable work? Or ten?

Let's add another twist: What if I reminded you that intentionally doing things that are uncomfortable pushes you outside of your comfort zone, and it teaches you new things about yourself that you cannot learn by doing only things that you enjoy? What if you learned that doing one day of every ten doing something you don't enjoy not only paid you 10x the value, but also doubled the value of the other work you did as well?

What about emotional and social value? What is the value of being recognized by the people in your life for doing something positive, or for reaching an achievement, or for a great contribution? Would you rather have everyone you know give you positive recognition for a full day, or have a full day off alone to read? How valuable is it to avoid rejection by someone you care about? Would you trade a day from work to avoid being rejected by someone you care about?

When working with people on productivity, there's a simple exercise to point out the importance of making value and values more conscious. Let's try it.

Quickly: Make a list of the things that are most important to you in your life. If your family is important, then write "family." If sailing is important to you, then write "sailing." If it's health then write "health." Make a list of the top 5-7 things in your life. Pause for a minute and write this out before going on.

Next, quickly write out a rough schedule of how you spend your day each day. What's your basic schedule like? As you look it over, mentally calculate how much time you spend each day doing each of the major things on the list. How much time do you spend commuting? Working? Watching news? Talking to people on social media? Reading books? Taking courses? Be brutally honest here, to get the most from this exercise.

Now look at your two lists, and compare them. What do you notice?

What most people quickly see is that they aren't living in line with their values. They might say that they value family, sailing, and health, but if you look at how they spend their day, they spend two hours each day reading news, hanging out on social media, checking messages, and chatting with people… and thirty minutes with their family. They might go sailing every three months. And they might be behind on their health regimen. What's going on?

Because most of us aren't consciously reviewing our values, and measuring different types of value against each other in an intentional way, we don't see this stuff. We forget what's important, and we get into routines of distraction and interruption, and ultimately waste too much of our lives.

AS YOU WORK WITH value, and you start thinking in different forms of value, it helps you to realize that you have more control than you think. Many of the models we'll cover in the next sessions are designed to help you get more clarity about what value is, and how to get more of it in your life.

As yourself each day: "What is value?" And then notice what it feels like as you are experiencing value in different domains of life, and the trade-offs that you make between areas of value.

Another Valuable Mental Model

Because it's important to really imprint the distinction of what a model is, and to get it on as many levels as possible, let's use math as model example.

In order to learn math, you must first learn a set of basic building blocks. First you learn the number 1. Then you learn 2. Then 3. Then 4. Then up to 9. At each point, you learn that there is a number that can stand as the symbol for the amount of things you have in a group. You learn that instead of thinking of the individual apples you have in each hand, you can say "I have 2 apples." Numbers become a mental shorthand for thinking, writing, communicating.

Around this point, you can also start to grasp the number 0, to stand for none. Once we learn these ten digits of 0-9, we can then start using them in sequences and combinations. We can put 1 and 2 together, and get another number: 3. Or, we can take 3 of something, remove 2 of them, and have 1 left.

This represents another leap upward one order of development from just learning the digits. It's not obvious at first, but moving to basic addition and subtraction is a higher order ability. It's a higher order **model**.

Once we can do basic addition and subtraction, and we "get" how it works, we can then make another intuitive leap. We can take a group of 3 of something, and ask "what if I had 3 groups of 3? how many would that be?" - and because we know addition, we can then take 3 and 3 and 3, and put them together, and get 9. This, obviously, is the foundation for multiplication.

We can take a group of 9 of something, and ask "what if we broke our group of 9 into groups of 3s? how many of those groups would we have?" - and because we know subtraction, we can subtract 3 a total of three times, and see that the answer is 3 groups. This is division.

Again, we have moved to a higher order of operation, of thinking, of symbolizing, and of ability. We are using a higher order **model**. Just as employee moves to self-employed moves to business owner, each using the previous level skills and time horizon in a higher order way, this new set of conceptual operations gives us a broader and more extended view.

What is important to remember here is that if you don't learn individual numbers, you can't do addition. Just like you can't tell someone what time to meet you for dinner if you have never learned about how to tell time, you can't do simple calculations without numbers.

Once you learn the digits, and have something that can stand for simple quantities, you can then start using them in sequences and combinations. Once you use them in sequences and combinations, you're at a higher order. Then once you learn those sequences and combinations, you can use **those** in sequences and combinations, to climb higher. This is an essential aspect of using models that I'm trying to convey. They come in levels, and they build on each other.

As you learn the following models, notice how they fit together, and can be used in combinations, just like numbers and mathematical operations. It's this combinatorial power that allows you to make big breakthroughs when discovering, creating and analyzing opportunity.

The Pareto Principle

"80% of your results come from 20% of your efforts."

Vilfredo Pareto was an economist who lived in Italy 100 years ago, and he noticed a hidden pattern that has become a cornerstone of success "the literature" and in practice. The mental model that has become known as the Pareto Principle is possibly the most iconic mental model, and also possibly the most valuable. We'll examine it here.

Pareto looked around his life, and noticed a pattern: That 80% of the land was owned by only 20% of the people... but also that 80% of the peas in his garden were in 20% of the peapods. This pattern seemed to be consistent across domains.

Pareto said that "for many events, roughly 80% of the effects come from 20% of the causes."

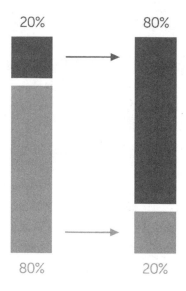

What this also implies is that 20% of your results are coming from 80% of your efforts. When you stop and really consider the implications here, they are profound.

One implication is that you can essentially stop doing 80% of what you do, and you'll keep getting almost the same results. If you dedicate some of that time and effort to doing the 20% that gets you most of the results, you can literally multiply the success that you have.

One of the many ways that I have used this model in my life is in the way that I eat. Several years ago, I was reading about health, and I learned that some foods have more nutrients in them than other foods and some foods have fewer nutrients in them. Many of the foods we eat, like white flour, white rice, white sugar… and fats like refined vegetable oils… have had all of the vitamins and minerals systematically stripped away, leaving essentially only the pure sugar or fat. Then these are used as ingredients in many of the dishes that we eat every day (you know, the ones that taste really really good!).

I then reasoned to myself: If some foods contain more nutrients per calorie than others, then there are probably a handful of foods that contain lots and lots more nutrients, or multiples of even something in its natural state that has all of its vitamins and minerals left in. After doing some research, I discovered that foods like the vegetable kale, and the fruit blueberry, and the grain black rice, have far more nutrients and antioxidants, than average foods. When you go and look at the comparisons and "do the math" it is really quite astonishing.

So I took this information, and I designed a green shake that includes about 10 different raw organic greens, plus diverse omega fats in their natural form, plus blueberries, plus fiber, plus a bunch of other ingredients to boost its nutritional value. I then added natural flavorings and natural sweetener (stevia) to make it taste good. I wake up every morning, and make a huge pitcher of this for myself and my family, and I also put one in the fridge to have as my afternoon meal. I typically eat 4 meals per day, and this green shake is my meal for two of them.

And this means that twice a day, every day, I give my body probably the same level of nutrients that the average person gets in several days on a typical diet. More importantly, it starts me off on a healthy track each morning, and it puts me into a healthy mindset. It gives me a couple of hours of sustained, clear mental energy. And it keeps me healthier.

The key is that I started out by asking "What are the foods that have the highest nutrient density?" In retrospect, it's kind of obvious to approach food this way.

This is just one way that I've applied Pareto to my life.

Here are more "physical" and health examples: Brisk walk for 30-60 minute every day. Take a vitamin pack with dinner every night, with supplements recommended by a nutritionist. Sleep until I wake up each day to be fully rested. Take breaks through the day to rejuvenate.

These are little "20%" things that give me huge returns. When you look around your life with the lens of looking for the 20% that gives you the 80% returns, it makes everything make a lot more sense. It also gives you permission to let go of the activities, patterns, habits, relationships, thoughts, and other aspects of life that are not delivering high returns to you. It helps you become more adaptive - and more attractive - to think this way. It makes you more of an evolutionary human, and it inspires you to prune your life and processes in order to become sharper, faster and more efficient.

I consider the discoveries that you can make by asking what the key 20% is in a domain of life to be a way of locating "found value" all around. When you stop doing something that was in the 80%, and you use that time to do things that are in the 20%, you multiply your success.

REMINDER: Download the "Opportunity Companion Guide" to Get Your Summaries, Checklists & Exercises

This book has an **Opportunity Companion Guide** that goes along with it, which you can download for free. It includes key chapter summaries, implementation checklists, and written exercises - plus extra chapters and other bonus material. Go here to get it now, so you can review the summaries and start implementing what you're learning:

OpportunityBonus.com

The Opportunity of Learning

Future-Proof Knowledge & Skills

WHAT'S THE MAIN PROBLEM with the higher education system? It's that most of the education tracks that you can take in a traditional college or university will teach you things that will be obsolete by the time you graduate and try to use them.

What's the solution? It's to identify those skills that become more useful and valuable over time, and that will grow with you as you evolve in your life and career.

I mentioned that I learned to play the guitar from my father. When I was in middle and high school, I also learned to play the trombone. I invested probably five years into learning to play the trombone.

I am grateful for this knowledge and these musical experiences and skills, but I also wish that I had learned a different instrument as well when I was learning music. Can you guess which instrument it would be?

I wish I would have learned to play the keyboard. Why? Because as music changes and evolves, the keyboard is the musical instrument platform that is "native" for making music in the digital age. The keyboard is the future-proof musical instrument.

I introduce the concept and model of "future proof skills" here for your consideration, as I believe that it's one of the most important conceptual shifts we can make as we build our opportunity model.

I once read that something like 85% of people who graduate from college never work in their field of study (and this isn't to mention those that drop out, who don't graduate). How many people do you know who got a degree in something like psychology, or history, or political science, or even business or marketing, who never "used it" in the real world? We all know many, because this is the typical outcome.

If you drill down past the level of degree, and into more specific layers of skills and techniques that people learn, I would say that the stats are even worse. Most of the things that people learn in jobs just don't "transfer" on to the next level of a person's life. They don't contribute to the next order of work. They don't make the person who is now an employee better at what they're going to be doing when they are self-employed, or better at being a member of an adaptive and healthy family. This is a tragedy.

Instead, what we need to learn are skills and knowledge that are FUTURE-PROOF. We need to learn things that become more valuable over time, and not less valuable. We need to learn things that will be more in-demand, and that will be worth more in the future.

For many years, I have worked in the online education space, and taught courses on topics like coaching, online courses, digital products, marketing, productivity, entrepreneurship and of course dating and relationships. Later in this book, we'll dedicate a section to these business models, as I believe that they are so important to learn for the future. These skills have become more and more valuable to me over time, and I recommend that people get started with these models if they are starting an online business.

As you develop your ability to find and create bigger and bigger opportunities for yourself, remember that the skills and knowledge that you acquire open the doors to those next-level opportunities. As you choose what to learn next, run a layer of thinking that asks "Is this knowledge or skill likely to get more valuable in the future? Will this knowledge or skill increasingly open doors to more opportunity?"

If the answer is yes, then you're likely looking at something that is likely future-proof. If not, then it's worth a long, hard consideration to decide if this is something that you really want to invest in learning and doing. Focus on learning skills and knowledge that are future-proof. It will pay off for you in the long-run.

Experiential Learning

Speaking of learning new skills and knowledge, the best way to learn something new is by doing it. Many people make the mistake of thinking that they can learn something simply by reading a book or watching a video. Of course, there is great value in reading books and learning from videos, but this only gets you part of the way to what I would call "real learning."

Memory is a form of learning. But it's nowhere near the higher potential levels of learning. If you only have a fact or piece of data that you've memorized, then what you have is an "idea about how something works." If instead you go into the real world and actually try out the idea, and get some feedback on how it works in the real world, you will achieve another level of imprinting. This level is called "experiential learning." When you go and implement an idea, and then actually experience the feedback (whether positive or negative), your mind learns in a different way.

Wyatt Woodsmall often says "knowledge plus experience equals understanding." This is a profound insight, that's worth writing down and reviewing regularly. By taking the knowledge, and then putting it to use or implementing it, you get messages back from the world that offer either validation or invalidation of your hypothesis. When a person sees the actual outcome of a test or an experiment, they become convinced in a different way than reading it in a book, or seeing it in a video.

The key is the feedback. It's having something "out there" come back and show you that your idea either worked or it didn't. You can read books about riding a bike all day long, but until you go try it, you don't have any idea what it's really like to learn to balance. It's only when you have the "ah ha" of actually balancing that the "click" happens, and you actually get it.

Another thing that Wyatt Woodsmall says is that "learning equals behavior change." If your behavior hasn't changed, then you haven't learned. This is another reason why experiential learning is so critical.

Great dancers don't learn how to dance by reading books about dancing, and then thinking about it all the time. They go and actually dance. Further, if you study great dancers, you'll learn that they also use a key tool for getting feedback: The mirror. They watch themselves as they are dancing, so they see what they look like in real-time visually.

Once you are able to accomplish something in the real world, and turn knowledge into results, then you also begin to achieve self-esteem in the domain as well. You become more confident about your ability, which has a powerful effect on your motivation and your courage. You become more bold, and more willing to invest yourself in projects, because you believe in yourself.

Many people come to me to learn marketing. I typically recommend that they start out by doing one-to-one sales in order to learn more about customers who would be likely to buy what they want to sell. Why would I recommend this? Because if you do your own sales, you will get high-quality experiential feedback from real people. You will accelerate your learning by probably 10x over jumping in directly to the marketing, and you will imprint the knowledge and the skill at a much deeper level. Most of the great marketers I know when through a phase of their career where they did live sales, with real people. I don't think that it's a coincidence.

When you learn through experience, you also build a much more powerful model in your mind. You develop a more sophisticated understanding of how the dynamics of the situation work, and you learn what to do when things go wrong... and when they go right... to keep your project on track.

Competence, Then Integrate

As we move into the future, we will find ourselves needing to learn more and more new skills. We will then use them as parts of our overall personal and business toolkit to produce value and create results in life. I believe that there is too much of an emphasis on "mastery" of skills, and not enough emphasis on just learning a skill to the point of competence, then moving on to learning the next one.

When you learn a skill to the point of competence, so you can do it consciously anytime you need, and then you integrate that skill with the others you know, I believe that you develop more efficiently in the long-run.

One of the hazards of learning a new skill is becoming overly-identified with the role or image that goes with the skill. If you see interviews with rock musicians from the 1980s, you'll see that many of them are still wearing the same clothes, telling the same stories, and trying to be the same image of a rock star from decades ago. They took the skill and the role a little too seriously, and the swallowed the hook, line and sinker. They actually bought into the idea that they were that image, rather than seeing rock star as a phase they went through on their way to somewhere higher in life.

I just saw a great video of Kip Winger, who was one of the hair metal rockers from the 80s with his band Winger (I love Winger, by the way!). He went on after his heavy metal career to learn how to score contemporary classical music, and was eventually nominated for a grammy. I really admire him for going beyond his "rock and roll role" and becoming something more.

The trick here is to learn new skills, to the point where you are competent at them, and then to start using them in combination with your other skills. Learn about eating a healthy diet, practice to competence, then integrate healthy eating into other parts of your life. Learn about entrepreneurship, start a business, then integrate it into other parts of your life. Learn about fashion, then start dressing better, and then integrate this ability into other areas of your personal and business life.

You may want to take some of your pursuits much deeper, and go for higher levels of skill and achievement. But when your strategy is to learn skills to competence, then to integrate and transcend, you will even learn the skills that you become a master of differently. You'll be remembering to integrate what you learn with other skills, and develop other aspects of your life. And you won't get stuck the way others will in roles, images, cultures, and ego trips.

Skills and knowledge then become tools in a bigger project, and means to bigger ends. They become vocabulary terms in a bigger conversation. They become notes in a bigger composition.

Another important thing starts to happen when you learn to the point of competence, then start integrating competencies together into your life: You become much more powerful in the domain of creative imagination. Once you develop a skill, through experiential learning, to the point of competence, you can then "mentally model" the skill. You can imagine doing the skill in your mind, and have a much more accurate ability to imagine, design, predict, and plan. You have a much better sense of whether or not a situation that requires that skill will have a positive outcome, because you can imagine all of the steps more clearly. This is actually the most important reason for learning to competence. Once you do, you can imagine more complex processes in your mind, and have a far more accurate ability to know what will work and what won't.

Once you have several of valuable skills learned to the point of competence, you will be able to imagine relationships, systems, businesses, investments, and much more with a far higher degree of accuracy.

When I sit down to do a marketing project, I can imagine all parts of it. I can think through what it will take to work out the main idea, how long it will take to write the copy… record the audio or video… design the site… create the email follow-up campaign, and much more. Why? Because I've done each of these things myself, and I am competent with them. I have a sense of what each step takes, and I can budget my time and attention in a way that makes me much more efficient when working on marketing projects.

Again, when you learn a skill to the point of competence, a very important thing happens: You have now installed the model, and you can THINK with that model of understanding, and use it in combination with the other skills and knowledge that you have. You can plan much more complex projects with a higher degree of accuracy, and you can intuitively guess whether or not bigger projects will be likely to work in a way that someone who doesn't have competence in each of those areas can never do.

When you take this approach, you begin the path to becoming a "modern polymath" - or a person who has skills in several valuable domains, who can think through how each domain works, and find connections between them. This is an incredibly valuable way to approach personal and professional development, and we can all do it now that knowledge about so many different domains is so freely available online.

Learning for a Higher Purpose

The future is about learning a new skill quickly, and then using it in combination with your other skills, and for higher and higher purposes, as you develop as a person and as a professional.

When you learn something, it's important to learn as what you are learning is going to be part of an olympic performance, or part of a PhD thesis, or like it might be the key that opens the door to your highest dreams and success. Each thing that you learn is going to become a part of something that you can't even imagine right now when you reach the next level in your life and career.

I was always a "hunt and peck" typer, until I went online and started chatting with women. Chatting online was great, because I didn't have to risk rejection in person. I noticed that when I was chatting live with a woman by text, that it would often take me too long to type what I wanted to say as a response, or make a joke that I wanted to make. So I decided that I was going to need to learn to "touch type" in order to flirt better. What better motivation could I have? So I learned how to type f-t-f-t without looking, and then f-r-f-r, and so on. After learning to type, I was able to flirt much more effectively when chatting. Sometimes the only way to be witty is to be able to respond quickly. And this was the incentive I needed to finally learn to type as an adult.

A few years later, when I realized that dating advice was in high demand, I wrote a book called "Double Your Dating" using a pen name.

I wrote the entire book in three weeks. How? Because by then I could type super fast. I would never have imagined that learning typing would be used later to write a book, but that's the way it turned out.

When I was in my teens, my dad taught me to play the the electric guitar, and I got a small home recording studio setup. I learned how to record and produce music for myself and for my bands. Years later, I went to work for a live seminar training company, as their audio visual engineer. I had no experience doing seminars, but my background in music gave me what I needed to figure out how to handle the sound system and recordings. Again, I never would have guessed that my music and recording background would be used later in a seminar context.

Then later, after releasing my book of dating advice, I did my first live dating seminar. Because I had seen how it was done, I borrowed a video camera, and had a good friend audio record the program. We used this audio and video footage to create my first in-depth training course, which doubled my business the day I released it. I never would have done this without the musical and audio-visual background. And I could never have guessed that what I learned as a teenager would be used to produce an audio and video course 15 years later.

When my wife and I first got together, we had a lot of conflict. As the conflict continued, and we worked together to figure out how to manage our emotions, we both learned "emotional regulation" techniques from teachers and therapists. A few years ago, my daughter was born. As she has grown, she went through a phase where she would throw "tantrums" for five or ten minutes at a time some days. It's challenging to stay cool and calm when one of these is happening, but fortunately I had been practicing with my wife through our conflicts, so I already had a lot of the tools. I now tell friends that the power struggle in romantic relation-ships is preparation and training for the power struggle in parenthood, and it's a blessing.

As I built my businesses, each time I encountered an area of business that I didn't know something about, I would get a book, or go to a course, or hire a consultant, or talk to friends who were entrepreneurs to learn what to do. I later created a series of courses to teach others how to build and scale their businesses. As I was doing that, I started investing in very early stage startup companies (that might typically have only a few people working for them). As I worked with these companies, and the founders would ask me for help with things like hiring, marketing, design, and growth I realized that I knew the answers to the questions they had... because I had studied it all myself. In fact, I found that I knew more than I needed to know in order to help them grow their companies rapidly. I had no idea that the business lessons that I learned would be used in this way later.

When you learn something, learn like it's going to be used for something big in the future. And this will represent an ongoing opportunity for you as you develop in your life.

REMINDER: Download the "Opportunity Companion Guide" to Get Your Summaries, Checklists & Exercises

This book has an **Opportunity Companion Guide** that goes along with it, which you can download for free. It includes key chapter summaries, implementation checklists, and written exercises - plus extra chapters and other bonus material. Go here to get it now, so you can review the summaries and start implementing what you're learning:

OpportunityBonus.com

Mindsets for
Seeing Opportunity

The Growth Mindset

DR. CAROL DWECK SAYS that some people believe that the world and everything in it is relatively fixed or set. For example, they would consider their life situation and intelligence level to be fixed, and they would invest time and energy to verify or document their level of intelligence, rather than investing time to increase it. These people have what Dweck would call a "Fixed Mindset."

Some people, on the other hand, believe that the world and everything in it is changing and evolving. They believe that they can change themselves and their situations. They would consider their intelligence level to be flexible and modifiable, and would invest time and energy working to develop their level of intelligence, rather than investing time to verify or establish it. These people have what Dweck would call a "Growth Mindset."

If you fundamentally believe that things are fixed in place, and that there's no use trying to change yourself or your situation, it's going to much harder to find and create opportunity for yourself and those you care about. Opportunity requires you to "believe it before you see it" in a certain sense. You must move through the world with a faith that opportunity is going to be there for you. This thinking requires you to believe that people change and evolve and that circumstances change and evolve.

If you find yourself feeling stuck in life, ask yourself if one of the root causes is a sense that things don't change, people don't change, and situations don't change. If you can see this pattern in how you perceive reality and how you think about your life, then start studying the sciences of change and evolution. Evolutionary biology and developmental psychology provide powerful models for how bodies and minds evolve through stages of life, and provide excellent referential frameworks for looking at other important domains.

Look back through your life, and remember the moments where you had to grow and change in order to go to the next level. Notice how growth was the key that opened the doorway to your higher potential.

If you're already a growth mindset type, then develop your ability to learn and change in domains of your life that you may have overlooked in the past. Often, we will unconsciously have an area of our lives where we believe that things are "fixed" (maybe health, relationships, happiness, or spirituality), and not realize it consciously. Look through your entire life to see how you can grow and evolve. This can represent the potential for huge opportunity personally, interpersonally, or spiritually.

Also, as you add the lens of opportunity to your life more consciously, I recommend watching for people who have a growth mindset, and add more of them to your social group and business projects. They will help create a "growth mindset culture" around you that pulls you even higher, faster.

Unique Genius

Each of us is born with a different genetic makeup, with a different arrangement and combination of brain centers, into a different family, in a different culture... and we each have different experiences growing up. These all combine and integrate into one personality, one persona, one person... YOU.

The more I study how we are each individually composed of these multidimensional genetic, family, cultural, and experiential elements, the more profound people become to me.

We each have dozens (or maybe hundreds) of different functional centers in the brain. Some of them are for senses, like sight or sound. Some of them are for language, both interpreting and communicating. Some are for organization. Some are for memory. Some are for analysis.

What's interesting about this is that each of us has a unique combination of different sizes of these areas. One person might have a larger visual center, while another might have a larger language center, and another might have a larger part of the limbic system or emotional center. Each brain is like a custom computer, with a unique combination of processor, memory, speed, sensors, communication systems, etc. This is just one of the things that contributes to the amazing diversity of ways of seeing, experiencing and interacting with reality that we humans demonstrate.

I believe that each of us has a "unique genius" - a way of perceiving and experiencing the world, that no one else has. When you combine and layer the genetic influences, family influences, cultural influences, and experiences that we have, it all adds up to a unique way of being in this world.

Unfortunately, most of us haven't had someone show up in our lives and say "You have something that is uniquely special, a way of seeing the world that only you can understand, and a gift that is important and valuable to us all." And we definitely didn't come up through an education system that was built upon this fundamental premise.

I don't mean to be negative about the education system. It has given us incredible benefits. But things are changing in dramatic ways right now, and the model of "mass assembly-line education" to prepare people for "mass assembly-line work" is in its final hours. It's exciting to be living in this modern environment, because we are waking up to the unique value that each person brings to the world, and we're starting to think differently about how to educate and integrate each of the miraculous people that are born on this planet.

As you build yourself into an opportunity discoverer and developer, it's useful to study some of the various personality models. Models like the Myers-Briggs system, the Big Five from evolutionary psychology, the Enneagram system, or the Kolbe model offer insights that are often profound. Some of these are more "woo-woo" than others, but I've found that each of them brings unique and valuable insights when they are studied and used for self reflection and interpersonal relationships. As you study different personality models, you start to realize just how unique your personality is, and you start seeing more clearly which aspects of reality are obvious to you - that aren't to other people.

I walk through the world now assuming that most people can't see most of what I can see. This is a very different stance than I had through most of my life. I used to assume that things that were obvious to me were obvious to almost everyone, and that people who didn't see these "obvious" things were not trying, or they were being lazy, or worse... that they were stupid.

As I have spent more time with diverse people across varied domains of life, and I've learned how to ask the right questions, I've found that each of us has a unique genius that is essentially invisible to the person who has it, and usually also to others around them. It's so natively a part of who we are, that we don't notice that it's there.

In many cases, we've either suppressed or exaggerated our unique genius (and also our shadow or unique blind spot as well), and this complex is what we call our "personality" or more typically "me."

But if you persist, and can get past the superficial levels when getting to know another person, what you'll discover is that they have a way of seeing and understanding a part of reality that is profound and astonishing.

They might be an "interpersonal genius" (like my wife is), who has an almost psychic way of reading social situations, and doing or saying what is needed to help a group of friends or family to function better as a unit. Or they might be a "logic genius" who can take complex situations apart and break them down into component parts in their minds, and instantly see how to make a process more efficient. Or they might be a "physical genius" who can look at something and know instantly how to build it at home, from scratch. Or they might be a "flavor genius" who can taste a dish and know all at once what the ingredients are and how they are prepared in order. Or they might be a "musical genius" who can listen to a piece of music, and play it note-for-note on an instrument.

Science is a good place to look for examples of this concept. Within the domains and branches of science, you have sub-domains and specific areas that become quite fascinating. And then you have people who learn multiple domains, and cross-pollinate or hybridize these domains, and come up with new things.

A key insight for me was realizing that if you're the smartest person in some super-niche area of life, that this is the first time in history when you can go out, look around the planet and at the projects and needs that are emerging, and find the place where your unique genius can be recognized, used and put to work. Now, you can do something that you have absolute passion about, and something that also produces a lot of value.

If you're not sure what your unique genius is, keep looking. And if you know what it is, continue to keep looking as well! Keep refining, clarifying, and using it in different situations to hone and develop it. This is the zone where you will find more success and fulfillment, and where you can help others and the planet best.

The Critical Counter-Intuitive

When I was in my early 20s, I went to the Lane County Fair in Oregon, where I grew up. There was a carnival game at the fair that you could play to win a huge stuffed animal. I watched as one person after another tried to win the game, but consistently lost toward the end. It involved holding a piece of metal and moving it through the game without it touching anything. As soon as it touched something, a buzzer went off and you lost.

I watched as the people who were working at the booth would demonstrate how "easy" it was to win. I watched with my own eyes as they demonstrated the winning move, but one after another, people walking up would lose their money.

I stood there at the game for hours, fascinated by this dynamic, becoming more and more determined to figure out how to win the game. After trying the game, and losing myself, and then observing more, I realized that there was a move that you had to make right at the end of the game that was against what people would instinctively do. You had to turn the piece you were holding in one direction in order to win, but the "intuitive" thing to do was turn it in the other direction, which would end up losing you the game.

Once I realized where the "trick" was, started closing my eyes, and imagining playing the game, and doing the correct move at the end. I would watch others play, then close my eyes and imagine playing perfectly. Finally, I tried the real game again, and won. I felt like I had conquered an important challenge. It was the counter-intuitive move that made the difference. It took mental rehearsal and practice in my imagination before I could actually do it in real life - when I was in the moment and under pressure.

When I was in my late 20s, and studying the dating and mating game, I noticed a pattern when observing men who were naturally good at attracting women: Many of the things that they did were completely outside of what I would even consider doing or saying to a woman. They would tease or joke around with an attractive woman, or even make fun of her within minutes of meeting her - whereas I was so terrified to talk to a woman that the idea of making a joke seemed inconceivable. Sure enough, when I started being more playful and having more fun when talking to women, it worked like a charm. But again, this is something that I wouldn't have thought of doing in a million years on my own. It was radically counter-intuitive.

When most people decide to lose weight and get into better shape, the first thing they think of is exercise. They think that they need to start going to the gym in order to lose weight. But when many people try losing weight this way, they are disheartened to see their weight often **increasing** instead of decreasing. What's going on? After talking with many trainers, bodybuilders and fitness experts, I've learned that 80% of weight loss is about diet, not exercise. And that when you start exercising, you add muscle, which typically makes you heavier. The body says "things are getting harder, conserve weight!" Turns out that if you want to lose weight, it's about what you're eating. Exercise is important to health as well, but the game of losing weight is about what you eat. Very counter-intuitive.

As I have continued studying success in different domains of life, I have seen this pattern over and over. Whether it's in health, relationships, business, success, spirituality, the pattern goes like this:

The next step on the path to success is usually not obvious, and it's typically counter-intuitive.

This is what I call the "critical counterintuitive." It's the counter-intuitive move that's critical to success. When you know this, it makes finding those non-obvious next steps in life much easier. As they say "expect the unexpected." When you actually expect the next step toward success to be something that's not intuitive to do, it frees you to try things that are way outside the box. And it gives you permission to be very experimental.

In NLP, they say that if what you're doing isn't working to get you closer to your goal, stop and try something else, because anything is likely to work better than something that doesn't work.

Opportunity is often hiding behind something that looks like it could never be the way forward and upward. But like a hidden pathway, or a secret doorway, we must be willing to experiment with new experiences, new relationships, new ideas, and new combinations of things in order to discover it. Remember that the next step on the path to success is not obvious, and typically counterintuitive.

How Much is Too Much?

Thomas Leonard, the author of the book The Portable Coach, recommended several strategies for increasing success in life. He said to look at the things in your life that you're "tolerating," and then to eliminate them to free up mental energy. If you're tolerating a lot of interruptions, set up your life so that you eliminate them. Turn off ringers and alerts, and stop answering your phone when it rings, and you'll program people to stop interrupting you (and you won't hear the interruptions in the first place). He also recommended to look at places in your life where you run out of things regularly and have to spend time re-stocking, and to build a reserve of them so you always have extras around.

Simple ideas, but very valuable. I have used these strategies to free up a lot of time and attention in my life. Once you free up attention from things that were robbing you, and then you stock up on things that you use regularly, you can move through life in a more efficient and streamlined way.

But I've also noticed that many of us are investing our energy in creating a level of reserve that is not productive. In fact, it's maladaptive, and ultimately counter-productive.

I'm talking about the person who gets into good physical shape, but then has to become a bodybuilder in order to feel good about themselves. Or the person who has to go on a date with a different person every night in order to feel validated. Or the person who achieves financial independence, but then spend the next 20 years trying to become the richest person they know.

I read some research that suggested that the more money you have, the more you worry about money. I can be an anecdotal piece of evidence for this myself, as it has certainly been true in my life. The logic to explain this phenomena goes like this: The more money you have, the more you have to lose. And we humans don't like to lose things. So we worry more about it when we have it.

The more you have of something, the more others will envy you, as well. It can become a burden on your social relationships to be the successful one. The Notorious B.I.G. said it best: "Mo money, mo problems." I had a friend several years ago who had owned a massive estate earlier in his life. He told me that he had one person on his staff whose only job was to travel around his property and change broken sprinklers. He eventually gave up the big home and big staff, and he moved to a condo in a highrise building. He said it was much better to not have to worry about managing a big staff and all of the hassles of the estate.

I'm not suggesting here that you should stop having big goals or dreaming big dreams. But what I would like to suggest is that we must learn to "satisfice" instead of to "maximize" when we are dreaming our dreams, and setting our goals.

Once you get past a healthy reserve in any area of life, you have to start adding an extra layer of thinking and management in order to manage that reserve. A bigger part of your mindshare goes to worrying about losing it, and to managing how others perceive you as well. It's an interesting experience to have.

My recommendation is to start looking at opportunities through the lens of building a healthy reserve, that you're "satisficed" with, and then move on to another area of life, and build competence and success there. Once you achieve a vibrant level of physical health, then go to work on your relationships. Once you have your relationships in order, go to work on your financial life. Once your finances are handled, go to work on building a family. You can do these in any order, but remember to keep building a successful life, and not just one area of your life.

If you get too "top heavy" in a particular domain, you will start to experience the burden of an over-reserve. While some of this is OK, too much is mentally and emotionally debilitating. It's a counter-intuitive dynamic to watch for in your life as you pursue opportunities.

Strengthen Your Strength & Your Weakness

Peter Drucker recommends to build your career and business success on your strengths. I believe that this is the correct approach to business and money success. You want to take what you're good at, and then find a way to develop that into a value-creation skill set that you can use in the world to produce value, money, assets, and wealth.

As you encounter and create opportunities in your life, one of the key questions to ask yourself is "Will pursuing this opportunity help strengthen my strength?"

If it will, then it's a double opportunity. For example, if you've discovered that you're good at sales, and you have an opportunity to take a sales role working for a company that you admire, then it's actually an opportunity to not only succeed, but also to grow professionally as well.

The opportunity to strengthen your strength is so valuable that you should also consider putting yourself in situations and signing up for experiences that will develop this strength even more - even if you're not paid.

My business partner James offered to come to work for my company doing sales for two months for free when he first started with me almost ten years ago. Why? Because he knew that this would be the best place to develop his talents. He became our top salesperson. Fast-forward to now, and he has worked his way up to becoming my business partner.

Part of the work in identifying your unique genius is to find out what you're great at. It's then up to you to develop your gift or natural talent into a powerful strength that you have used in various situations to produce value.

As you move through your life, it's important to notice where you are naturally talented, and then to develop those talents by learning from the best, and challenging yourself at higher and higher levels. Your strength is likely where your business success will flow from.

Just as developing your strength is key to success professionally and in business, developing your shadow or your weakness is key to success in your personal life. Let's say that you are naturally a more rational type, but you are uncomfortable in social situations. By strengthening your thinking ability, you will develop your skills and potential in business. But by strengthening your social skills, you will develop your ability to have better relationships.

Many people avoid developing their weaker sides, because it is often uncomfortable. But a little bit of progress in your shadow area can have a profound effect on your entire life, often far more than working in the domain where you are naturally talented and comfortable.

If you have been neglecting your physical health, your emotional life, your rational side... or not developing your ability to create success, build relationships, or follow your purpose... then it's likely that you feel a big hole in your life in that domain. You might feel shame, or self-consciousness, or even terror. When you finally take on this domain, and find people who can explain it to you and help you grow there, it has the potential to dramatically impact the quality of your entire life.

In my life, I always avoided conflict. I didn't have a natural sense for social relationships, and I didn't know what to do if someone got upset in a friendship or work relationship. My wife has taught me that conflict is actually natural in relationships, and that it can be resolved by intentionally confronting it and working with it. This has led to incredible breakthroughs with friends, family and work situations. By working on weakness, I have so much more confidence with friendships and relationships, and I can relax more when I'm in social situations.

Strengthen your strength, and your weakness. These are two of your biggest opportunities in life.

Thinking, Planning, & Living in Longer Time-Horizons

As you develop in the world of career, business, money and investing, the time-frames that you think in become longer. Robert Kiyosaki points out that we typically go through the following sequence in relationship to business and money:

1. Employee
2. Self-Employed
3. Business Owner
4. INvestor

As an employee, your horizon is the work you're doing today, and producing positive results in the moment. You could be thinking past today, about getting a raise or a promotion, or even what your next career move might be, but most of your consciousness is concentrated in the short-term. You do your work, and you get a paycheck.

If you strike out on your own and become self-employed, or do contract work, you take on new responsibilities and new risks. You now have to learn and focus more on getting paying customers and clients, and you also have to follow up with them in order to get paid. It might take you a month or two to get a client, then a month to do a job, after which you might send an invoice, and then it might take another month before you receive your pay for the work. You have expanded the horizon and business cycle that you are operating within from a couple of weeks to maybe a few months.

If you start a business that produces and markets a product or service, your time horizon extends even further. You must invest to create your product, hire people to handle various roles in the business, risk money up front on marketing to generate leads, then follow up with those prospective customers to get them to buy from you… and keep following up to turn them into long-term customers who continue to be profitable. As a business owner, you might start thinking in cycles of 6-12 months or longer, as you make investments in new projects and then receive the returns much later.

If you then take the developmental next step to become an investor, the time horizon stretches out for years. You might invest in a stock and hold it for several years. Or buy a piece of real estate and intent to rent it out for a decade. I have investments that I made between five and ten years ago in startups that appear to be doing well, but I won't know until they experience some type of exit whether or not my investment has paid off. These types of time horizons can be scary, as your capital is locked up in an investment that may or may not work out, but you just have to stay with it until you discover what happens.

If you have children, the time horizon stretches out for decades, and for entire life-spans. An early investment in extra time and attention with your child can pay off spectacularly in terms of a feeling of secure attachment and self-esteem in your child later.

I find this expansion of time horizon to be one of the more interesting and challenging aspects of opportunity. As you develop in your life, and begin seeing and thinking in longer and longer cycles in different domains, and feeling what they are like experientially, you are growing as a human being.

Only through experience do you see what the long-term impact can be in saying something hurtful or mean, or doing something that damages your reputation. And only through experience do you see what an incredible difference it can make in the life of another person to take the time to understand them and help them get to the next level of their own development.

As you work with this material, and you seek out and creatively experiment with opportunities in different life domains, begin thinking in longer time-horizons… observe the longer cycles… learn to dance with the longer-term implications of the decisions that you make.

Making a decision today that you won't know the outcome of for years or decades involves a huge sense of responsibility. Most people become very uncomfortable when faced with making a long-term financial decision, or making an investment that they won't know the result of for ten or twenty years. And rightly so.

If you haven't learned how to think in time-scales of months, then years, then decades, you don't develop the models and intuition to guide you when faced with decisions like these. It feels like standing on the edge of a cliff and making the decision to jump off, not knowing whether or not you'll sprout wings and fly on the way down. It can be scary.

This is why it's so important to work with the ideas, tools, and models that I've assembled here, so that you can start to see bigger patterns as you grow in life, and to think and plan in longer and longer time scales and cycles. Practice making predictions about how things will turn out in various domains of your life, in order to develop this long-term sense.

An exercise that I find particularly valuable is to intentionally notice what different lengths of time feel like. Set a timer for one hour, then go to work on a project and focus until the timer goes off. When it does, stop and reflect for a minute or two one what one hour felt like physically, emotionally, and conceptually. Then try it with two hours. Start noticing what the time period of 24 hours, or one full day feels like. If you have a routine that you do at the same time each day, leave yourself a reminder to take a minute to check in with yourself, and notice what it felt like to live in that space of 24 hours. If you do this for several days, you will imprint or map an intuitive sense of one a full day feels like.

Continue expanding this to three days, a week, two weeks, a month, three months, and a year. I remember in one of Shad Helmstetter's books he told the story of seeing his grandfather each year around the holidays, and his grandfather would take him for a walk, and snap his fingers and say "another year has gone by, it's what you do between the snaps that counts." That always stuck with me, and it's exactly what I'm talking about.

Peter Drucker advises that each year you should invest the time to make a plan for that year, and then at the end of the year invest the time to carefully reflect on your plan, to see what you did and didn't accomplish. This type of ritual also helps you develop an experiential intuition around what a year feels like and about what's possible in a year. It also develops your ability to imagine what you can actually accomplish in a year, to make you more productive and effective in the bigger picture.

My wife Annie and I go to Burning Man every year. We met there in 2009, and it has been a ritual for us to return annual to experience what we think of as the coolest event on the planet. We orient and organize our entire year around being at Burning Man around the first of September. The ritual of going to Reno, Nevada a few days early to acclimate to the time-zone and to shop for supplies... and then waking up before dawn the first day to drive into Burning Man... gives me a chance to reflect on what another year feels like in my life. The event also offers me the opportunity to unplug from technology and experience new and novel ways of thinking about life, community and society. I often get my best insights and ideas when I'm at Burning Man, and it has become a sort of defining yearly family ritual.

I recently realized that in my life, I have made a major change every ten years since I was sixteen. At age 16, I dropped out of high school, got a car and a driver's license, and started sleeping at friend's houses much of the time. I went to a local community college, and tried to pursue a career as a musician and jewelry maker. At age 26, I moved from Oregon where I grew up to San Diego, California to pursue a career in marketing. Another huge move for me, and a time when I went from making very little money to being able to afford a nice apartment (small, but nice) and a nice car. At 36, I started teaching entrepreneurship and marketing full-time, and transitioned out of teaching dating advice, which I had done for about five years. This was a major shift for me, and involved a lot of risk and change. At age 46, I had a huge revelation about my relationship with my wife, and I let go of a lot of anger and resentment that I was holding towards her… and settled into my relationship in a more permanent way. After eight years of being together, it really clicked for me that we were now merged into one entity, and that I was never going to be alone or on my own again. This insight about the 10-year cycle in my life was a revelation, and it allowed me to really understand and get a sense of what a period of ten years **feels** like.

In 2009, I went to my high school 20-year reunion (I dropped out of high school early, but I went to the reunion anyway!). It was one of the best times I've had in my life. I had not seen most of the people there in the twenty years, and it was an enlightening experience for the entire weekend. What was particularly interesting was to reflect on what twenty years **felt** like.

Warren Buffett and Charlie Munger are famous for talking about how patient they are as investors. They often say that they will wait years for the right investment opportunity, sometimes sitting on billions of dollars in cash… just waiting… for the right opportunity.

You really have to believe in yourself and in your ability to find and create long-term opportunity if you're going to approach life this way. Think about it. If you had a billion dollars in cash, would you personally spend most of every day reading, studying the market, and looking at potential opportunities… until just the right one came along maybe a year or two down the line, before investing? And would you invest with the expectation that you were going to hold that investment forever?

Who would you have to become in order to do something like this? And what would your life experiences have to be in order to approach things this way, have this level of patience, and then also have the courage to make an investment this big when the right opportunity presents itself?

What we're talking about here is a type of self-esteem, a sense of your own knowledge and confidence, and a well-thought-through system for analyzing and selecting opportunities. Character aspects and skills like these are only built through experience, and with intention. You have to intend to do it, and then use the days, weeks, months, years, decades to practice… so you can discover and then recognize a great long-term investment when it comes along. Otherwise, you're easy to fool, or too afraid to make a decision and commit, or both. You build this type of self-esteem and develop greater confidence in yourself by playing the game of life in longer and longer time-frames.

REMINDER: Download the "Opportunity Companion Guide" to Get Your Summaries, Checklists & Exercises

This book has an **Opportunity Companion Guide** that goes along with it, which you can download for free. It includes key chapter summaries, implementation checklists, and written exercises - plus extra chapters and other bonus material. Go here to get it now, so you can review the summaries and start implementing what you're learning:

OpportunityBonus.com

Where & How to Find Opportunity

Finding Opportunity at the Edges

WHEN YOU LOOK AT the origin stories of the most famous entrepreneurs, you also often find that they discovered opportunity at the edge of acceptability, culture, and even legality.

Steve Jobs started out building "blue boxes" - which were devices you could use to make free (illegal) long-distance telephone calls from phone booths. Steve also famously used LSD, and said that it was one of the most important experiences of his life (Apple's software and user interfaces bear the distinctive mark of psychedelically-inspired design).

Google was built on things like being a better pornography search engine, and on placing advertisements in their search results that most people didn't know were paid ads - that sent money to Google if you clicked on them. YouTube was built on content that was being published illegally by hoards of users. Uber was built by doing things that were illegal in many of the cities in which they operated.

Mark Zuckerberg's original college software project was called "Facemash" - which was a site that allowed you to rank the attractiveness of other students at Harvard. He was accused of violating privacy, copyright, and security rules.

Each of these early "experiments" went on to lead to massive success for each of the enterprising entrepreneurs involved. Each was vindicated that what they were building was ultimately worth the risks, because they were seeing the future in some way that others weren't.

When I wrote my first book, Double Your Dating, I was teaching men about how to succeed with women and dating. There was something about this that felt edgy, and risky. It still does. The war of the sexes is real, and teaching men how to go from socially awkward to charming and attractive requires some courage. People are sometimes offended by the advice that I offer men, but that's part of the price you have to pay to do something innovative (and fortunately, most of the stories I hear from men are stories of success finding partners... marrying the love of their lives... building families, etc. so the long-term payoff has been overall very positive).

If you want access to the biggest potential opportunities, you must we willing to dance on the edge a little more than most people. It takes courage to believe in what you're doing enough to risk offending people, or doing things that are "about to become legal," but the lessons of history are filled with stories of entrepreneurs who did just this, and won in the long-run.

Later, we'll learn about increasing the number of tests, experiments, and small bets in your life and business, and how in the long-run this turns out to be a good strategy. For now, remember that if you want to discover and develop the biggest opportunities, it will require you to be at the edge of your comfort zone, and at the edge of the comfort zones of potentially a lot of other people as well.

But remember, that the edge is where opportunity lives. Learn to become more comfortable at the edge, and you'll find yourself surrounded by a lot more wonderful opportunities.

Opportunity Shopping

Does opportunity come to you, or do you have to go out and find it?

By now, you have probably noticed that I prefer to go out looking for opportunity, and that I take a proactive approach to opportunity discovery.

I think that the most empowering stance toward opportunity is that it is unlimited, and that it is growing all the time. But even though opportunity is abundant, we must go out and intentionally look for it, if we want to discover those opportunities that are best for us as individuals (and even those opportunities that are best for groups and communities that we are members of).

It's a balance that we must strike. We must know that opportunity is everywhere, but we must also going out and look for it. It's about seeing opportunity all around, but only selecting and developing those opportunities that are best for us. It's about keeping an open mind about doing new things, but also focusing on those opportunities that will bring the most benefit.

Annie and I were in Boulder Colorado recently, and we were in a part of town that we were unfamiliar with. It was about 9 PM at night, and dark outside. We saw a grocery store, and decided that we would pick up a few things if it happened to be open. As we walked around the outside of the store, we couldn't quite tell if the store was open. The lights were down low, and there were only a few cars in the lot. We walked toward the front door, thinking more and more that it was probably closed, but as we got closer, to our surprise, the front door opened automatically.

As we walked in, it was obvious that we were likely the only ones in the store. They were about to close for the night. We walked to the fresh produce section. It had been freshly stocked right before we got there. Every shelf, every rack, every table was full of fresh fruits and vegetables. Refrigerated cases were packed full of brightly-colored chard, beets, and leafy vegetables. Tables and bins were stacked high with strawberries, apples, squash, onions, and every other imaginable fruit and vegetable. I stood there looking around, not even knowing where to start. It was the greatest concentration of fresh, beautiful, amazing produce that I had ever seen. In a flash, I imagined what it would be like to bring a prehistoric human into this store with me.

I imagined taking someone who spent most of their day looking for food into a room like this that had enough food to feed everyone in their tribe many times over... food that was grown using the best methods, using the highest quality seeds, most of it organic… then picked when it was perfectly ripe, washed, and prepared for display to make it appear most attractively. My guess is that this prehistoric human would have been awestruck, and possibly overwhelmed by the sight. They might have gone to get their family and friends, and just sat in the middle of the room laughing at the sight! I stood there in that room looking around, and realizing that this level of concentrated diverse opportunity was completely outside of what we humans would have encountered in our day-to-day lives.

And this has become a metaphor for how I think about the increasing opportunity that's all around us. Most of us can walk or drive to a town or a part of a city where we have essentially unlimited options for high-quality, freshly-prepared gourmet food. We can shop through an unlimited number of fashionable, low-priced clothing options. We can access almost anyone online to learn things and engage in dialog. We have a choice between millions of songs, videos and movies to watch. It's a lot to deal with.

The produce in that grocery store is there every day, for anyone who goes there looking for it. In order for that store to be a real opportunity for you, though, you have to have a vision of what you need and why you need it. You have to know what types of meals you're going to prepare, and which of the foods you need as ingredients. Then, when you walk in, everything makes more sense.

When you know what you're trying to do, then it becomes easier to work with the myriad of different items that you'll encounter. Of course, as you walk through the grocery store, you'll also see new options that you weren't considering, and sometimes one of them will jump out at you as something to get as well. But you're approaching the entire situation with a selective eye.

Another aspect of the metaphor is the stance towards the availability and the abundance of the resources in the store. If you walk into the store thinking that you're an unlucky person who isn't deserving of the food inside, you might walk through without even looking around.

Maybe you think that the food in this store is "too good for you" and that you're the kind of person who only buys groceries in the discount grocery store across town. You might walk into this store with a friend, and be internally mocking everyone who is shopping there… and miss out on new ideas and new foods that could be very beneficial or enjoyable to you. The way you experience the grocery store is related to how you see yourself, and how you see life.

As you go looking for opportunity, and as you begin designing your life to optimize for increasing the quality and quantity of opportunities that you encounter and produce, I think that it's important to maintain a stance toward that opportunity the way you would walking into a grocery store full of groceries. You don't need it all, and you don't want it all. In fact, there's so much that you can only hope to leave with a tiny, tiny fraction of what's there, to bring back to your world and use in your life.

This grocery shopping metaphor helps us get a felt sense or transmission of how to approach and work with the opportunity that is available to us in our lives. There's more out there than you could ever possibly need or use. So much, in fact, that you can't even look at or consider most of it.

Opportunity is often found gathered or congregated in particular places, the way groceries are found concentrated in grocery stores. If you go to these places, you'll find it as abundant as you'll find vegetables at the market. When you find it, relax a bit, and don't get too excited or overwhelmed. Remind yourself that this is the way things are, and that it's up to you to discover and create the very best opportunities for yourself and for those you care about.

When you spot an opportunity that looks exciting, lean back a little bit, take a few breaths, and remind yourself to be selective. Don't let the over-abundance of opportunity overwhelm or immobilize you. If you find yourself getting too excited, take a break and go do something to distract yourself, then come back later with a fresh mind.

When you go shopping for opportunity, bring a short list with you, and stay open to seeing something amazing that you didn't anticipate. And be selective. Curate the best for yourself, and you'll find opportunity growing in quality and quantity around you for the long-term.

Go Out Looking

I grew up in a rural town in Oregon, about 30 minutes outside of the local city of Eugene. My parents were hippies who grew up in Brooklyn, New York, and their idea of "making it in life" was to live on a farm. So they left their home and their families in their early 20s, with a 2-year old child, and they moved to Oregon. We had very little income, and my family was on and off of government assistance as I was growing up.

Maybe once or twice a week, we would go "into town" - meaning we would drive to the city of Eugene. My father was someone who did not have the ability to pass by a "garage sale" sign without stopping. I grew up going to second-hand stores, garage sales, and junkyards regularly.

My father would pick through everything, and usually find something to take home with us. Every once in awhile, he would find a treasure. He would often buy broken televisions, and then bring them home and fix them. One time, he found a personal computer in a second hand store for a few dollars.

When I was in my late teens, I continued this pattern, and I would stop at garage sales and second-hand stores myself. One day, I stopped at a garage sale and found a stereo system with a large pair of speakers. I asked her how much for the set, and she said "a hundred and fifty dollars." I was into music and stereo equipment, and I knew right away that the speakers alone were worth thousands of dollars. I was so happy when I got those speakers, and I enjoyed them for years.

Another time, I went into a Goodwill store in Eugene, and found a set of cassette tapes produced by a real estate seminar speaker that I had recently seen speaking on stage. I couldn't believe my luck. Instead of the normal price of probably $100 or so, they were one dollar!

I took those tapes with me to my job, and I listened to them while I was working. I got so many creative ideas from those audio sessions. In fact, I went back several times to that same store, and a few weeks later found another set of tapes from the same person, again for a dollar!

I was so impressed with this teacher, that I called his company, and started making friends with his telemarketers on the phone. I eventually talked the company into hiring me to do audio-visual for their seminars, and this opened the door for me to learn about sales, marketing, and information products... which changed the course of my life.

You have to go looking for opportunity!

I mentioned earlier that I went looking recently for a new headset to use for calls. Lately, I have been frustrated with my computer headsets. I have multiple expensive headsets, but each of them has a problem. My $350 wireless headphones that I love won't work with some programs for calls. My fancy USB headset that was also expensive makes a hissing sound. My earbuds work pretty well, but the microphone hangs low and isn't good for recordings. I finally decided a few weeks ago to find a better solution. I went online and read reviews, and bought a few new models to try.

After trying them all out, I found one that I love: The Logitech H151. It plugs straight into my headphone jack, and it always works, with every program, every time. It doesn't need an adaptor (like my USB headset), it doesn't need to be recharged, and it's comfortable. But the real surprise was the sound. I am into audio equipment, and I own a few pairs of expensive headphones. The stereo headphones in this headset are wonderful. I was shocked when I heard them. I can actually listen to music on them, and have a great experience. And this headset was twelve dollars! A tiny fraction of the cost of my other headsets.

In my life, I have found that when it's time to find a solution, or get something done, or reach a goal, if I go out looking, I will find the opportunity. It's always there. But you have to go looking.

Being proactive in life is a winning strategy overall, and it's doubly true when it comes to opportunity.

Opportunity Spotting

Build a Lucky Self Image

"Build a lucky self-image by noticing where you are lucky."

IS LUCK RELATED TO success? Researchers did a fascinating experiment. They asked people to read a newspaper, and count the number of photographs inside. People who described themselves as "unlucky" took two minutes to count all the photos. People who described themselves as "lucky" came up with the answer in a few seconds.

How could this be? On the second page of the newspaper, there was a big advertisement, with headline that said "Stop Counting, There Are 43 Photographs In This Newspaper." It was deliberately designed and camouflaged to look like an ad. The unlucky people didn't see it.

Richard Wiseman, the psychologist who was doing this research, said: "Unlucky people miss chance opportunities because they are too focused on looking for something else. They go to parties intent on finding their perfect partner, and so miss opportunities to make good friends. They look through the newspaper determined to find certain job advertisements and, as a result, miss other types of jobs. Lucky people are more relaxed and open, and therefore see what is there, rather than just what they are looking for."

Wiseman went further, and created what he called "luck school" and had people do exercises for a month to practice behaving like a lucky person (seriously, this is real!). A month later, he went back and interviewed the subjects of the experiment, and guess what? 80% of them were happier, more satisfied with their lives, and... yes, they were luckier.

A few tips on how to practice making yourself more lucky: Follow your intuition more. Add more variety to your life. Look at the bright side when things go wrong.

My favorite method for building a lucky self image is to consciously look through my life at how many lucky things happen. I do it when things go the way I want them to, and when things don't go as I want them to. I do this with even painful and traumatic experiences from my childhood. This might be stretching things a bit, but I have gone back to consider how growing up with a father who was sometimes violent was lucky for me, as I have seen how that kind of behavior plays out, and I can now choose to live my life in a more peaceful way - having the benefit of experiencing how destructive violence can be to relationships and families. I know not to be violent with my own child, because I know what it feels like. In a way, this is lucky, as I would gladly go through unnecessary pain to prevent my child from having to experience it.

Each of us is the tip of an unbroken chain of miraculous humans, who were each the 1 in 500,000,000 or so sperm that were made that day... that made it to the egg at exactly the right moment to spark the genesis that we call life. If you follow the theory of evolution, this would be approximately a quarter of a million ancestors (!) between you and our last common link with chimps, for example.

This 1 in 500,000,000 LUCKY BREAK happened to every one of those quarter of a million grandmothers and grandfathers before you. That's like winning the lottery a quarter of a million times in a row. And that's just going back 7 million years. Life has been around for billions of years on this planet. The magnitude of lucky events and convergences that has synchronized to result in you being born are astronomical. It's basically mathematically impossible that you or I are here, right now. And to be born at the dawn of the age of the internet, when poverty and war are at all time lows, and lifespan and success are at all time highs... even more lucky.

The big insights here are that lucky people are happier and more successful, and that you can actually turn yourself into a lucky person by practicing.

They say "count your blessings" - and as you're pursuing opportunity, make sure to remind yourself daily of how lucky you are. You're going to need it as the number of opportunities that you pass up and miss increases exponentially, and you need proactive tools to keep your optimism high!

Opportunity Signals

As you drive down a road, you will see road signs that indicate that you are approaching a curve, or nearing an exit. As we accelerate into the Creativerse, there are tell-tale indicators that you are in a domain, or a time, or a situation that is likely to be rich in opportunity. In my experience, opportunity comes in waves and cycles, and there are hints, clues, signals, and warning signs when you're near it.

There are two main signs to look for:

1. Change
2. Stagnation

When a system is going through change, you are in new territory, and many things are unpredictable. Many or most of the people involved in a system that's changing do not know what's going to happen, and most of them are waiting for someone else to figure out what's happening, and what everyone should do. This configuration represents opportunity because a system going through change is often in chaos because it's reorganizing in order to break through to a higher level of organization on a different level. As the internet was being adopted in the 1990s, it was a chaotic mess (an exciting mess, though!). No one could have anticipated the reorganization that would come through platforms like Amazon, Google, Facebook, and others.

When a system has stopped changing, and has stagnated, it's likely that the people involved have become complacent and lazy. They often believe that everything is going to stay the same forever, and that they are entitled to things being stable and predictable for the long-term. This represents opportunity because new, creative, innovative entrepreneurial types will eventually discover these stagnated pockets of reality, and seek to use modern ideas and technology to reengineer and make these domains more dynamic and efficient.

In my experience, most people become confused, fearful, and conservative when things start changing rapidly. Because they haven't been anticipating, preparing, and mentally rehearsing for cycles of change, they become disoriented.

On the other hand, most people become lazy, complacent, and over-confident when their situation stays the same for too long. They haven't been mapping cycles of stability and change in their lives enough to know that stability is a platform for development and preparation for your next move in life. They essentially stop orienting beyond what they know, and get locked into a groove, going down a road that doesn't go anywhere in the long-run.

When change comes, it usually represents a massive wave of opportunity for those who are ready. And it's often not exactly what you'd think. When gold was discovered in California, the legend is that it's not the gold miners that got rich, it was the people selling picks and shovels. Like a surfer, you must read the water... prepare yourself... position yourself... and be poised as the swell comes... to catch that wave and ride it in.

When change comes, it creates opportunity for many people in many different roles. I am obviously very biased towards entrepreneurship, but a lot of people have also produced a lot of value and gotten rich by going to work for enterprising companies in new and emerging industries. Early employees at technology startups sometimes become millionaires because they chose the right company to work with.

If you are the type of person who prefers working in a more supportive role, then you can use this knowledge to watch for the signs of opportunity in a domain or industry, and then to go and find a group of superstars who are building a great company. I read somewhere that there are 150,000 millionaires in San Francisco. Most of these people did not get rich by starting companies. Google has likely produced several thousand millionaires alone.

I encourage you to take it seriously when you see the signs of change coming, and to realize that it represents a huge wave of opportunity for many people. If you know how to read and surf the wave, you can be one of those people.

Look Beyond Business & Money

In this book, I am focusing most of my energy on business and financial opportunities. I do this because it's a place to focus that is very motivating for most people, and it offers a way to both learn about opportunity and also improve a key area of life. It's a synergistic way to learn and practice these models and tools in life.

But remember that this is only the beginning. Our biggest opportunities in life are typically in domains other than business. Business is a means to an end. As we look more carefully at our lives, and ask more direct questions about what we really want, we can start to see that there are even bigger, more fundamental opportunities for us to watch for.

Ask yourself these questions, now that you are more familiar with the nature of opportunity, and notice what comes up for you:

Where is the greatest opportunity with my body? How can I avoid and prevent sickness and pain, and create more energy, health, and vitality?

- Where is the greatest opportunity with my emotions? How can I avoid sadness and anger, and create more happiness, joy, and fulfillment?

- Where is the greatest opportunity with my mind? How can I avoid boredom, and create more learning, growth, and meaning in my life?

- Where is the greatest opportunity in my environment? How can I avoid failure, and create success and surroundings that inspire me?

- Where is the greatest opportunity with my relationships? How can I avoid rejection, and build loving and collaborative relationships with friends, family and business partners?

- Where is the greatest opportunity to make a contribution? How can I end suffering and create success and joy for all people and all life?

REMINDER: Download the "Opportunity Companion Guide" to Get Your Summaries, Checklists & Exercises

This book has an **Opportunity Companion Guide** that goes along with it, which you can download for free. It includes key chapter summaries, implementation checklists, and written exercises - plus extra chapters and other bonus material. Go here to get it now, so you can review the summaries and start implementing what you're learning:

OpportunityBonus.com

Social Models of Opportunity

The Leading Fringe

WE'VE LEARNED THAT FINDING opportunity is about seeing opportunity. It's partially in the way that you look at reality, and partially in the situations that you encounter.

As I have studied and learned about different domains of life, I have found myself in very different groups of people, and very different cultures. If you hang out with a bunch of entrepreneurs, it's very different than hanging out with a bunch of people who are preparing for natural childbirth... which is very different from hanging out with a bunch of artists... which is very different from hanging out with an indigenous group of people from another continent.

As you get to know different groups of people who have come together around different passions, and purposes, and places you can also begin to see what I think of as one of the most interesting things about cultures. It's that each culture or subculture sees reality in a unique way.

I read an article about the dying out of languages around the world. It suggested that each language is a record of a unique map, model, or paradigm of the world and how it works. When you start thinking of it in that way, then the loss of a language becomes a much greater tragedy (as long as you're one of the people who values different ways of seeing reality, that is!).

When you immerse yourself in a group of people and a subculture that is passionate about something, you learn a new way of thinking about and approaching **everything**.

If you delve into the world of music, and surround yourself with performing musicians, you find yourself with a group that values expression and entertainment. If you go to work in a science lab, you'll find yourself in an environment that values research, measurement and rationality. If you spend time in a social worker's office, you'll find yourself in a culture that values empathy and charity.

Each of these domains is what we're calling a subculture - meaning a subset of the greater national or regional culture that they are a part of. Subcultures, to me, are like little laboratories that experiment with new ways have relationships, collaborate, compete, succeed, learn, evolve, communicate, and much more.

The "cool part" of being a in a mix of diverse subcultures is that each subculture has a different way of doing things. They are optimizing for a unique set of values, or a particular set of outcomes, and they have tweaked and tuned their reality model in order to best produce that outcome (they often don't realize that they are optimizing for values and outcomes, but if you look closely, you'll see it).

Therapists live in a model of reality where things work better when you get into the other person's perspective and feelings, seek to understand their emotional life, and behave supportively as they move through difficult changes.

Artists live in a model of reality where things work better when you creatively express what is yours alone to express, in your unique way, without worrying about whether or not everyone approves of what you're doing (and often being inspired and motivated when others don't like what you're doing!).

Entrepreneurs live in a model of reality where things work better when you look for business opportunities, then select the best ones to act on, test, and develop into valuable businesses, money, and assets.

And within each subculture, you will discover a smaller group that is at the leading edge of evolution in that particular domain. I call this smaller group the "leading fringe." They are leading, because they are way ahead of the world in evolution in their domain. They are also living in a kind of "fringe reality" where they tend to be living experimentally relative to everyone else, even in their domain.

And there are always a handful of evolutionary leaders in each leading fringe subculture who are essentially living in the future. These are the people you're looking for. These are the ones who will give you the download about where things are going in future of their domain (and often other areas as well). I love these types of folks, because they bring a new way of thinking that is typically radical and distinctive.

If you enter one of these niche subcultures, and practice their speciality with them, you can not only learn a valuable skill set and approach to realizing a particular values set in life, but you can also acquire something much more fantastic and valuable. You develop a new prism for seeing life.

It's when you start layering and combining these ways of looking at the world that they open up entire worlds of opportunity. When you take a model you've learned in one place, and you use it in another very different place, you can become very innovative and potentially successful.

Jeff Koons, the artist who creates massive metallic balloon dog sculptures (one of which sold for $58 million, the record for the most expensive work by a living artist ever sold at auction), started out as a commodity trader on Wall Street. He later emulated Andy Warhol's "factory" concept by hiring dozens of assistants to create the art pieces that he imagined and designed. If you listen carefully to how Jeff Koons communicates about his art, you can almost see the brilliant commodity trader in there, thinking about what would be the most valuable commodity for the art market. He learned to look at the world through the lenses of a commodity trader and an artist, and the results speak for themselves.

Tony Hsieh, the CEO of Zappos, started out studying computer science in school. Then he launched an advertising network. Then he started an investment fund. Then he became CEO of Zappos, an online shoe company. I have known Tony for many years, and what always blows my mind about him is how he keeps learning about new areas of life and business. He is fascinated with building culture, to the point where he is known as an innovator in the area. He has also taken on an ambitious self-funded project to revitalize downtown Las Vegas. Multiple lenses all working together to innovate in new domains.

I was a long-haired guitar player in the late 1980s. Later, I went into real estate, where I started to study sales. I then went to work doing audio-visual for a seminar company. I then went on to learn direct response marketing. Then I learned how to be successful with women and dating. As I moved into each new area, I met people who understood that domain, and I learned about how that part of the world worked. But I also brought with me the lessons learned from previous domains.

When I became an audio-visual tech for the seminar company, they were making poor sounding audio recordings. Because I had played live shows and recorded albums as a musician, I was able to bring that lens with me to this new seminar environment. By looking at the "recording a seminar" situation through my "playing a show and recording an album" lens, I was able to immediately see where the opportunity was to improve things (by getting better microphones and recording equipment).

When I was a real estate agent, I started to study sales methods and systems. In the process, I discovered NLP (Neuro-Linguistic Programming) which teaches that if you want to understand more about a person, it's important to understand their beliefs about the world. Later, when I was learning how to get a date or a girlfriend, I made friends with diverse guys who were naturals in this area of life. Because I had learned about beliefs in NLP, I knew to ask them about their models of the world. This led to many huge insights that helped me become confident in this new domain.

When I started teaching dating advice, I first wrote a book, which became successful. Because I had worked for a seminar company, I looked at the growing business through that lens, and knew that my next step was to do a live seminar. I recorded that first seminar, and it became my first audio and video course.

Each of these experiences that I had, and each of these subculture "worlds" that I entered in my life, taught me different lessons - and most importantly - different and useful ways of looking at things. These lessons have become more and more valuable to me through my life.

I find that people who have moved around in their lives become a part of different subcultures, who have learned different skills and different ways of looking at the world. I find these people to be much more interesting, adaptable, and creative than those who haven't done this in their lives. If you've been in your environment for too long, maybe it's time for you to join a new community.

In order to pursue this as a strategy, you must acquire the taste for being a beginner in novel situations. It can be stressful and sometimes embarrassing to be the only one in a group who makes "newbie" mistakes. But it is so worth the extra effort and emotional bravery required.

As I mentioned, I met my wife Annie at the Burning Man festival, which is in my estimation the "world's capital of intersecting diverse subcultures." It's a place that's designed on many levels for personal and collective experimentation. You can dress up in feathers for breakfast, attend a seminar on permaculture, then mingle with Silicon Valley venture capitalists at a talk on psychedelic research.

Myriad diverse subcultures from all corners of the culturesphere come to experiment with novel ways of living, thinking, communicating, expressing and collaborating. If you haven't been, and you're "that type" of person, then get yourself a ticket (and come see my wife and I speak when you get there!).

By immersing yourself in leading fringe subcultures, and finding the visionary leaders in those spaces, you learn new ways of seeing and understanding how everything works. You imprint new paradigms and values sets. You access aspects of your own potential that can be discovered and developed only inside of these diverse contexts. And you gain access to opportunities that are completely invisible to most people.

Your Opportunity Network

Networks create opportunities. If you're part of what we might call an "evolutionary network" in a particular domain, you will increase the number of opportunities in your life.

When you hang around innovative people who are experts at manifesting the reality that they want to see, you plug yourself into a powerful source of knowledge, ideas, experiments, collaborations and news. As this information streams through the network, you have a much better chance of seeing it and understanding the implications than others who are not embedded in the network.

Networks collect valuable information. Individual niche networks contain people who have spent their lives studying, experimenting, and figuring out the best way to do things in their domain. When you become a member of one of these networks, and you intentionally approach it as a willing student, you can receive an incredible amount of value very quickly.

As you become a member of multiple networks, and connect with others in multiple networks, this effect becomes exponential. The real power is at the intersections. Because most people only stay in their own network and their own little comfort zone, they don't experience the highest potential of their knowledge: Transferring and using it in a different domain.

It's when you take knowledge from one domain, and use it in another, that sparks fly, and great opportunity emerges. This is another reason why it's important to continually expose yourself to new groups of people, have new cultural experiences, and experience new ways of doing life.

I have had a lot of fun building my network in my life, and seeing the surprising and amazing results of putting different types of people together... and then watching what happens.

I did a series of events called MetaMind, and I invited about 100 people to each of them. Many of the people I invited were from the online education and coaching worlds, and some of the people were from other diverse domains like art, science, philosophy, psychology, futurism, etc. Each day, we would have presentations and group discussions, many of which were focused on what is happening in the online education and coaching world.

I remember one conversation that was centered around estimating what would happen in the future of the online education industry. As each of the people in the discussion shared their experiences, ideas, and predictions, something magical started to happen. We started to creatively imagine an educational model that involved taking parts of the traditional "university model" of education, and combining it with elements that we were all learning about in our individual teaching, training and coaching businesses.

We envisioned a new role emerging, of the "virtual guidance counselor" who would be familiar with all of the highest-quality online courses from different teachers, and who would also be trained in professional coaching methods. These people could help individuals understand their personality types, then match those talents to growing needs in the business landscape, connect them to the best online training courses, and then coach them through the process.

It became obvious in that moment that this was a role that was going to emerge in the future, and that it represented a huge business opportunity. So far, I haven't seen it become reality, but it's one of the best business ideas that I've heard. Maybe you're the right one to do it. (Or maybe our company will do it someday, or maybe we can even collaborate on it!)

Sitting in the middle of that group discussion put me at the heart of a fascinating network of people, and as each of us contributed ideas for a potential business model, it just became more and more valuable. This is an idealized example of the value of being part of a network of people who are good at finding and creating opportunity, but it gives you a sense of what's possible.

I've had hundreds of conversations like this in my life. Each time, I marvel at the emergence of insights, ideas and innovations that comes from bouncing ideas around between diverse minds.

I also like to attend conferences for niche domains of interest and practice. I find that events that have up to several hundred people tend to be the most interesting. I'd say that the sweet spot is from a few hundred to maybe a thousand or so max.

To me, this is the range where you're getting a group of people who are passionate, but it's still early enough in its development that you are learning something that's relatively new and fresh.

I can remember attending the first "Singularity Summit" in San Francisco. There were maybe a few hundred people in the group. As I sat there hearing people talking about computers achieving human level consciousness and extending lifespan indefinitely, I knew that I was hanging out with a creative group of humans! I now have many friends from that world, and I find them to be some of the most interesting and creative people I've ever met. Those small conferences are where the subcultures are crystallizing, in many cases. If you can find them, go.

Ultimately, you must build your own opportunity network. And you must approach the building of your opportunity network with intention. There's a huge serendipity element to opportunity, and to the building of an opportunity network. But there's also great value to be gained by thinking about your social network as being a brain that is designed to produce opportunity for its members and for itself.

And again, keep an eye out for the visionary creative thinkers in each domain that you involve yourself in. They will often be essentially "invisible" to you, because their way of looking at reality will seem essentially alien. They have been off on their quest to understand their dimension of reality for so long that they are often unrecognizable.

A Silicon Valley venture capitalist famously called Steve Jobs a "renegade from the human race" when he met him. Steve was 21, had ripped jeans, and was walking around their garage workshop with bare feet. That's the kind of thing you're looking for.

I remember going to Burning Man in 2012 with a group of friends, and walking into the art gallery created by Android Jones. I will never forget seeing this man, dressed like a shaman from another dimension, standing up on a small riser, lighting what looked like a brass bowl of something... then holding a small machine and pointing it at the bowl. As I got closer, I realized that he was lighting a large metal bowl of incense, and then using a small **leaf blower** to circulate the scent of sage through the gallery.

Android has turned out to be one of the most fascinating people I've ever met, and I think he's also the most innovative visual artist alive today. You wouldn't know this immediately if you had seen the "inter-dimensional art shaman" stoking the cauldron of incense with the leaf blower, but in retrospect it makes perfect sense. (Thank you, Android, for designing the cover of this book!)

Often, the thought leaders in these fringe cultures and niche networks dress in an unusual way, or they have their own style or mannerisms. Or sometimes they have no apparent style at all. The visionary leaders in these domains are often unconcerned with participating in normal "consensus reality" - so they may not cut their hair, or might live off the grid, or in a house with 20 other people, or perhaps they have their own cult. They're often surrounded by controversy (or at least rumor).

What I'm trying to do here is widen your peripheral vision, soyou start considering more diverse and interesting people as part of your opportunity network.

Further, if you are part of several of these networks - especially if you're the only one that is the connection of those networks - then this becomes a multiplier. You recognize an opportunity relative to one domain, and then you look through your conceptual lens of the other domain, and see how they could be layers or hybridized in order to create a new and novel opportunity.

And instead of this happening just on the mental model level, which tends to be more of theoretical manifestation, it starts happening in a more real-time way. It's when you see opportunity emerging across more than one domain simultaneously, and you start seeing intersections, that things become really interesting.

In the early part of 2017, I started getting getting a lot of messages from friends and people in my network asking me about blockchain and cryptocurrency. I had been casually following the rise of bitcoin and the blockchain, but something happened in early 2017, and it really started to hit a critical mass in the consciousness of my different networks. Entrepreneur friends were asking about it. Artist friends were asking about it. Personal friends were talking about it.

A couple of friends invited me to attend a live event on the topic, and when I went there I saw three other people I knew within a few minutes. What stood out to me about this topic was that it was hitting the radar screens of very different types of people, all at once. It was interesting to many different industries and groups.

As I have spent more time attending events, making new friends, and learning more about the new paradigm and values system that is emerging here, I have realized that this is more than just the emergence of a new technology. It's also the emergence of a new culture, with a new set of values. Already, many new opportunities have come into my life by connecting to these new entrepreneurs and visionaries.

As you build your opportunity network, focus on finding people who are at the intersections of multiple networks. Look for the musician who knows the other musicians, but who also hangs out with technology geeks and foodies. Look for the architect who is the innovator in the group, but who also hangs out at the chess club and the windsurfing meetup. Look for the investor who has an investment mastermind, but who also loves going to art openings and who has a Burning Man camp.

And keep building your opportunity network with new, diverse, interesting people who are connected to multiple networks. Your opportunities will increase exponentially as a result.

Mastermind: The Ultimate High-Leverage Tool for Self-Evolution

I'd like to share what I believe is the highest-leverage model and tool for change and success that I know of. This is the idea of the "mastermind," that I first learned about from Napoleon Hill, in his timeless book Think & Grow Rich.

I want to emphasize again that this is the highest-leverage model that I know of for personal change and success. Of everything I'm sharing here in this book, nothing has the direct sort of shaping power and influence that a mastermind has.

If you want to change, and become something that you are not, then this is the way to do it. It probably has five or ten times the leverage of any other way of influencing yourself.

In fact, Napoleon Hill said directly and clearly that no one can have great power and success in life without a mastermind. So not only is it a path to becoming who you want to become, and achieving what you want to achieve… but if you don't use the power of the mastermind, then it's essentially impossible to realize great success in life.

Hill defined a mastermind as "Coordination of knowledge and effort, in a spirit of harmony, between two or more people, for the attainment of a definite purpose."

I will explain my way of thinking about a mastermind. To me, a mastermind has the following qualities. It's a…

- Group of people
- High achievers
- Meeting regularly

- Sharing and supporting each other
- Working purposefully
- Collaborating
- Let's take these one at a time.

GROUP OF PEOPLE. This is key. There's something about our natural "imitative learning" function that is highly influenced when we are observing another person, ideally in-person, who is a living example of what we are trying to learn or develop within ourselves. Just a like a child learns from who you are and not from what you're saying, we adults also learn from a sort of direct transmission that happens when we are in the presence of another person. It's a kind of "tribal wiring." This effect is so powerful that we must be very careful who we expose ourselves to, as other people influence everything from our self-image and self esteem, to our model of how the world works to our beliefs about reality itself. If we are in the presence of someone with a negative self image and pessimistic beliefs, these will imprint upon our psyches without any conscious effort or even awareness, in most cases. When you then put yourself into a group of people who all share particular ideas and values, it creates an exponential multiplication effect of influence that is essentially irresistible. Social psychology has shown over and over again, in many different types of contexts, that a group of people can influence an individual to do things that are completely against what the individual would have done if they were alone. When you use this knowledge intentionally, and you assemble a group of people that is consciously designed to influence you in a direct way (because you have imagined where you want to go in life and want to use the ultimate technology for shaping yourself) this knowledge becomes profound. Key to the mastermind: It's a group of people.

HIGH-ACHIEVERS. Because we are influenced so directly and powerfully by others and by groups, we want to intentionally select people who will be the most positive influence on us and on our direction in life. My experience and my teachers have shown me that one way to identify people who will perform well in the future is to look at how they performed in different situations in the past in their lives. Many people give up when they face obstacles, or setbacks. Or they stop trying when challenges arise and the going gets harder. When forming a mastermind, look for those who have consistently achieved success in their lives, in domains that you admire. Ideally, the people you select will have already achieved success in the domain that you want to achieve success in yourself. By intentionally selecting high-achievers for your mastermind group, you stack the odds dramatically in your favor, and in the group's favor.

MEETING REGULARLY. As your group begins to form, you will notice that a sort of "collective intelligence" begins to emerge. The more the group can work together, the more this becomes obvious to everyone involved. In a sense, this is what's meant by the word mastermind. It's like taking a bunch of minds, and plugging them into a network, and using them as building blocks to create something on a higher order. You could imagine each mind becoming a neuron in a brain that thinks on higher levels. Meeting regularly is a key to the emergence of this phenomena. I have been in masterminds that meet weekly, and masterminds that meet quarterly and masterminds that meet every 6-12 months. It's not necessary to meet often in order to benefit, but my experience is that if you meet more often, you benefit more. Whatever you do, make sure to meet regularly with your mastermind, because the value and quality of what happens goes up with each successive meeting.

SHARING AND SUPPORTING. The spirit of the mastermind is a one of contribution and support. You will likely get even more than you give, but the "trick" to this being true is your willingness to give to others and the group. Because of the direct influential power of the mastermind context, as soon as this process of giving begins, it turns into a virtuous cycle, and it influences everyone to give. Supportive environments benefit everyone on multiple levels. They increase happiness, from the social interaction. They increase a sense of well-being. And they increase inspiration, in my experience. If you're a more independent personality type, practicing giving and receiving support in your mastermind. By supporting each other on many levels, it can bring you magnified benefits in your relationships, family, and overall life - not to mention your business.

WORKING PURPOSEFULLY. A mastermind is more powerful if it has a purpose. Just like an individual becomes more focused when they have a purpose, the group becomes more focused as well. If you have a mastermind meeting and you just "hang around and talk" you might enjoy it, but you'll only generate a fraction of the value that you could have with a purpose. You can have a "tactical" purpose and you can also have a "strategic" purpose. In one of my masterminds, we each take turns on the "hotseat" - and we share a challenge or an opportunity that we have in our business. The rest of the group then takes 30-45 minutes giving that person specific feedback and advice to help them. This is more of a "tactical purpose" that gets everyone focused.

As an example at the strategic level, my wife and I went to a gathering of friends who were having a celebration. As part of the event, three members of the group performed of a long-form visionary poem. They had asked everyone in the group to share what their unique gift was, and what their vision was for the world, and then they wove all of the submissions from their members together into a powerful shared vision. It was incredible to listen as the entire group's voice was combined into one collective vision.

COLLABORATING. Collaboration is built on the recognition that each of us brings unique gifts and individual talents to the group and to the mission. As you work with people who have specific types of genius, and you work together in various situations, you begin to discover ways to work in pairs, small groups, and larger groups more effectively. To me, collaboration is special because it implies multiple people who are different, but who are also aligned and synchronized, and who are operating as one emergent entity. When you're collaborating, you are in the domain of 1+1=3 or 1+1=11. As your mastermind continues to evolve, you will see these magical moments emerge where the group is acting with one mind, and one body. Watch for those moments where something emerges that could not have come from one person alone. I was reading recently most great scientific innovations that are attributed to individuals are actually the result of collaborations, when you look closer. The key to collaboration is to find people who have different types of intelligence and skills, and then to figure out how to work together as a team, and how to turn differences into complementary pairs and combinations. Remember when you meet someone who sees the world in a very different way that they might make a great collaboration partner!

Organizing a mastermind is organizing a group mind. It's setting up the conditions so that a collaborative higher-order intelligence can emerge. When that happens, windows of opportunity open in higher dimensions for each of the member of the group. The mastermind represents concentrated transformational energy, and concentrated opportunity generation potential. Each of us should be a member of at least one mastermind at all times, in my opinion. It's the fastest, highest-leverage way to transform yourself and your success that I know of.

REMINDER: Download the "Opportunity Companion Guide" to Get Your Summaries, Checklists & Exercises

This book has an **Opportunity Companion Guide** that goes along with it, which you can download for free. It includes key chapter summaries, implementation checklists, and written exercises - plus extra chapters and other bonus material. Go here to get it now, so you can review the summaries and start implementing what you're learning:

OpportunityBonus.com

Opportunity Estimation

BECAUSE OPPORTUNITY IS MULTIPLYING for all of us, we need to have a first line of consideration, so that we can quickly choose which opportunities are worth investing the time to look at more deeply, and which to let go by without wasting our time.

Most of us, in my experience, do not give potential opportunities an "optimal initial consideration." What I mean by this is that when an opportunity either presents itself, or is within reach, we don't take a few moments to do some quick mental math to determine the real potential of the opportunity.

Further, because different types of opportunities have implications for different parts of your life, it's important to stand back and consider what a potential opportunity could mean to the bigger picture of your life…

In this section, I'd like to share the models that I use when doing a first pass at considering an opportunity. These models are relatively simple, and that's part of the point. For initial estimation, we don't need a deep dive. We just need to know whether or not what we're looking at **deserves** a deep dive.

The skill of quick estimation is one that becomes more valuable and more efficient with use. Use these models with each opportunity, and practice them. The more you use them, the more automatic they become.

We'll start with a couple of insights about how we get off track when estimating, then we'll dive into the techniques for making quick estimates to figure out whether or not an opportunity is worth considering in-depth.

Emotional Estimation

It turns out that we humans are not very good at estimating how things will make us feel in the future. We assume that winning the lottery will make us happy forever, or that losing a limb will make us depressed forever. But this isn't the case. If you look at the studies, you'll see that after an initial boost or drop in happiness from a particular result in life, we tend to return to our original levels - even if we get a huge windfall or suffer a tragedy in life. Lottery winners and people who are disabled in accidents return relatively quickly to their original level of happiness, which says a lot about human psychology.

This tendency to assume that reaching a goal will make us permanently happy (or that suffering a setback will make us permanently unhappy) tends to color our ability to initially estimate or perceive the implications of an opportunity to our lives. We get excited about things that actually won't result in long-term benefit to our lives, or we avoid things that we perceive as having too much risk, rather than taking a more objective look at the possibilities before letting emotions get the best of us.

If you see an opportunity, remember that you will only be temporarily fulfilled by a success, and also remember - very importantly - that if you go for it and fail, it's not the end of the world. You'll recover emotionally, and move on.

Value Myopia

Each of us has a unique way of assigning value to things in life. Because this is our lens for estimating and evaluating things, it is essentially invisible. It's like a colored contact lens that we wear on the eye. It's so transparent that we forget that it's changing our vision dramatically.

The way we value things determines much about our perceptions, thoughts, decisions, actions, and results in life. I believe that each of us has a "native" way of perceiving the world.

In my model, based on the triune brain model, we tend to be either more attuned to the physical-material domain, or more attuned to the emotional-social domain, or more attuned to the conceptual-idea domain.

If you're more a physical-material person, you're going to be looking at opportunities through a more physical, pragmatic, practical lens. If something doesn't seem like it can be done, or like it can be done easily, you might drop it from consideration immediately. You might not look deeper to see if it might be worth the extra effort, because it could yield some benefit in another domain of life (like feeling more fulfilled, or learning a new model). You will be measuring the value of an opportunity by the tangible, pragmatic, "real" results that it can deliver.

If you're more of a emotional-social type, you'll be unconsciously viewing opportunities through more of an emotional, relational, affiliation lens. If you perceive that the opportunity might create social tension, or make someone feel bad (including yourself), you might not even consider it. Or you might get hung up on an opportunity that you think will make someone feel happy, not seeing how much it will cost you in other areas. And you would likely not take into consideration how this opportunity might bring you tremendous benefit physically, or as an achievement, or help you learn conceptually, or to realize your purpose.

And if you're more of a conceptual-idea type, you'll be unconsciously looking through a more rational-logical lens. If an opportunity doesn't "make sense" to you initially, it might never even be considered as an opportunity. Or let's say that the potential opportunity involves going through cognitive dissonance or might lead to you changing your world-view. Something like that might be avoided completely, as it has a big unknown attached to it. Or maybe the opportunity would lead to a huge improvement in your social life, or your health, but these never even hit your radar because you've only got your "rational lens" on as you're scanning.

We each tend to use our own unconscious values lens and system when estimating the risks, costs, rewards and benefits of an opportunity. While this is obviously a strength that each of us has, it also represents a huge blind spot. And we need to compensate for this by widening our estimation of the value that an opportunity or possibility could bring to our lives.

My mother tried to persuade me to have a child since I was a teenager (really). I always felt offended that she was pressuring me continually through my life. I imagined a child as being a bad logical choice for me, as I liked having my attention for my own purposes, and I didn't like the idea of a screaming brat making my life miserable.

Well, fortunately I ultimately got the message that a child could bring something powerful to my life in a dimension that I couldn't even imagine… thanks to my wife. After having my daughter, I can now see how blind I was to the potential value of the "family opportunity." I couldn't estimate it, because I didn't have the experiences and frame of reference to know what the benefits could be. I was looking at the possibility through a rational lens, rather than seeing it through the prism of emotional fulfillment and enjoyment in life.

Every day, I have a type of fun playing with my daughter that was absent from my life before that. I have learned a new level of self-regulation and a new level of living as a self-aware role-model. I have seen myself being loving and considerate in situations where I assumed that I wouldn't be able to handle the needs of another. These experiences have developed my self-esteem, and my overall satisfaction and fulfillment with life in ways that I could not have even imagined.

As you move through life, remember to be willing to put aside your native way of looking at and valuing reality, and to learn new ways of estimating the viability of an opportunity.

The Power Of Estimation

Over the past few years, I have become much more interested in intelligence, and understanding what it is and how it works. The deeper I go, the more I come to believe that intelligence is primarily about **using maps or models of the world** in order to better understand, interpret, and predict. If we feel that we understand something, we'll have more confidence to act, to take risks, to try things, and to find our way forward. If we learn how to interpret the events that are happening and the experiences that we're having, we can orient and situate ourselves better in the swirling layers of change that are happening around us. And if we can predict better, we can arrive at what will happen in the future before others, and we will have a great advantage.

Prediction is quite the paradox. The idea that we can know what will happen in the future is a mind bender. I just read something written by a reputable scientist who said straight up that no one can know what will happen in the future, and that even trying is futile. In a sense, this is true. But in a sense, it is also very limiting.

I personally think that it's better to walk through reality believing that you can develop your innate ability to know what will happen in the future.

I also believe that it's useful to sometimes believe things that aren't absolutely true or accurate, if they help you realize an important value in life, have better relationships, make a bigger contribution, or achieve your purpose. My wife takes this much further. She thinks that beliefs should be created real-time to help you move through the domain of thought, and then be released immediately to make room for whatever is true next. To her, it is as if beliefs were makeshift bridges across an experiential gap, generated for an immediate purpose at hand... not to be dragged forward into our future identity, past their expiration date. In her words, "Beliefs get stale fast, and we can always make newer, better ones with the latest data." If she weren't the most brilliant person I know, and my greatest teacher, I might think this was overly weird. As it is, I think that it's almost too weird, but I'm trying to develop more of this quality in my own thinking, and it seems to be helping!

The point is that there are many different ways to approach thinking, understanding, explanation, reasoning, decisions, communication, and prediction. And none of them is the "right" one, the "best" one, or the "only" one. If you want to adapt more rapidly, develop more efficiently, and evolve to your highest potential so you can get the outcomes you want in life and be more interesting and attractive to others, then it's important to learn diverse ways of relating to your experiences in the world.

Now that we just went down that rabbit hole, let's pop back out to talk about estimation again. I think the practice of estimating how things will go in life is very valuable. It's important to not only estimate, but to also check back in after events happen, to see how the estimation turned out, and to refine and tune our estimation and intuition systems.

It's also important to engage in collaborative estimation practices with friends, associates, and groups of people, to study prediction in the context of a group dynamic. Things change when you and others are under the influence of the social entity or the group mind. By practicing estimation on these different levels, you get a much better insight into what it is and how it works.

Wyatt Woodsmall taught me about the philosophical idea of "teleological causation." Telos is the ultimate end of something. It can be thought of as the end state that a person or process is moving towards. Aristotle apparently introduced the idea that an outcome could actually become a cause. This is a unique situation that happens in human minds when we set a goal (an outcome or end state) in our minds, then go to work to create it - the goal having then become the cause of the outcome. Teleological causation is another mind bender, because it inverts the way that we intuitively experience reality as happening.

I watched a documentary about Werner Erhard, the founder of EST, where he discussed being friends with Richard Feynman, the legendary physicist. Werner said that he learned a lot of things from Feynman, but remembers one thing that Feynman learned from him. Werner told him that there were some things you could only learn by creating them. This stuck with me, as it's a new way of thinking about learning.

Werner is well-known for teaching people to stop "putting their past in their future" and just repeating what had already happened in their lives. In his experiential courses, they walk people through the process of creating a place of pure possibility in their imaginations, and then starting to invent new things to put in that imagined space for their future.

Another mentor of mine, Gerry Ballinger, regularly used the metaphor of standing in front of a giant canvas, and painting the story of your life. Most people look at the past, at what has already happened, and what has already been painted. They stand close to the canvas, looking at the past, and then continuing to paint the same story, patterns, and events over and over. Instead, he would say that we can stand back, and look over our other shoulder and realize that there's a huge blank canvas in our future, and we can paint anything we want there.

The self-help and new-age movements have extended these ideas even further, suggesting you can have anything you imagine, and that if you believe something enough, it will appear as if by magic. I tend to stop short of the "magic wand" theory of manifestation, but my aesthetic falls somewhere in the middle between "it's impossible to predict the future" and "imagine a new car in your garage and it will be there when you get home."

As I mentioned earlier in this book, I like the idea of the Creativerse, and I think that it's very empowering to migrate into this paradigm of reality, and to live more and more from and into this way of being. Like anything else, you can become overly weird or attached to these ideas, so you have to be mindful as you do it. But what I'm saying here is to start noticing your beliefs about the future, about predicting the future, and about estimation.

The more we can estimate what is going to happen in a particular situation, then watch as things happen, and then review after they happen to see how our prediction matched up to what actually happened, the better.

Estimate how much your purchases will cost when you're shopping. Estimate how reaching a goal will make you feel, and for how long. Estimate how much more energy you will feel in your body after exercising. Estimate how a meal will impact your ability to think and interact with others.

As you learn new models, use them to estimate what will happen. I was fascinated maybe ten or fifteen years ago or so when I heard Ray

Kurzweil explaining how solar, wind and other renewable forms of energy would completely replace fossil fuels in the coming decades. When he was making these predictions, solar and other renewables were less than 1% of energy production, and they were far too expensive to be considered viable by most people. But Ray pointed out that renewables were doubling every two years, and that, according to his Law of Accelerating Returns, that even this was accelerating, so they would be doubling in a shorter and shorter amount of time in the future.

Well, fast-forward to now, and almost 70% of new power-generation installations are solar and other renewables. We still have a long way to go, but the point is that it's often hard to see what's happening if you are using old models of thinking, or going "on intuition" alone. As a tip, if your models of estimation don't involve compounding and cumulative growth, then you really can't see what's coming with any kind of clarity.

So start estimating more. Estimate how things will go in the physical world. Estimate how things will impact your energy. Estimate how an event will make you feel. Estimate what will happen in relationships. Estimate how something will change your thinking. Estimate what will happen in culture and society.

I've developed a practice of using percentages to assess how likely an outcome will be, or how likely it is that I'll do something. For example, if a friend asks if I can come to their party a month from now, I rarely say yes or no. Rather, think about what might be going on in my life then and then offer them a percentage, "I estimate a 35% chance that I'll make it." I try to be as honest & accurate as possible. My friends often laugh at this, but they also appreciate the effort and the honesty.

And remember to check back as the outcomes are happening and after they happen. Notice how you will tend to only notice those places where your predictions and estimates were correct (this is confirmation bias). But look deeper, and use this process of going meta to estimation and prediction as a gymnasium to work your mental muscles and your imagination.

Practice Estimating Within 20%

As we become more entrepreneurial, and live more entrepreneurial lives, we realize that we will have to take more responsibility for our outcomes in life… if we want to create the lives and lifestyles that we want for ourselves.

Taking personal responsibility comes down to saying "I am in this situation largely because of the decisions, choices, thoughts, beliefs, relationships, actions that I have had, made and taken in the past. I choose to assume responsibility for where I go and end up in the future, and what my life and lifestyle become."

But this isn't the kind of dynamic where, once you do it, everything goes exactly the way you want it to. As you take more responsibility in your life, and you also realize that it's very challenging to create the reality that you want to live in, you get a sense of the challenge that it also is to get good at estimating with any kind of confidence.

As a help and support to this endeavor, I recommend that you add what we might call a "meta estimation." And this is the idea of being happy if you get your estimation within 20% of what actually happens.

If you can estimate an outcome, whether it be how long it will take you to walk from one place to another, how much a home-improvement project will cost, or how many people will want to buy your new product… and be thrilled if you get within 20%, it frees you in an important way conceptually.

Too often, perfectionism and paralysis of analysis cause us to go into recursive loops of fear and hesitation. We get the feeling that if we can just go and think about it all over again, and plan some more, or get some new insight, **then** we will be able to perfectly estimate and predict what will happen. And if we can do that, we can then relax and move forward. But this it's not possible to get estimates and predictions perfect, so we we get caught in the never-ending loops of trying to be perfectly confident before doing anything.

I think that a lot of this is left over from the basic model of competitive education & keeping a job, that's set a context for so many of us. In those situations, the entire path was planned out, the twists and turns were known, and the description of "success" could be known with some level of confidence (at least by the teachers and bosses). If you didn't do things "the right way" then you got a lower grade, or a lower paycheck (or you were expelled, or fired). The benefit of this is the systematic transmission of verbal and mathematical literacy to billions of people. But the cost is the programming of conformism and "playing it safe" to the point where many people never develop their creative ability to imagine, design, and produce the outcomes that they are capable of in the world.

This underlying pattern manifests when we try to estimate an outcome in some domain of life, and find ourselves stopped because we don't want to be wrong, or look bad to others. In many cases, it's just easier to do what you've done in the past, or to imitate what others are doing, than to deal with the cognitive and emotional stress of imagining things going differently, then being wrong, and losing what you have or being rejected by others.

To counteract this, I suggest that you adopt the attitude that if you can estimate within 20%, that you've achieved something important in life. Of course, you will sometimes be way off in your estimations, and sometimes you'll be much closer than 20%. But that's not what's important. The key here is to start with the assumption that getting within 20% is excellent. This helps relax perfectionism, and paralysis of analysis, and frees you up to start doing "mental math" a lot more often, and fine-tuning your process as you go.

This is practice of doing "quick estimations within 20%" is particularly valuable with business and investing opportunities. I regularly use quick estimates and even quick spreadsheets to estimate how a set of business and financial investments might play out. Because these usually involve compounding over time, it's very enlightening to see how an investment might work out over several cycles.

As you develop in your life, you will notice that life in general becomes more complex. You go from doing a particular job to managing a group of people who are doing not only that job, but also other jobs. You go from being single to being in romantic relationships, and then to being a part of a larger entity called a family. You learn new lessons about how things work in the world that have much deeper implications. You start to see complexity in domains that you thought were simple. And this is happening across many domains of life at once, and across new domains that you didn't even know existed.

When you give yourself permission to make mistakes, and you estimate outcomes with the idea that being within 20% is a win, you can start dancing with these different challenges, and mastering them much faster. You start learning a lot more about yourself and your own process of learning and development. And you get better at seeing the future, creating the future, and working in collaborative partnerships with others to see and create the future.

When you estimate, consider it a "big win" if you are within 20%.

Assume a 20% Success Rate

When you become an entrepreneur, one of the major adjustments that you have to make early on has to do with how you estimate your chances of success. An example might be creating a new marketing campaign, or launching a new product.

What is the probability that your new advertisement is going to work? Or the probability that your new product is going to succeed in the marketplace? It turns out that success is less likely than most of us think.

In my company, we did an analysis of hundreds of new advertisements that we had tested over the past few years. In our analysis, only 1 out of 3 of them performed well enough to keep running. And keep in mind, my company was good at marketing and advertising. We had been doing it successfully for years. And when we wrote new ads, only 33% of them "worked" for us.

A mistake that I see people make in business continually is estimating their probability of success much higher than it actually is. I will talk to someone who wants to create a new product, service, or learning program, and after speaking with them for a few minutes I'll realize that they are assuming that what they are doing is definitely going to work.

What's the problem with being so optimistic? Specifically, the issue comes down to how much time, effort, energy and attention that you invest before actually testing out the idea on real customers. We'll discuss methods of testing your product and marketing ideas out on a small scale before committing major resources in a later section. But for now, the thing to do is test out your idea on real prospective customers before you decide to commit and go big. And just know that there are ways to "pre-test" your product and marketing ideas before you waste too much time on something that's likely to not work.

When you are estimating the potential value of an opportunity, multiply that value by 20% to get a more realistic projected value. Most things that we try don't work out in business. By remembering this, it reminds you to run early validation tests, and to develop those things that show promise, and not just those things that you're excited about.

Again, practice estimating and predicting how things will turn out in different areas of life. The more you can do it, and check back in to see how things turned out, the more you can develop your powers of predicting and creating the future.

Estimate the probability of a new business or marketing experiment

---

REMINDER: Download the "Opportunity Companion Guide" to Get Your Summaries, Checklists & Exercises

This book has an **Opportunity Companion Guide** that goes along with it, which you can download for free. It includes key chapter summaries, implementation checklists, and written exercises - plus extra chapters and other bonus material. Go here to get it now, so you can review the summaries and start implementing what you're learning:

OpportunityBonus.com

Opportunity Evaluation

IF AN OPPORTUNITY MAKES it past your first level of estimation filters, this means that it warrants a closer look, and a more careful analysis of potential.

One key to evaluating an opportunity is to use multiple models to appraise, estimate and predict potential future value (and potential future costs or losses). Remember, as a general rule we unconsciously use our "native" way of perceiving and measuring value when looking at opportunities. But this leaves much of the picture in our blind spot, and it leads to missing many big potential opportunities as well as missing potential dangers. Use several of these models when seriously evaluating an opportunity. It will give you a type of perspective that will reveal far more about an opportunity than just using one lens or prism to view it.

Return On Experience

We will discuss the calculation of return on investment (or ROI), but I'd like to discuss what I think is probably my favorite model for evaluating an opportunity, that is a relative of ROI. I call it "return on experience" and I think that this model is going to become far more important as we move into the Great Acceleration over the coming years.

The idea here is that:

- We can't afford to have experiences that we don't learn from anymore. Things are changing too quickly, and wasting time doing things that we don't learn from is putting us behind.

- If you are having an experience that you aren't learning from, you have two basic choices: 1) Do something else, that you do learn from or 2) Do the thing you're doing in such a way that you learn from it.

- What you learn from an experience is at least as important as the experience itself. These lessons, when imprinted as conscious reference experiences and models, become the building blocks of development and innovation in future situations.

Most people don't choose their next projects, jobs, or learning experiences based on what they will need to know several years into their future. Instead, they do things that are "interesting" to them, or that are "available" to them, or that entertain them, or that distract them.

The learning element is not seriously considered in the context of optimally positioning yourself for several chess moves ahead. And the tragedy here is that most things learned now will not be valuable in the future.

When I am evaluating an opportunity, I am always asking: "Will pursuing this opportunity grow me as a person, build valuable relationships, and teach me skills that will become more and more useful in my future?" If the opportunity is only going to be about money, but will take my time and attention, then I'm not interested. I have passed up many opportunities to make a lot of money that just didn't fit my values set.

Right now, as I write this book, I am working on a few projects and pursuing a few different opportunities.

One of them involves learning and teaching mental models. As you have noticed, I am explaining a bunch of mental models as part of this book. My involvement with mental models has been very valuable to me, because it has forced me to practice teaching at a higher level. When teaching a model, you are not just teaching information. You're teaching a better way to hold information. And even though this is harder, and more challenging, I think it's worth it to practice this skill for several years in life. I believe this ability is going to really be useful later in my life, especially as my daughter grows up and starts learning how to make her way in the world. It's also going to be valuable to just about everything else I can think of in my future, because having mental models to use as prisms to view and create various dimensions of my life… physical, emotional, conceptual, cultural and spiritual… will produce a richer and more meaningful experience. My work with mental models has been a "hobby" for the past few years, but I'm starting to teach in this area more and more, and I think I will wind up building a business in this area as well.

Another opportunity I'm pursuing is building a technology platform to discover and share news about the future. As you've probably noticed, I find futurism fascinating, and believe all of us need to learn the basic "futuring" skills that have been discovered and developed over the past several decades. The idea of creating software to help people find, share and collaborate around futuristic news is very challenging and interesting to me, and I believe that by working on this project I will learn and practice several skills that will be incredibly valuable to me in the future I want to create.

Another project I'm working on is partnership-based leadership. My wife Annie and I have been collaborating on this topic for several years now. Most of the leadership models from the past several decades have a built-in assumption that individuals should be positions of management and leadership. Many of these models are highly valuable and useful, but it has occurred to my wife and I that when you learn how to lead in partnership with another, the entire game changes. The leadership role then has access to two diverse perspectives, which gives it a higher-dimensional or "binocular" vision unavailable to merely one individual. This collaborative-partnership-as-leader model holds the possibility of making more holistic and trustable decisions that optimize for many more variables.

Annie and I try to carry out a "debrief" every time we have a conflict, to reflect & see how each of us contributed to it. This has led me to many powerful insights in my life, including the decision made a few years ago, to work with partners on all of my business projects into the future. What I am learning from being in partnerships is truly profound, and I know that the experiences I'm having are preparing me for the collaborative future that is coming up fast.

The common denominator of these experimental projects and opportunities that I'm pursuing is their **return on experience.** I have a high level of confidence that what I'm learning from each of these enterprises is going to be worth a lot more than potential money. In fact, so far these projects have not produced a lot of financial profit. I'm optimistic that they will at some point, but I am not attached to it happening, because I know **the lessons I'm learning are more valuable than money.**

One conceptual doorway that this type of thinking opens up is the consideration of different types of experiences in life as being potential bigger opportunities than a business or financial opportunity. I approach life believing that my biggest opportunities will be in domains that are not directly related to money. They are in domains of things like health, energy, fulfillment, meaning, love, relationship, purpose, and contribution.

Of course, I pursue financial opportunities and business opportunities. I am working on several of these right now. But if you look more carefully at how I choose the business and money opportunities to pursue in my life, you'll see that I'm doing it more for the learning than for the money. If the money works out, that's great. But as an entrepreneur, I know that most things don't work out exactly as I planned, and so I'm keeping this return on experience as my highest value, and using it to make the big decisions and commitments.

As you seriously evaluate opportunities in your life, estimate the return on experience. Choose those opportunities you'll learn the most from, that will teach you skills, models and abilities that will become more valuable in your future.

Opportunity Cost

Warren Buffett, the self-made billionaire, and likely the most successful investor in history, says that the most important consideration when making an investment isn't the return on investment. Instead, it's the **opportunity cost**. Opportunity cost is a counter-intuitive potential "expense" that most people don't consider when choosing an opportunity or investment, or estimating their ultimate returns.

When we are in the presence of what feels like a great opportunity, it can emotionally and psychologically abduct us. We start fantasizing about all the wonderful things that will happen, and getting high on our own emotional state. We imagine the positive outcome we want (or avoiding the thing we fear), and then we start getting attached, and "taking ownership" of the result before it actually happens. This process tends to put blinders on our imagination, and keeps us focused on that one opportunity.

Opportunity cost is a fascinating way of approaching a potential opportunity, because it takes a completely different view. Opportunity cost assumes that there are several other opportunities that are available, where we could invest the same time, energy, effort, attention and other resources… and that we need to consider what the potential outcome would be for those opportunities as our most important consideration. Whenever we say 'yes' to one thing, we are saying 'no' to a million other things.

I was talking with my friend Dr. Geoffrey Miller, the evolutionary psychologist. We were discussing the topic of children inside of inner cities, and how they are growing up with unrealistic expectations of being sports and music stars, and getting rich by playing games and making songs. Geoffrey commented that none of these kids have had someone sit down with them and explain the real probabilities involved, and how fierce the competition is for so few spots in the "make millions playing sports" game. Instead, he said that if a kid grew up parking cars in a parking lot, and saved up for several years, and then bought a small parking lot, and ran it well, then bought a few more parking lots over time with their profits, that they would probably have a hundred times the probability of becoming a millionaire. But because owning parking lots isn't sexy, none of them will ever learn about or consider it. This is an example of how invisible opportunity cost can really impact the course of a life.

When an opportunity comes your way, sit back and seriously consider the other opportunities that you could pursue with your time, attention, and resources. Don't choose an opportunity just because it's there. And don't get attached to an opportunity, because many more are coming, and it's probably not very likely that it's going to go exactly the way you want it to go. This helps you develop a more abundant attitude, and gives you the patience to wait for the big ones. Remember, if this one doesn't work out, there will be another one right around the corner.

Return On Investment

This is possibly the most common way to appraise or estimate the potential for an opportunity. The idea is to predict the potential reward that you will realize by successfully pursuing an opportunity, and then divide by the cost or investment required to achieve that reward. This is your return on investment.

If you buy a piece of real estate for $200,000, and put $40,000 down, then your initial investment is $40,000. If you later sell the property for $400,000, and you net $200,000 after expenses, you have made a 500% return on your investment of $40,000.

This all sounds easy enough, but wait a minute... how will you make the payments between when you buy it and sell it? And how much will it cost to maintain that property? And how much is the real estate commission you'll have to pay when you sell? And what if the market crashes, and you can only sell it for $300,000 in the future?

Return on investment is usually a lot easier to calculate at the end of an investment or business opportunity than it is at the beginning! But it's a highly useful model to use when estimating the value of an opportunity. I recommend that you use it as often as possible.

Things get really interesting when you start estimating the *emotional return on investment,* or the *learning return on investment* of an opportunity. Or how about the *cultural return on investment,* or *character return on investment,* or *spiritual return on investment*?

When estimating return on investment, remember to start with the potential return, then multiply by the probability that you will succeed. If you have a potential return of one million dollars, and you estimate that your chance or probability of success is 20%, then the estimated value of this opportunity is $1 million multiplied by 20%, or $200,000. If, for example, you could invest $20,000 and this would essentially buy you this 20% chance of getting $1 million, then this is mathematically a 10x return on investment. Most individual investors would probably not take this bet, because they don't want to bet on things that only have a 1 in 5 chance of paying off. But if you really think this through, then these are exactly the kind of bets that you should take in life.

Peter Thiel is famous for placing lots of small bets on things that have a low probability of success, but a very high payoff. He has made investments in all kinds of "alternative" domains, and done very well as a result. Do the math when you're calculating ROI, and you'll start to see these opportunities all around you.

One way to get an even more granular estimate and perspective of ROI is to use this model:

Risk x Probability x Expectancy

Can be stated simply as: "Estimate the value of an opportunity based on what you are risking times probability of success, multiplied by the factor of iteration." I learned this way of thinking from Van K. Tharp, the investing guru.

Risk is what you will invest or spend. It's your time, effort, energy, money and other resources. It's called "risk" because it's what's at risk. If you invest, and don't get anything back, you have risked and lost your investment.

Probability is your chances or odds of success. Most people assume that their chances of success are either much higher or much lower than they really are. This is why some people spend years working on something that doesn't work out, or they don't even try because they assume that they'll never succeed. For most estimates, it's good to begin with 20% as a rough general starting point (as we learned in the last section).

Expectancy has to do with the results you'll achieve after you do many iterations or steps in your process. This model comes from the investing world, where your ultimate return is calculated by combining and aggregating the net result after you've made many different trades. Another good example of this is playing poker. In poker, your ultimate result or expectancy is what happens after playing many hands. You can lose most of the hands, but if you win the right hands, you can win the entire game.

So again, the formula is:

Risk x Probability x Expectancy

If you have $10,000, and you decide to invest it in the stock market, you have to decide how much of it to risk on each of your individual investments. You also have to calculate the probability that each of your investments will grow in value. You also have to calculate the total return that you expect, when you combine all of these elements together.

If you listen to some of the billionaire hedge fund managers and other successful investors, you'll notice that they tend to invest in both things that they expect to go up in value, and also things that they expect to go down in value. Why would they do this? Because the things that they expect to go down in value are their "hedges" - meaning that these are things that, if the market turns against them and goes the opposite way they expect, will pay off in a magnified positive way, and save them from losing their money.

So an investor might invest $8,000 of their $10,000 in stocks that they expect to go up, and distribute that $8,000 among ten different stocks. But they might also then take the $2,000 that's left over and invest it in gold and options, which they expect will go way up in value if some of their other investments experience a huge drop in value.

By using a Risk x Probability x Expectancy model, they will be optimizing for the overall return on investment, and also protecting themselves from catastrophe at the same time. This is a more dimensional way of thinking about risk and return than most people are using, and by using this model I'm suggesting, you'll be able to make better choices, and select better combinations of opportunities.

And speaking of risk, one of the most powerful transmissions of this way of thinking has come to me through the board game Risk. If you haven't played it, then I recommend getting it and then rounding up a few friends and family members (and plan for a couple of days of intense learning!). For the past two years, I have played at Christmas when my wife and I go to her family's house. The designer of that game has really captured the essence of the ups and downs of the real world, and created a fun way to practice using a model like this one that we're discussing.

In the game, you plan your strategy, and you place bets of various kinds. But then there is the "random" element of rolling dice, and of opponents that you must form alliances with and defend against when they form alliances against you. And because the game involves many rounds of turns, and decisions that must estimate and balance short-term and long-term implications, it shows you how strategy and chance work together to produce outcomes.

When appraising and evaluating an opportunity, calculate Risk x Probability x Expectancy. It will give you a much more dimensional perspective on the value and likelihood of success.

REMINDER: Download the "Opportunity Companion Guide" to Get Your Summaries, Checklists & Exercises

This book has an **Opportunity Companion Guide** that goes along with it, which you can download for free. It includes key chapter summaries, implementation checklists, and written exercises - plus extra chapters and other bonus material. Go here to get it now, so you can review the summaries and start implementing what you're learning:

OpportunityBonus.com

Opportunity Selection & Negotiation

WE HAVE COVERED APPROACHES for preparing your mind for opportunities, spotting opportunities, and for estimating the value of potential opportunities. Once you find one that looks right, sounds right, feels right, and makes sense, and all of your ways of calculating value line up, then it will be time to actually commit to that opportunity.

A moment of decision in life can be one of our most psychologically stressful experiences. The word "decide" is built from the suffix "cide" - which means to cut off, or to kill. It's related to words like pesticide, homicide, and suicide. Not very inspiring! Yet, in the moment of decision, we must cut off other possibilities, and potentially kill off other opportunities.

If you pay careful attention, stress often accompanies decisions of all types. The mind has to deal with the cognitive dissonance of potentially making a huge mistake, or missing a huge opportunity resulting from a different choice. The brain, pound for pound, uses the most energy of any organ in the body. I suspect one of the reasons it uses so much energy is this cost of decision-making.

I still think about decisions I made in the past where I missed out on big opportunities that were right in front of me. Sometimes they haunt me. But I remember decisions I made that led to accidental opportunity. Each of these possibilities creates a present awareness of what's at stake when it's time to make a decision in life.

Somehow, knowing that decisions can be very stressful helps me. It reminds me that when I feel hesitant, nervous, or fearful… or excited, optimistic, or greedy… that this is all normal. It gives me permission to relax a little bit, and allows me to go meta to the situation and look at it from a higher perspective.

WE'RE ALSO LEARNING MULTIPLE models and methods for finding, creating, appraising, selecting, and acting on opportunities, which adds to the complexity.

In this section, we're going to look at mindsets and methods for selecting your best opportunities, and doing it in a way that's less stressful, and more efficient and natural. Use these tools and models to select the very best opportunities for yourself and your future.

Evolution is About Adaptation & Selection

When people think of evolution, they tend to think of the "adaptation" side of evolution. Animals moving through a dangerous world, needing to move quickly or be eaten. Nature red in tooth and claw, and all that business.

But we forget that evolution is also called "natural selection" - and that selection doesn't mean only "selection pressures" but also "being selected" by another one of your species… in order to mate and reproduce.

If you go look around in the animal kingdom, you see a lot of strange things that don't seem to make sense at first glance. You see huge tail feather displays on male peacock and giant antlers on male deer. Darwin was confused by these exaggerated body parts, because they appeared to be counter-productive to the survival of the animals that carried them.

But Darwin also gave us a huge insight into what was going on here. In his work, he discussed "sexual selection" -which is a big part of the word selection in "natural selection."

Exaggerated ornamentation is usually observed in males when it exists, and evolutionary scientists tend to agree that it allows females to select the most robust, healthy and genetically fit mates more easily.

If you're carrying around a massive rack of antlers, then you probably have great genes, lack diseases or parasites, and have been able to find enough food to grow them. If you have long tail feathers with lots of eye spots on them, then you have great genes, lack disease or parasites, and have been able to run and fly faster than the things that want to eat you (even with the extra disadvantage of a few feet of feathers hanging behind you to grab onto!).

And if females love exaggerated ornaments, then they'll tend to mate with the males who have the most exaggerated ornaments, leading to the theory of "runaway" feedback loop, where the ornament (fitness indicator) just keeps extending further and further, as females select for it more and more.

The point here is that evolution is just as much about being choosing and being chosen (sexual selection) as it is about survival and adaptation. You can be born, survive to adulthood, and have a boatload of other positive qualities. But if you are not chosen by a mate, and you don't reproduce, then your genes don't make it into the lottery for immortality, and your genetic line ends there. The stakes are high, and animals do a lot to select and be selected by the best possible mates.

The term "selection pressures" means that you not only have to adapt to your environment, but you also must deal with the pressure that comes from needing to be selected in order to find a mate. And that's serious pressure!

In the animal kingdom, biologists have noticed that it's mostly females doing the selecting. Being married and having a daughter has shown me first-hand how powerful a woman's selection power is in real life.

I also know a thing or two about this, because in a past life I was the #1 dating guru for men, and I discovered that the "secret" to success with women was to stop acting like you didn't deserve to be selected. If you want to be successful at attracting a mate as a man, then you need to attract her. It's a completely revolutionary mindset for most men who have challenges with women, but it can also create a radical shift for a man when it's properly understood.

To sum up: Selection is a big deal. If you want to succeed in life, you need to **select** great opportunities, and you need to be **selected** as a great opportunity.

But there's another side to this as well. Many animals, and many humans, specialize in sending signals that make them appear to be one thing, but they are actually another. Counterfeit ornamentation, fake signals, and convincing camouflage are common in both worlds.

An anglerfish has an extension that sticks out of their head, which holds a small bulb at the end. These are actually bioluminescent in most cases, which means they light up in the dark. A small fish swimming at night sees the light, swims toward it, and then has a huge set of teeth devour them from the darkness. Not so fun, if you're the prey. (And by the way, scientists think that the "light lure" also serves another function - to attract mates - which is interesting to contemplate).

One of my favorite attractions at Burning Man is a giant mobile nightclub that has been built (I think) from a school bus. It is almost entirely covered in psychedelic lighting that creates pulsing waves of complex color patterns. The incredible contraption features a small dance floor that sticks out in front, ahead of the driver, where dancers can step up and dance. From far away, you realize the entire thing is a giant fish, with fins and a tail. If you look closely at the dance floor in the front, there are fake teeth, with a giant disco ball hanging above. When it all comes together, you realize the designers have created a massive anglerfish on wheels. This giant mobile disco drives around Burning Man, stopping to pick up and drop off dancers, luring them to its dance floor with a magical psychedelically-lit disco ball. This is a personal favorite example of selection in action!

Curate

In our evolutionary past, we had far fewer options than we have today. If you were hungry, there were no restaurants, grocery stores, or delivery services available. You had to go out looking for something to eat, or consume what you stored up previously. Walking into a grocery store full of fresh produce displays more abundance than any historic king could have dreamed.

The point is we now live in a very different reality from the one we were designed for, at the animal level. I think it's important to make intentional mindset upgrades when it comes to the moment of selecting an ideal opportunity. This prevents "opportunity overload" and the making of rash decisions or regrettable mistakes. There's an interesting new word that has been emerging onto the scene in various domains. It's the word "curate." I hear more and more people using this word in diverse contexts. Google trends show that the interest in the word curate is growing dramatically in the past decade as well.

What does it mean to curate? Originally, the word mean to "care for" or "be responsible" for something, and it also has historic religious overtones, implying caring for souls. To curate is to select certain elements from a wider array, as in an art gallery, music festival, or social event.

If you curate an art gallery, you select the pieces of art that will be featured in the gallery. If you curate a social event, you select and invite the people who will be attending. Curation implies taking responsibility for the overall production, and seeking out and selecting those elements that contribute to the best experience for everyone involved. It also implies creating a setting or a mood, aligned with a particular aesthetic.

I think that the explosion of options in the world contributes to the rise of the use of this word and concept of curation. When you have many options, you don't have to pick just one, and you don't have to limit yourself to what's readily available. You can go search the world for the best, and then from the options you find you, select the right combination to create the atmosphere, the tone, and the outcome that you want.

I am part of a Burning Man camp called "Camp Mystic." I curate much of the art we feature in our event space. Others curate the musicians, the live speakers and the performances. The camp leaders act as "meta curators" to coordinate all of these various mini-circuses happening, in order to bring it together as a unified, streamlined experience.

By the time we have the entire camp set up, it becomes something extremely intentional & special. When you walk into a space that has great lighting, great art, great music, great performances, and great people, it puts you into a certain state of mind that excites and inspire you. Even though it's out in a dusty desert, and much of the setup is improvised from whatever is available, it's clear and obvious that intention goes into making the space welcoming and mind-expanding for everyone who visits.

Because I curate much of the art we hang in our camp space, I feel a responsibility to make sure that it's the best. And so each year, I look across what has been produced by all the visionary artists in the previous year, and I select a few new pieces to feature in our gallery. I then add them to the collection of already-great pieces, and keep building a wonderful collection. I know there are always far more options than I could ever use, so I'm careful & selective in my process. I'm very selective. I often have to do a lot of extra work to contact an artist, get their permission to use one of their art pieces, then have it printed on special material so that it looks good in our semi-outdoor desert gallery. But it's worth it in the end, because we feature some of the best visionary art in the world, and when it's all displayed it creates an unforgettable impression on all visitors.

I believe it's important to "import" this curation mindset into your pursuit of opportunity in life. Remember you're not selecting opportunities in isolation, and you're not going to only have one chance at selecting an opportunity. You have essentially unlimited choice available to you, and you will be selecting opportunities as a way of life into the future. So start thinking about how to create a system for curating those that are the very best.

AS YOU SELECT GREAT opportunities in life, you will build a "collection" of them, and some will start to pay off in wonderful ways. You will start seeing how the right combination of successes in life brings you something higher and more interesting than just winning once in one domain.

As an opportunity curator, you'll build a collection of wonderful opportunities in different domains of life. You'll look for opportunities to become more healthy and energetic. You'll create opportunities to build relationships with people you admire. You'll pursue opportunities to create meaning in your life. You'll collaborate with others on opportunities to live your purpose, and make a contribution in the world. As these all begin working together as part of one life, you'll see how they synergize and create a higher-order emergent success that cannot be achieved by succeeding in one area alone.

To embrace the curation mindset and to begin approaching reality as an intentional and conscious curator, you must transcend or go beyond the mindset of "deciding." You must see that each decision is actually a choice, and that you have lots of options.

If you ever feel like you have "no choice" and your decision is being made for you, take a time-out, and ask yourself if this is really true. Sure, once in awhile you'll find yourself without options or choice, but this is the kind of thing that we just don't have to deal with most of the time in life. Use the tools that you're learning to generate lots of opportunities so that you always have options. Next, when you face a situation where you feel pressured to decide... or feel stress because you know the decision you're about to make has big implications for your life... take a few breaths. Put it in a wider perspective or bigger context, see that your life is a progression of steps, and that this choice is one of many. Most of the choices we make in life are not "life or death" - and many of them can be made by using the tools we're learning here. If you remember to use a multi-model approach, you can make great progress.

Ultimately, what we're learning about here is moving up a level, and approaching opportunity as a curator. You're creating a "gallery of opportunity" in your life, and you want to walk in, look around, and see that you have many choices... several of which are potentially great for you. When you start designing your life in this way, it can give you back a lot of that energy unconsciously wasted "worrying about decisions" - and frees up our attention for more important things.

We're not deciding. We're choosing. And we're not just choosing, we're curating.

If you don't have enough great options to curate, then take a time out. Go add good options to the mix, so that you're choosing and selecting, not deciding. Then, from those options that you generate yourself, select a promising mix of them to seriously consider.

Curate your opportunities; curate your life.

Wait, Wait, Wait, Commit!

Money burns a hole in my pocket. I'm not sure if this is because I grew up poor, and there was never enough money around, or if it's just "the way I am"... or maybe it's the culture I grew up in. Or maybe a combination.

In any event, I have a hard time just sitting on money, and not using it. When I was younger, I carried credit card debt for many years. In my early 30s, I had about $30,000 worth of credit card debt. Fortunately, I had invested a lot of this money in books, seminars, and education. But it was still there. And a lot of it, to be honest, was because I couldn't stop myself from spending the money.

I have met a lot of other people who have a similar "problem" with money. Part of the problem, I now believe, is that we forget that better and better opportunities are coming in the future, so we take whatever is available in the moment. Probably another tendency left over from our prehistoric foraging days. If you have resources, you have to use them, or they'll go bad or be taken by someone else.

Warren Buffett and Charlie Munger are very impressive, not only in their success, but also in their patience. I have already mentioned that they will sit on a huge pile of cash for years if they don't have a wonderful opportunity to invest it in.

Their mindset is: Wait, wait, wait... commit!

They are looking for one good investment idea per year. Often, they don't find one, so they hold on to billions of dollars in cash, waiting for just the right opportunity to come along.

This might sound like a paradox, or possibly like it doesn't go along with some of the other things that I'm saying here in this book. If there are lots of opportunities around, and more coming in the future, why not just invest your resources in the best of what's available? This is where a bit of artistry is needed. Yes, there are lots of opportunities around us right now. And yes, there are exponentially more coming in the future. But striking the balance between acting now and waiting for just the right opportunity for you is important.

Warren Buffett and Charlie Munger invest in the long-term. They think in decades and lifetimes. When you start looking at the implications of compounding interest, capital gains, and long-term accumulation, you see just how important it is to choose the best opportunities possible.

After fifteen years of making investments, if I had it to do all over again, I would have made half as many investments, and held on to the cash I had and waited for better opportunities to come along. I would have waited years, in some cases. If you have to figure out how to hide the money from yourself, do it! (I'm half kidding here, but save up your capital, and wait for those great investments, seriously.)

Warren & Charlie often mention that it's not just the waiting, but it's also the **courage and nerve to make a decision and commit** when you see the right opportunity. This combination of patience plus action when you discover the right opportunity is a winning long-term strategy.

Another benefit to this approach is that it encourages study and research. It incentivizes you to really understand the investments that you're looking at.

Warren Buffett recommends not to invest in things that you don't understand. This is one of the best pieces of investing advice that I've ever received. If you're going to be betting a lot, you want to be as sure as possible that your investment has a high probability of paying off. And the surest way to know this is to understand what you're investing in.

But overall, remember the mantra:

Wait… wait… wait… commit!

How Many "HAPS" Will This Opportunity Give You?

When you're selecting an opportunity, it's important to calculate not only the financial return, but also the personal return that you're going to potentially receive (as well as the personal price of being involved with the opportunity).

Opportunities will come and go. You'll win some, and you'll lose some. And while the chances are that a particular opportunity isn't going to be the one that changes everything for you, some opportunities can cause you to become stressed, depressed, or very unfulfilled.

I'd like to propose that you estimate the potential of any particular opportunity using what I call "Holistic Actualization Points" or HAPS for short. It's a score that you personally estimate, between one and ten, that is an estimate of how much this opportunity will contribute to your overall long-term personal actualization.

If an opportunity doesn't contribute to the quality of your life, and to your own personal growth, then is it really an opportunity? If it's going to drag you down, or become an emotional burden, is it something that you really want for yourself?

My wife uses the term "haps" to mean happy. She says "That gives me the HAPS!" when she's really happy about something. Because we're talking about the dimension of actualization and fulfillment, I felt that this was a wonderful feeling to incorporate into the term.

If the opportunity is to start a new business that might make you a million dollars, but it's doing something that you will hate for the next ten years in order to get there, and it won't grow you very much, then it's probably a 1 or 2 on the HAPS scale.

But if the opportunity is to join a new mastermind that you'll be paying to be a member of, and traveling to three times per year... that will help you become a better parent... and you have a strong intuition that this is going to make you and your family stronger... then it might be a "7 or 8 of HAPS."

Note that the first example might make you a million dollars, and the second example would cost you money and time... but the second one will bring you so much more fulfillment and actualization in the long-run.

I have seen many people get involved in opportunities just because they thought that it would make them money, but who wound up feeling trapped and unhappy with the reality of their situation. They knew going in that they were doing it just for the money, but they didn't really take time to calculate the cost to their esteem and to their spirit.

Another reason to consider giving each opportunity you encounter a HAPS score between 1-10 is that the opportunities that we are going to encounter in the future are going to become more diverse. We will encounter more and more opportunities to develop our health, our emotional resilience, our businesses... to travel, to build diverse relationships, and to learn knowledge... to find our purpose, to contribute, to evolve spiritually. And when we discover these opportunities, we will likely have to compare very different opportunities in order to decide where to place our attention and invest our time.

How do you compare an opportunity to take up a new exercise routine that will take 30 minutes per day but give you more health and energy... with an opportunity to join a new men's or women's group that will provide you with emotional support and create an environment that will grow you spiritually?

How do you compare an opportunity to invest $10,000 into the stock market vs. investing the $10,000 into an education program that will help you launch and grow our own business?

HOW DO YOU COMPARE an opportunity to do something that will improve your relationship with your children to an opportunity that will provide your family with a nicer place to live?

These are complex decisions, and they are typically stressful. Many people will just shut down when faced with big decisions that have implications this wide and deep in their lives. Others will get so excited about one new opportunity that they won't consider the opportunity cost, or take the time to look into the other things that they could be using their time, energy, attention and resources to invest in.

By considering the long-term implications of an opportunity, and how that will contribute to your own personal growth and actualization, then giving it a HAPS score, you have a simple, intuitive way to score one opportunity against another.

Someone approached me recently with an opportunity to invest in and advise a technology startup. The entrepreneur is smart, and the business idea is solid. As I considered the investment and a role in the business, I realized that it wasn't something that would challenge me, as I have done several things like this in the past. It wouldn't grow me very much as a person or as an investor, even if it made a lot of money. It would probably have a HAPS score of about 3 or 4 in the long-run. And that's not enough to get my attention right now in my life.

My wife and I have been discussing teaching a series of classes on romantic relationship, intimacy, collaboration, and conflict resolution. The more we discuss it, the more I see how valuable the material would be to others, and the more I believe that this would challenge my wife and I to go to the next level in our own relationship. I don't know if it would be successful financially, because I don't know if the way we think about relationships would resonate with a wider audience. But the personal and relationship growth alone would probably give me a HAPS score of 8 or 9, so this is something we're going to do soon.

As you consider an opportunity, don't let excitement blind you to the wider implications of your involvement with it. Always ask yourself "how much will this contribute to my overall actualization as a person and as a success in the world?" If getting involved with this opportunity will lead to a lot of personal growth and development, then score it higher on the HAPS scale, and include that in your calculation of the value of this opportunity. Again, you're looking for opportunities that will deliver a high level of **H**olistic **A**ctualization **P**oints in the long-run of your life.

If it's going to be a drag on your enthusiasm and your spirit, then be very careful. Very rarely is it worth it to do something just for the money, fame, success or power... if it's going to cost you your happiness and self-esteem.

Another way to use the HAPS score is to calculate how many HAPS you will lose in a particular domain if you commit to a particular opportunity. If you have the prospect of starting a new business, consider how it will impact other areas of your life. Right now, I have a daughter who is going to be turning five years old soon. Writing this book (along with other business projects) has taken a lot of intensive time and effort, and I haven't seen her as much as I would have liked over the past few months. Not spending as much time with her has cost me HAPS in that domain of my life. Overall, I feel the investment is worth it, but by feeling the cost to my emotions and my conscience I am fine-tuning my sense of what an opportunity will mean in my life. In the future, I will likely not take on as much as I have lately, because it's important for me to have more time available to spend with my wife and my family.

Remember the question: "On a scale of 1-10, how many HAPS will this bring me?"

Checking in With all Levels of Your Being

When you are the verge of actually making a choice, and selecting an opportunity for your "opportunity portfolio," take a moment to check in with the different levels of your being.

As you're making your decision about which opportunity to take on, check in with yourself at these three levels:

INSTINCTIVE CHECK. This is checking in with your gut. Make sure you are in a calm and relaxed environment, close your eyes, and take a deep breath. Feel down into your stomach, and in the core of your body. Does this opportunity feel right? If so, your body will expand in response to the question, rather than contract. Use your body's openness or closedness as the indicator of an intuitive yes or no. There are an estimated 100 million brain cells in the gut, and many believe this provides us with the "gut sense" most of us have. By checking with your gut, you check in with an ancient sense of personal wisdom.

INTEGRITY CHECK. This is a check that makes sure the opportunity is aligned with the rest of your core values. I define personal integrity as the alignment of thought, feeling and action. Ask yourself: Does this opportunity align with my life, my values, and how I want to feel? The real implications of most opportunities don't reveal themselves until you're deep into the project. Search your intuition to ensure your values are in alignment with the opportunity you are considering.

HIGHER SELF CHECK. Each of us has a latent higher self, a conscience, or something like a super-ego. If you don't relate to these terms or ideas, then just try imagining a more actualized future version of yourself. Try to get in contact with the more transcendent aspect of your consciousness, and move your perspective and identity to that place. Once you are in touch with that aspect of yourself, ask from there: Does this opportunity support my highest selfe and the transcendent values I stand for?

In his book "Flow" the psychologist Mihaly Csikszentmihalyi draws a distinction between the idea of happiness and the concept of joy or enjoyment. He describes joy as a more encompassing, long-term fulfillment in life. The experience of enjoyment typically includes some happiness, although not always. You can enjoy something that is even frustrating, as long as it is so interesting it keeps you fully engaged.

What we're after are opportunities that put us into the flow state as we pursue them. This leads to a deeper engagement, that develops our intelligence and creative spirit. As you're tuning into these levels of your intuition, remember you want to choose an opportunity that's going to be great for you as a person, as an individual, as a family member and at the soul or spirit level. An opportunity to make twice the money, but have half the joy in life, isn't usually worth it.

Marie Kondo, recommends going through your home or office and touching each item, then asking the simple question "Does this bring me joy?" If it does, keep it. If not, then get rid of it.

Your joy is important.

I did a series of counseling sessions with Dr. Nathaniel Branden, the man considered the father of the idea of self-esteem. In the first session, as he asked me questions about what I was trying to do in my life, I answered by explaining how the different projects I was working on would contribute to others, and help the world. After listening to me for awhile, he asked: "But what about you? What about you being happy?" This led me down a path of consideration that has been fruitful in the development of my own joy in life.

In his work, Dr. Branden defines self esteem as the feeling of confidence that you can cope with the challenges that come up in life, plus your feeling of deserving happiness. Just as evolution is composed of adaptation plus selection, self-esteem is composed of confidence plus deserving happiness. You need both if you want to have a fulfilling life.

The key here is to avoid unconsciously undermining your trust and confidence in yourself by choosing opportunities which are at odds with your values. This will only create friction later in your life.

To put it another way: Don't sabotage your future self. Instead, make choices that grow your sense of confidence about being able to handle the challenges that will come, along with your feeling of deserving happiness.

Opportunity Negotiation

When I was in my late teens, I would often buy and sell second-hand guitars and musical equipment. I would look for bargains, and then fix or clean them up to use or sell or trade later. Even though most things I bought were in the tens or maybe hundreds of dollars, I noticed patterns.

One thing I realized was that if I was buying a guitar for a hundred dollars, and was able to negotiate twenty dollars off the price in the last few minutes, that I was effectively making hundreds of dollars per hour during that little window.

If it took me five extra minutes to save twenty dollars, I was making four dollars per minute, which is $240 per hour. At that point in my life, I was earning in the range of about $6 per hour at my job, so saving twenty dollars was like getting back over three hours of my time for free. If I could save a hundred dollars, it was like getting back a couple of days of my life.

I eventually developed a little system and script that I would use when buying things. I haven't thought about this in years, but as I sit here writing it's coming back to me just how useful this script was. Here are the three questions I would use:

1.   "How flexible are you on your price?"

2. "What's your best price right now?"
3. "Would you take $100 in cash?" (As I held out the money.)

Let's say that I was at a garage sale, looking at a set of speakers that I wanted to buy. Maybe the speakers had a sticker on them that said that the price was $200. I would decide how much I wanted to pay for them, and then prepare the cash in one pocket of my pants. We'll assume for this example that I was willing to pay $100 for the speakers. I would then put $100 in one pocket, so it was ready to go.

Once I was ready, I would say to the owner that I had a question about the speakers. If I had any specific questions about the condition, or the functionality I would ask those first. Then, when I was ready, I would say:

"How flexible are you on your price?"

This indicated that I was interested, but also that I was going to negotiate. It is an open question, and often a seller would say something like "I'm pretty flexible, and I'll make you a good deal" or something similar. If this happened, I might know to offer even less than what I was first thinking. If the answer was "Not very flexible, I think this is worth it and I'm pretty firm on my price" I would continue to the next step. I would ask…

"What's your best price right now?"

This would send the message that I'm serious, and ready to buy now. We're talking about money, and getting to specifics. Again, if they suggested in some way that they would accept a price that was lower than I had already decided I'd pay, I would often offer even less, to see if I could get a better bargain. If they said "I'd take $50 for those speakers if you want them" then I might say "Would you take $25?"

At this point, it's obvious that I'm going to buy them, so it didn't hurt to ask! Sometimes a seller would just want to get rid of something, and they would almost give it away.

But let's say that the owner of the speakers looked at them and said "I'm asking $200, and the lowest I'd go is $150" then I was ready with my final offer. I would take out the $100 in cash, fan it out so they could see that it was $100 total, hold it out to them and say:

"**Would you take $100 in cash?**"

There's something about having the money right in front of you that is very persuasive. And many times, a person selling an old pair of speakers that they didn't care about would take the money and say "You have a deal!"

Ten or so years later, when I was in my late 20s and learning how to meet girls, I developed a similar approach. At this point in my life, I had no idea how to start a conversation with a woman, or what to say if I was having one. Women seemed like aliens to me, and the process of meeting a woman was a complete mystery.

As I made friends with a diverse group of men who had more natural intuition and skill around women, I had several major revelations. One of them came from watching men start conversations with women they didn't know, and then get a phone number or contact information within a few minutes. That looked like magic to me, so I continued investigating until I figured out what was happening, and I was able to replicate it myself.

What's interesting is that the process often involved a bit of negotiation.

Let's say I was talking to a woman at a bar on a Friday night. Maybe we met standing in line, or ordering a drink. After a few minutes of conversation, I might go back to talking with my friends. Before I left, I would say "Hey, do you have email?"

If she said "Yes" then I would take out a pen and a piece of paper, and say "Here, write it down for me." Most of the time, if the conversation was going well, she would write down her email. I started by asking for something that was low-risk to give to me. Then, while she was writing her email, I'd say "And write your number there, too." Many times, she would just keep writing, and I'd leave with a name, email and phone number, all in a few minutes.

But sometimes, a woman would stop, and look at me, and say "I don't even know you." To which I would respond "It's OK, you can give me your number... I'll only call you ten times a day!" This would typically get a laugh, and then a written phone number. Sometimes the banter would continue on for a minute or two, with me continuing to tell her that it was going to be fine to give me her number, but only if she agreed not to call me all the time once she had mine when I called, and continuing to joke arund. She might want to connect via social, or send me a text, or sometimes take my number or contact info instead.

But I learned through experience that I often had to **negotiate** to get a woman to give me her contact information! And I also had to be ready. I bought a wallet that had a pen built-in, so that I was always carrying something to write with. This in itself was kind of interesting, because the pen I had was a conversation piece in itself (a space pen, which comes in all kinds colors and finishes).

These examples might seem small and relatively insignificant at first glance, but each of them represents me going through a particular type of situation over and over in life, and realizing something important: If I was ready in the moment to negotiate, I could create a much more favorable outcome for myself.

I am fascinated by watching people miss opportunities in their lives. It's not something I enjoy, but it's kind of like watching a car crash... you can't look away. It's painful. But you can learn a lot.

Most of the time when a person wants something for themselves, but they don't go after it... then persist until they get it... and negotiate to get the best deal possible... it appears to me that it's fundamentally a self-image and self-esteem issue. They didn't grow up learning that they deserved to have what they want in life, and they didn't develop the skill and ability to actually get the things that they want.

Neuro-Linguistic Programming has an interesting maxim:

> **"Possible in the world and possible for me**
> **is a matter of how."**

This essentially means that if it's possible for one person to do something, then anyone can do it if they learn how. I like this general approach to life, and most of the time you'll find that believing this will help you learn and achieve at a much higher level. (Sometimes, what's possible for one person or group isn't possible for others because that person or group has a special advantage or unique genius that you don't have. But if you generally believe that anything is possible for you, and you seek to learn how those that are the best do it, you can almost always make great progress and enjoy many of the benefits of success that the best enjoy.)

In this case, we're discussing the topic of negotiation, and I would like to suggest to you that it's worth it to pay careful attention to the moments in life where you are "making a deal" or setting up a transaction. In those often brief windows of time, there is an exponential multiplication in the benefit and return you can receive on your effort and investment. If you typically make $50 per hour in your life, and you're negotiating the salary for your next job, you might make an additional $5,000 in yearly pay by negotiating for another hour in the right way. This is a 100x increase in your typical hourly income, and it's a very big deal to take it when the window of opportunity is open for you.

As you begin using the mindsets and tools in this book to increase the quality and quantity of opportunities in your life, keep an eye out for these special high-leverage moments. Prepare yourself to discuss price and terms, and to negotiate for what you want in the agreement.

If you're negotiating to hire someone, or to go to work for a company, or to collaborate or partner with someone, there are more reasons than just money to do this. If you don't negotiate a deal that really works for you in terms of time, money, working relationship, and expectations, you can quickly find yourself unhappy, unfulfilled, or even feeling taken advantage of. If you get to this place, it's likely that you didn't carefully consider what you wanted and needed, and you missed your opportunity to negotiate and ask for it up front.

If you are interviewing someone, and want to hire them for your company, ask them if they will come to work part-time for a couple of months to do a project as a consultant or contractor. This gives you a real-live experiential impression of how the person behaves in actual working situations, and it can sometimes save you a lot of time and money by seeing actual performance rather than just hearing talk of performance.

If you are negotiating for a service or buying media, ask what the price is if you buy a lot more than you want right now. Indicate that if what you're testing out with them works, you would like to scale up in the future (if it's true, of course). Often, a company will give you a better rate up front if they believe that you could become a big purchaser down the road, and using this to negotiate up front has both saved me and made me a lot of money.

In real estate, they say "you make the money when you buy, not when you sell." This means that your profit will be determined by the price that you negotiate when you purchase, not the price you negotiate when you liquidate. If you can save ten thousand dollars by negotiating for another day or two, was that worth it?

One of my cousins has built up a portfolio of rental homes over the past few decades. He told me something maybe twenty years ago or so that stuck with me. He said that if you call up ten people who are advertising their homes "for sale by owner" and you ask each of them if they'll take twenty percent less than their asking price if you pay cash, that one of them will probably say yes. It's an interesting way to start a conversation, isn't it?

Warren Buffett and Charlie Munger have a philosophy when it comes to buying companies. Warren says that he used to look for "good businesses at wonderful prices" but then Charlie came along and convinced him to buy "wonderful businesses at good prices." If you're buying the best, you don't need to always negotiate bargain basement prices. A good price is good enough. But if you read into this, you can still see that there's a spirit of negotiation in there. "Wonderful businesses at good prices." As I move through my life, I really see the wisdom in waiting for the best, and in buying one great thing rather than a bunch of "just OK" things.

As you practice negotiation in different domains of life, you will eventually see a pattern that some call the "wanting it tax." If you want something too much, to the point where it becomes obvious that you are needy or desperate, the price goes up dramatically. We could probably spend an entire book on a topic like this one, as it involves more general animal drives and status dynamics, plus a lot of psychology. But for now, it's useful to mention that if you're about to initiate a transaction, make an offer, or negotiate a deal, get yourself to the point mentally and emotionally where you don't NEED the thing that you're acting to get.

Look at other options. Create other ways to do it in your mind. Figure out alternative ways to achieve your outcome. And demonstrate to the other person or people that you're interacting with that you are stable and self-sufficient. In negotiation, there is a famous phrase: "Negotiate with one hand on the door" - meaning to always be acting like you're about to leave the negotiation, in order to convince the other person that you have other options and might walk away. This is going a bit too far, as far as I'm concerned. But it's worth remembering as a concept, because negotiating with one hand on the door also results in you not having to pay the wanting it tax.

I'd like to also clarify something here. When I talk about being ready for the moment of striking an agreement, or asking someone to do something, I am not suggesting to take advantage of another person's situation or weakness, and to profit at their expense.

If I'm buying a pair of speakers from someone at a garage sale, and offering them $100 less then they are asking, I am not putting them into a compromising position or financial situation. If I'm asking a woman for her phone number and then joking around with her to convince her to give it to me, I don't lie and say that I want to cast her in a movie and make her a star.

Don't take advantage of people who are in unfortunate situations, or lie in order to get a better deal in life. Negotiate in good faith, and play the game in a fair way.

I have been studying marketing for many years and I use powerful persuasion and influence techniques when I create my sales letters and videos. I really believe in the tools and training that I offer to people, and I have invested years to create programs that will change the life of anyone that goes through them. This gives me a lot of confidence to pitch my products.

But I don't actively target people who are in financial hardship and promise to make them rich with the push of a button. I don't go looking for people who are desperate, and convince them that all of their problems will be solved if they just give me the last of their money.

I think that it was Napoleon Hill who introduced me to this poem:

"I bargained with Life for a penny,
And Life would pay no more,
However I begged at evening
When I counted my scanty store;

For Life is just an employer,
He gives you what you ask,
But once you have set the wages,
Why, you must bear the task.

I worked for a menial's hire,
Only to learn, dismayed,
That any wage I had asked of Life,
Life would have paid."

—Jessie B. Rittenhouse

If you prepare yourself for the moments of negotiation in life, you can bargain for a lot more. And if you do this over weeks, months, years, and decades of your life, the compounded gains really start multiplying and adding up. The windows of opportunity that open at negotiation points can be some of the biggest that you encounter in life. Be ready.

REMINDER: Download the "Opportunity Companion Guide" to Get Your Summaries, Checklists & Exercises

This book has an **Opportunity Companion Guide** that goes along with it, which you can download for free. It includes key chapter summaries, implementation checklists, and written exercises - plus extra chapters and other bonus material. Go here to get it now, so you can review the summaries and start implementing what you're learning:

OpportunityBonus.com

Opportunity Design

THE MORE I HAVE worked with opportunity in my life, the more I realize that an opportunity is really a collaboration between the conditions and circumstances that converge in your environment, along with the way you use your mind and actions to take advantage of it.

It seems strange to speak of the "creation" of an opportunity, or the design of an opportunity, as opportunity typically seems to be more of a "happy accident" than something that an individual person or group can manifest intentionally.

But let's talk here about a few of the ways that you can approach creating and designing opportunities in your life. This way, you can have more of the types of opportunities that you want to have, and you can have higher quality opportunities that are a better fit for your personality, your goals and your skills.

Creating

At the beginning of this book, we discussed the idea of living in the Creativerse, and seeing reality as being a fundamentally friendly environment for the emergence and creation of innovative new things.

One of the benefits of doing art in some form is this continual experience of starting with empty space and building something... or starting with a blank page and drawing something... or starting with silence, and making music to fill it. I believe that each of us should be continually involved in at least one creative practice in life, as it shows us at a deep, unconscious level that we are naturally-designed or purpose-built creators.

Creativity is a concept worth making a study of in life. I have been a student of creativity for many years, and I find that the more I learn about it, the more profound the idea becomes.

Some people think that creativity means coming up with original ideas. And some think that it means being artistically talented. I'll suggest that creativity is about first creating. Create is the root word of creativity, and when you're creating you are in a process of dancing between the world of ideas and the world of objects and relationships.

One of the best ways to practice creativity is to take something you learned in one place, and try it or apply it in another place. Use a recipe that you learned online at a party with your friends. Take a melody that you learned on piano and play it on a guitar. Try a conflict resolution technique you learned at work when you're home with your family. Teach an idea you learned in a book to someone who needs it.

When you do these things, you are being creative. You are using your mind to apply knowledge from one domain to another, using your thoughts to put things together in new ways.

Whether you practice creativity by making art, learning and applying knowledge, teaching others, or physically building things with your hands, I believe that it is fundamental to our happiness and development to have an ongoing practice of being creative in our lives.

When my daughter comes to say goodbye to me and give me a hug before she leaves, I remind her to be creative. Sometimes I'll say "try something new today" and sometimes I'll say "be creative today."

Again, even if it's just creating a drawing on a piece of paper of something we want in our lives, or making a melody that expresses how we feel, simple creative acts build our identity as creators. This is very important as it relates to opportunity, because once you develop the ability to create your own opportunities, you become far more sufficient in life.

The more that you intentionally practice creativity, the more you will have the experience of transforming one thing into another, multiplying resources, and manifesting outcomes that you first envision in your mind.

The domains of design and marketing are areas that can offer you these types of opportunities in business. When you design something, like a product, you assemble ideas, components, and models, and put them together into something that can solve a problem or deliver a result to people who need it. When you create a marketing communication, you combine psychological motivators with powerful communication techniques to attract customers to buy your product or service.

There is a sense of doing something mysterious, like an ancient alchemist working to turn lead into gold, when you do these things. Before, there was only a blank page, and now there is a design for a product. Before there was no customer, and now you have many customers coming to buy what you're selling. And the key resource was your creative ability.

Creativity is a transformer and multiplier of resources. It is part of our unique visionary power. Creativity envisions new ways of doing and being.

Design Thinking

As you build your esteem as a creator, and as you practice creativity, you will want to refine your ability to create things that are better and better. And this includes opportunities that are better and better.

To create great things, it's important to learn and practice design.

I'm not talking about interior design here (although it is one way to practice design). I'm talking about a place where you intentionally invest time and attention to imagine and architect the thing you want to create, considering as many of the important elements as possible, and fitting them together so that they work as one unit.

If you're designing a system, it would be about imagining how you would like the system to work, and then arranging the parts so that they are in balance and harmony together working as one emergent entity.

Some people specialize in design. Software developers are designers of code. Architects are designers of buildings. Composers are designers of music. Even if you are not primarily a designer in your life, it's becoming more and more important to learn the principles and practices of design, so that you can increase your ability to create what you want (including the design and creation of opportunities for yourself and those you care about).

Discodesign

Before we get into principles and techniques of design, I want to share a word I use when I think about design. It's a combination of the words "discover" and "design" - and the word is "discodesign."

Part of design is discovery. And part of discovery is design. You can imagine something in your mind, and then go try to create it in reality. Most of the time, it doesn't turn out exactly as you imagined, and you discover something. Maybe you discover that when you try to draw a circle to represent a person's head, that it looks like an oval. But you discover an oval on the page, and you then think "maybe I'll draw something different with this" - and you start designing something else to draw using the oval. The accident leads to a new creative discovery.

As I have built my companies, I have tried to follow the needs of people who wanted to learn things, always curiously asking them what they want to learn next. When I notice that a lot of people want to learn something specific, I then create a teaching program to help them learn how to do it, and they become customers.

As I was building a business teaching dating advice, I noticed that a lot of people started asking me not just about dating, but also about how I was building my business. This pattern continued to the point where I realized that I should teach people what I had learned about building a successful and profitable company that was virtual. This led to a very successful course called Altitude, where I taught entrepreneurs how to build thriving and growing businesses.

Teaching and launching this course got me interacting with a lot more entrepreneurs, which led to me discovering several other topics that they wanted to learn, which led to me designing several more successful courses, masterminds, and education programs.

Did I discover these opportunities? Or design them? It was some of each. It was discodesign. If you look closely, you'll see that there's always some discovery in your design, and always some design in your discovery.

Discodesign is part luck and part skill. It's part planning and part randomness. It's part random chance, and part conscious romance.

The mindset here is to learn and practice design along with discovery, and to see them as two wings on one bird. Discover as you design, and design as you discover. Discodesign.

Design Paradigms

You've likely heard the phrase "form follows function." It is sometimes spoken as if it was a rule of the universe, or an immutable law of design.

It's an amazing insight, and a wonderful summary of one way of approaching design in life. You think about the function, and then you make a design that will fulfill that function. The final form, or expression of the design, will then be following the general functional need.

Can you guess what type of person would have expressed a quote like this one? Any ideas about what this person might have done for work? Or who they might have been? I'll give you a hint: What would you create that would be best to design first by thinking carefully about its function?

Louis Sullivan was an architect who is credited with being the creator of the modern skyscraper. When you're building a skyscraper, you seriously need to think through how it's going to be used before you build it! And it was Sullivan that is credited with this quote.

Form follows function is a mindset of what we might call "pragmatic design." It's creating a design from the starting point of how it will function as the starting point in your mind.

I've heard this phrase echoed through conversations about design in several domains of life now. It's very useful, but it's not the end of the story.

Try these variations:

FORM FOLLOWS PLEASURE: Design something that makes you feel as good as it possibly can, and disregard practicality or logic.

FORM FOLLOWS BEAUTY: Design something that appears beautiful to you, without concern for other factors.

FORM FOLLOWS IMAGINATION: Design something that comes as completely as possible from your imagination, in order to practice manifesting what you see in your mind's eye. Art is a great place to practice this approach to design and creativity

When it comes to creating and designing opportunities for yourself and others, it's important to use many different approaches. A great opportunity isn't just a functional opportunity, it's also something that you enjoy, that makes you feel good, that expresses your creativity in some way.

As you practice designing things in your life, you'll work these different creative muscles, which will help you improve at creating better opportunities for yourself.

Visual Design Principles

As you develop your creativity, and as you develop your design skills, it's useful to practice every time you make a document, written communication, email, advertisement, or website.

Here are a few principles that I've learned along the way that can really help.

ALIGNMENT: Notice that the paragraphs and headers in this book are mostly left-aligned. This creates a nice visual edge on the left side, and it creates a professional appearance. People often center page designs without realizing that it makes longer copy hard to read, and unnatural.

SPACING: Look at the space between lines on this page. It is just enough to separate the lines, but not so much that it wastes space or gives the eye more work than necessary when shifting between them. I would typically add a little bit of space between paragraphs as well (and if you're reading a segment of this online it's probably there), but in the printed version of the book we decided to indent paragraphs rather than adding space between them to make it easier to read long blocks of text.

CONTRAST: Notice that the chapter titles and headings are much bigger and bolder than the body copy. Note that they are also a very different font. The body copy is "serif" type for style and ease of reading in long blocks, and the titles and headers are "sans serif" - also for style, but in this case designed to be easier to read in short blocks (big bold words are more legible, and grab attention, but you don't want to use huge bold type for longer sections, as it's bulky and inefficient visually). If you're using colors, use very different colors. Use a color wheel, and try pairing colors from opposite sides with each other, and notice how this creates a natural and pleasing contrast.

HIERARCHY. In English, we read left to right, and from top to bottom. Follow this natural "eye gravity" in your designs. Put your most important piece of information and visual element at the top, starting on the left. In advertising, use a headline that is larger and bolder, so it stands out and carries visual weight. Make the next thing you want the reader to look at the second biggest element on the page. If you have a picture at the top, put your headline below the picture. Then below the headline, use smaller type to communicate your main message. Big picture, medium sized headline, small body copy. This visual hierarchy is intuitive to use, because you look at the big thing first at the top (the picture), then the next-biggest thing second (the bold headline under the picture) then the next-biggest thing third (the small body copy under the headline).

PROXIMITY. Put things that are related to each other close to each other visually. If you have a picture and a caption, make sure the caption is directly under the picture, because that's where we naturally go to look for it. Put space between elements that aren't related to each other. And organize your visual elements into a handful of groups on the page, so that the design is simple and not confusing to look at.

FONTS. Don't use a lot of different fonts if you're designing a communication. One or two is enough. If you'd like to add contrast, choose one serif font and one sans-serif font, and use one for your headlines or subheads, and one for your body copy. Make the headline font bolder, and the body font lighter, and it will look better. Try different combinations until you have one that looks good. Then stick with it through your document. Notice that I am using a simple combination of fonts in this book, and how this brings a sense of elegance and professionalism.

THEMES. When you find a combination of fonts, sizes, colors, and other elements that works for you, keep using it over and over in your presentation or design as your theme. In programs and apps like Microsoft Word and Google Docs you can create "styles" where you pre-design how titles, subheads, body copy, footers, etc. will look, with all of the font size, color, and paragraph spacing chosen in advance. This is a great way to create a theme that you can then use over and over in the future (and you can do similar things with web design as well).

As you move beyond designing simple pages and websites, here are a few other principles to work with.

Make your design recognizable. If you're designing a book cover, spend a few hours and look at the covers of books that you think are well-designed. Note the stylistic details and conventions that are unique to book covers. If you're designing a website, take a few hours and look at the best websites in your industry, again noticing the stylistic details and conventions that are unique to websites. Books often have a title in huge print on the cover and a single image, but websites often have multiple pieces of copy and multiple images. If you make your book look like a website, it's probably not going to "feel right" - and it won't build trust and rapport when people see it.

If you're designing a house, look at great house designs, and pay attention to what makes something uniquely a "house design." If you're designing a car, notice what car designs have in common. This might sound obvious, but if you are going to design something, it's important to remember that others have often invested their entire careers (and sometimes generations of careers or longer) experimenting and working out how to design something in that domain. The conventions are often important for reasons that aren't obvious at first.

USABILITY. As you design, remember that the purpose is ultimately to be used. As they say "form follows function" and you want to make sure that you are always designing for final use. As you develop a design, do yourself (and your customers) a favor and observe people using your product or service. You will learn so much by watching people do things that you couldn't have anticipated. The way people use your design isn't going to be the way you think, so plan to spend time with people watching what they actually do. You'll learn so much, and discover many opportunities to improve (and often opportunities to design additional products and services as well).

REMINDER: Download the "Opportunity Companion Guide" to Get Your Summaries, Checklists & Exercises

This book has an **Opportunity Companion Guide** that goes along with it, which you can download for free. It includes key chapter summaries, implementation checklists, and written exercises - plus extra chapters and other bonus material. Go here to get it now, so you can review the summaries and start implementing what you're learning:

OpportunityBonus.com

Opportunity Testing & Validation

IT'S EASY TO MAKE the mistake of thinking just because you have a great idea, or a great design you think will work out, that you've already created a success.

Remember, entrepreneurs know that only 1 in 5 things will work out the way that they anticipate, and they need to get real-world feedback in order to orient and navigate to the next step.

In this section, we're going to discuss ways to test and validate your idea or product, before you waste too much time on something that isn't going to work out in the long-run.

Because we can mentally model and imagine how things work in the real world, we are in a continual process of trying to anticipate what's going to happen in domains where it really matters. And because business and investing in particular are about money, they typically really matter. So we're always trying to find new ways to anticipate what's going to happen, in order to best position ourselves to do things that create a lot of value, and produce a lot of success.

But as we think about what's going to happen and learn new skills and ideas, and then go to work to make products, marketing and businesses that work, we have to remember that the physical-material world doesn't work exactly the same way that our minds work. We have to remember that part of the job of the entrepreneur is to remember that thinking isn't perfect, and that ideas have to be tested out in order to see whether or not they will work.

Since ideas have to be tested, we want to find a method that works efficiently, and that doesn't waste time and money testing. And we must also go further, and adopt an experimental mindset. We have to start looking at ourselves partially as entrepreneurs, and partially as research scientists who are doing experiments in their labs to see if their theories are correct.

Physical Variation

W. Edwards Deming was a statistician and management consultant that applied statistical approaches to business and manufacturing. Through his books, I learned an important mindset and approach to testing and to business in general.

Deming and his followers recommended charting processes on a run chart. A run chart is when you measure something over time, and put a dot on a graph to show the measurements over time. It looks like this:

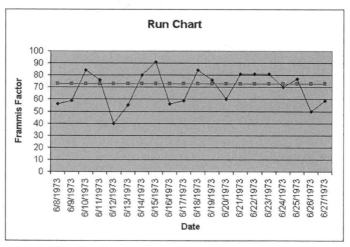

Source: Wikipedia

The line that goes "up and down" is the plot of measurements, and the line that is straight is the median, or the average. I believe that the simple run chart is one of the most innovative inventions that humans have produced, as it shows you a huge amount of information all at once, at a glance.

If you just look at a column of numbers, it's very hard to see whether the trend is up, down, or sideways. But one glance at a run chart, and you can see what's happening immediately.

In the chart above, the process that you're looking at is what Deming might call a "stable" process. At first glance, you might say "that doesn't look very stable to me" - but look again. If you look at the moving average of the entire process, it's flat. So what's going on?

Let's say that this is a chart that you keep daily of the time it takes you to commute to work. Let's say that the average time it takes you each day is 15 minutes. But some days it takes longer than others, and some days go faster. Sometimes there is a delay because of a train, or because it's raining outside. And sometimes things go quickly, because there are no delays.

If you chart the time it takes you each day, you'll see a pattern like the one on this chart. It will go up one day, and down the next. Or up a couple of days, then down a day, then up a day, then down two days, etc. Deming called this phenomena "physical variation" - it's the idea that the physical world introduces variation into processes that can't be anticipated, and in many cases can't even be known.

Some processes are "stable," meaning that if you chart them over time, you will see that they have an average that is stable and predictable. Some processes are not stable, and they can't be predicted with confidence.

If you're building a business, or a portfolio of investments, it's important to chart the processes in your business, so you can see how they are performing visually. This gives you the feedback you need to see whether or not something is working the way you need it to. Charting is particularly important when testing out advertising and marketing campaigns, to see how they perform over time. An ad might work well in the beginning, but then stop working as well over time, and if you're not watching the performance on a visual chart, you won't be able to see this.

Remember physical variation. Results go up one day, and down another, within a range, in all processes. This creates a distraction for a lot of people, because they see that results went down since yesterday, and then they go and spend hours looking for the reason why the numbers are down. Once they think that they've figured it out, they make a change, hoping that the numbers go back up tomorrow. If the numbers go up tomorrow, they think they were right about the change that they made, even though the change had nothing to do with it.

When you make changes to a system that is stable because you think that the system is unstable, this is what Deming called "tampering" with the system.

Let's say you're running a new advertisement, and you're watching the daily performance. After a few days, you notice that the results go down one day. You think that there must be something wrong, so you change the headline of the ad. Results go back up the next day, so you assume that the headline is what fixed things. Then the next day results go back down again, so you change the picture in the ad, and results go back up.

What's the problem with an approach like this? It's that each of the "down days" was likely not because something was wrong, it was because of physical variation of some kind. And when you then go and make changes to your ad, you are now tampering with the system, and potentially making things worse in the long-run.

When you make changes to a system that is actually stable, and then the system appears to respond to those changes, but what you are observing is actually normal physical variation, it will confuse and disorient you. Ultimately, it will hurt your confidence and self-esteem…

Testing

Jay Abraham has one of the best mantras that I've heard in business:

"Everything is a test."

The mindset is to remember that when you start a new process, or make a change to an existing process, you are running a test. And you have to be watching, and expecting to see changes as a result.

The change that you make might give you one result in the short-term, but a completely different result in the long-term. When you remember that everything is a test, it creates an atmosphere where you become less attached to outcomes, and more motivated to test things earlier, rather than later.

In a way, this is a very scientific mindset, as it encourages you do more than just think of good ideas. It leads you to also ask yourself how the idea could be tested out, and either proven or disproven with minimal wasted time, effort and energy.

Many people who are building businesses make the mistake of "falling in love with their ideas." They become convinced that their idea is going to work, so they don't actually test out their assumptions in the real world, which ultimately leads to big problems later.

David Ogilvy tells the story at the beginning of his book Ogilvy On Advertising of how the Ford car company ran an advertising test, where they inserted a new advertisement into a magazine. In this test, they ran the ad in half of the magazines, and they ran no ads in the other half. This is called a "split test" or an "A-B test" in business. When they went back later and measured their results, they had a surprise: The people who had seen their ads bought **fewer** cars than the people who had seen their ads. In effect, their ads had un-sold people on buying their cars.

As I was building my company, we hired someone on our marketing team who was leaving a company that had raised a large amount of money from venture capitalists. The company had designed and built their website several years earlier, and they felt that it was outdated and ugly. They spent a year of time and a lot of money designing a new website that was more modern and attractive. Their estimate was that a new website design would at least double their sales. Guess what happened when they launched the all-new site? Sales went down. Not awesome.

Tim Ferriss told me in an interview that he tested book titles before selecting "The Four-Hour Workweek." He ran pay-per-click ads, to see which title idea got the most clicks, then chose the winner based on which one people clicked on most. This is a great example of testing before falling in love with an idea.

Travis Kalanik, the co-founder of Uber, tells the story of making cold calls to see if people would be interested in being part of the Uber service. He looked up limousine companies in San Francisco online, and started calling them on the telephone to tell them about his idea. Out of ten people that he called, three of them were interested and said "let's meet." He took this as a sign that they had a good idea on their hands.

In our companies, we are constantly split-testing ads, marketing funnels, subject lines, prices, copy, and other elements. You can do a test by sending multiple subject lines to small segments of your list, then sending the winner to the entire list once you find it. Seemingly small things like this can give you 5%-25% better open rates, and sometimes more if you do them.

I have often done price tests for products, and found that higher prices actually work better. What a fun discovery this is when you make it.

The question to ask is: "How can I test this idea quickly?"

Call up potential customers, and tell them about your idea. See if some of them are willing to pay you up front for it. Send out a survey to your audience or list, and ask their opinion about your product idea, and what they'd be willing to pay for it. Do a live webinar, and teach some of your best ideas, then ask everyone at the end if they want to join you for an advanced version of the class that's paid. Run two versions of an ad, to see which one works better.

When you approach things this way, you are integrating feedback from real people in the real world into your design and development process. Silicon Valley has begun incorporating these mindsets over the last several years, and calling them things like "lean startup methodology" and "customer development." Check out the work of Steve Blank and Eric Ries for more depth.

Whatever you do, remember that "Everything is a test" so that you don't fall in love with an idea or opportunity that hasn't been tested out in the real world. By asking yourself how you can test each of your ideas, you also program yourself to think more steps upstream, and you develop the ability to model processes much better.

Trustable Data

As you begin testing and charting your results visually, you realize that there is another puzzle that needs to be solved: How do you know when you have enough data or feedback in order to make a call about whether or not something is "working" for you?

If you split-test two advertisements, to see which one works better, how many people need to click or respond to each in order to know which one is working better?

Bill Scherkenbach, a protege of W. Edwards Deming said something interesting once. He said that the most dangerous number of data points to gather is two. Two data points will almost always imply a trend in one direction or the other, but because you have so little data, there's also about a 50% chance that the direction that the two points imply is wrong.

If you measure how long it takes you to commute to work one day, and it's 15 minutes, then you measure it tomorrow and it's 22 minutes, then you chart these on a run chart, it will look like a trend going up very fast. But it's not. It's just that today there was more traffic than usual. If you take two data points, plot the trend direction, then start believing in it, you can get into trouble very fast.

Scherkenbach recommended that you typically need at least 30 data points, taken in regular intervals, on a chart, before you can start seeing what's really happening.

I recommend that you start by charting the following numbers every day on a simple spreadsheet (you can use Excel or Google Sheets for this):

- Visitors to your site
- Opt-ins or follows
- Sales

Every day, gather the numbers yourself, and put them in your spreadsheet. Then click the charting button to make a chart over time, so you can see the run chart. Finally, add a moving average so you can get a sense of which direction things are going on average.

If you do this for 90 days in your business, you will have a completely different sense of what's happening at a more fundamental level inside of your company. You'll learn on an emotional level not to let it bother you if traffic or sales are down a little bit one day, and to not get too excited if they go up a little bit one day.

You'll also be able to spot big shifts that indicate important under-lying changes as well. If opt-ins drops to zero one day, after being in the hundreds every day, then something is probably wrong. Your opt-in form might have stopped working, or maybe someone made a change to your design that broke the rest of the site. Or you might see traffic go way up one day, and wonder why... then go do research and see that your site was featured in a news story. This can lead to discov-ering strategies for getting customers and traffic that you may not have thought of before.

In order to trust your data and your reporting, you have to build it yourself, and do it over time. Different sites will give you different metrics, even for the same traffic. You might see Facebook report that 100 people clicked on your ad, but on your website you only have 87 visitors. What happened? By tracking your numbers daily, you'll go and figure out what's happening, and you'll learn how to estimate based on initial results and on changes in trends over time... and the entire system will make a lot more sense to you as you do this.

As you track, measure, and report your numbers, you can also start using online tools to make sure that your data is "statistically significant." This is the term that is used to describe a situation where you have enough data over time to actually be confident that what it is telling you is true.

For now, go and look up a "statistical significance calculator" and play around with it bit. Try a few few of them - you'll see that there are several free versions online. They are easy to use, and they tell you a deeper story about your data. The more you use tools like these, the more you start to understand how to read group behavior by looking at it through measuring and reporting lenses like these.

And by looking at your data every day, and charting it visually as well, this process will give you more and more insight and confidence.

Feedback

On a higher level, testing is about getting feedback. Feedback can be thought of as the result, or as what happens when you do something.

If you are playing basketball and you shoot the ball, you can watch as the ball either goes into the basket or doesn't go into the basket. Either way, you have received feedback about your shot.

If you take a test, and you score a perfect 100%, you have received feedback about your performance.

If you write an advertisement or make a video marketing piece, and you run a test to see how it performs, you will receive feedback about whether or not customers respond to it in the form of traffic and sales.

To think about feedback, think about the distinction between action and reaction. Feedback is the reaction.

It's not the part that you enact, it's what happens as a result. If an action is a cause, then the feedback that you get is the effect.

A simple example of feedback is looking in front of you as you walk. You put one foot in front of the other, and walk along a path. By looking out at where you are going, and seeing the movement of the environment all around, you can make adjustments to keep moving in the right direction, and stay on your path. If you accidentally walk the wrong direction, you can see that you are not going the right way, and you can change course to correct.

Imagine how challenging it would be to go for a walk if you didn't have sight. You would have to rely on other feedback mechanisms to help you navigate through the world. When you see someone holding a cane with a red tip in front of them, and moving it back and forth as they walk forward slowly, what you are typically looking at is someone who doesn't have vision, who is feeling their way through reality by using the cane to get feedback about what is in front of them.

Because we have these miraculous sensory systems of vision, hearing, smell, taste, and touch (not to mention many other more subtle perceptual systems and combinations of systems), we move through physical reality and receive feedback on all of these channels simultaneously. This feedback all0ws us to make subtle changes real-time, so we stay on track doing things like putting food into our mouths without missing, giving hugs to people we love, and reading lines of text smoothly and quickly.

But most feedback doesn't come real-time in life. One of the challenges with cause and effect, or action and reaction, or doing something and getting feedback is that many results or outcomes are separated in space and time from causes or actions. This is particularly true in domains like relationships, business, and investing.

Unlike putting a bite of food in our mouths, which is happening real-time, feedback in most domains typically comes from a very different place or in a different way than we expect.

People who take up exercise programs are often surprised to see that instead of losing weight, that they actually start gaining weight. The body stores more calories as dense muscle, but it doesn't shed fat, because it assumes that things are getting harder, and that it's going to need to not only build muscle, but also keep storing all the fat as well in case it needs it!

After working out for a month, it's not exactly encouraging feedback to step on a scale and see that you gained weight.

But people who start exercising are also surprised to notice that unexpected things start happening. They start sleeping better. They have more energy. They start feeling more optimistic and inspired over time.

Again, they receive feedback that is unexpected, and in ways that they could not have predicted.

Not only is feedback separated from actions or causes in space and time, but it is typically also separated in domain. Physical exercise now triggers better sleep tonight, and positive mood a week from now. If you weren't watching for these, and you didn't know that it's typical to start sleeping better and feeling happier when you exercise, you very well might never even put the two together.

This goes much further than almost anyone realizes.

Maybe you have worked hard for your entire life to become successful so that you can please your disapproving parents, only to find that when you finally "make it" they still aren't satisfied. You realize in a moment that it wasn't about whether or not you achieved success, and that it was actually about your parents feeling like they needed to always be acting as "parents" by telling you what to do. You were expecting to get feedback of praise and pride, but instead you received feedback of more disapproval. By considering what's happening, you can start to see through time-spans and layers of feedback that have come down through generations of family hardship, or millenia of religious or cultural shame.

What I am attempting to point out here is that reality gives us feedback each time we communicate, act, or don't act within essentially every situation that we find ourselves in. From our physical actions and inactions, to the things we communicate and don't communicate in relationships, to what we do in our businesses and investments, everything provides some level of feedback. The challenge is knowing when and where to look, and how to interpret what we see.

If we can get the feedback, it often gives us a key insight that allows us to learn better, understand better, adjust better, think better, communicate better, and take advantage of new levels of opportunity better.

If we don't get the feedback, we are essentially flying blind. We are missing the insight or the lesson from each of our actions. Even worse, we can become superstitious, in the sense that we assume that things that are happening around us that are actually the results of things we did days, weeks, months or years ago... are the results of things that are not correct.

If you exercise for a month, and then notice that you have actually gained weight, instead of finding the true cause (the body is building heavier muscle and getting healthier) you might make up a reason ("exercise doesn't work"), and then go off in the wrong directly completely.

Dr. David Kolb of Harvard wrote a fascinating book titled "Experiential Learning." Part of the idea is that real, true, deep learning is a result of having experiences, getting feedback, and integrating that feedback into your process. When you actually see, feel and experience how something works, you learn in a completely different way from reading about it, or having it explained to you.

The experiential learning that you receive by actually riding a bike is in a different dimension from the process of reading about riding a bike, or watching someone ride a bike. It can help to read about it, and to watch others, but there's nothing like learning by doing. This is why work-study programs and internships are such important aspects of the education experience in college and university. You get to see how things actually work in the real world vs. how they work in a classroom.

Opportunity is tricky. Because there's so much of it, and because most opportunities don't work out and become big hits in your business and your life, it's easy to mis-identify causes and effects, and to miss important feedback about what works and doesn't work.

When you move to test out an opportunity, or act on it, you want to waste as little energy as possible in the testing and validation phase. But you also want to get high-quality feedback, so that you notice whether or not your test or experiment is working.

You also need to have several different models for evaluating the feedback that you're getting, so that you don't misinterpret the feedback and make a decision that sends you in the wrong direction.

Observe Customers Using Your Product

One of the companies I have invested in is called Splash. They are an event platform where you can announce, organize and manage your live event easily. One day they called me and asked me to come to their office to see the new version of their system.

When I walked in, they gathered a team of about 15 people around me, handed me a wireless keyboard, and said "Plan an event using this new system."

I had never seen their new interface, and I didn't know where to start. I felt like they were really putting me on the spot, because there were a bunch of people watching me flounder around! But I went with it...

As I went through the process, the team had a conversation around me, discussing some of their previous assumptions, sometimes asking me questions, and sometimes complaining to each other.

I had a hard time figuring out how things worked. It was an emotionally challenging experience, to be making mistakes and not having things work, knowing that the team had worked hard to build this new system.

When we were finished, the team had seen how many challenges there were and how non-intuitive many of the elements were. We got together and said "We have to go back to the drawing board" - and we made a big list of things to tweak and change. As they started rolling out this new version, they had many challenges come up. It was a hard time for the company, because they were trying a lot of new things with this redesign, and attempting to solve a lot of different challenges in innovative ways.

But a few months later, Splash released an updated version of this new design that fixed most of the issues of that initial version. It was now the best thing on the market, and their company has exploded in size since they launched it.

They took the initiative to get some of the best feedback that you can possibly get: Watching a real person use your product or service. It's hard, but it's worth it. Watch your customers whenever you can as they interact with your product, service, company, team members, websites... everything. There is so much valuable information and feedback, just waiting for you!

Key Types of Feedback

As you get more feedback, you will have more intelligence about what is happening in not only your business, but also the minds and hearts of your customers and your marketplace in general. Here are the key domains to tune in to in order to keep your finger on the pulse of the feedback...

Prospects: Talk to individual prospective customers yourself, and learn more about them. Ask them about their fears, their desires, their wants, and their frustrations. Ask them about what they would like in a product or service, and what annoys them about what's currently available. Watch how prospects respond to your advertisements and offers, to see what is most interesting to them, and keep refining.

Customers: It's also very important to talk live to people who have actually purchased your products and services - the ones who have given you money. These people are a subset of all potential or prospective customers, and they will be different in important ways. Notice these differences, so you can learn about who is more likely to buy from you, and so you can learn how they see the world and how they make buying decisions.

Surveys: By doing surveys, you get a more general look at your prospects or your customers. Surveys are useful, but I want to warn you that most people want to skip talking to real people, and instead just send out a survey. Do both. Use surveys to ask large groups about their commonalities (age, gender, interests, wants, fears, etc.). You can ask your group everything from what they want to buy in a product to how much they are willing to pay for it, and you can learn a lot by doing it.

Sales: If you can't sell someone your product 1-to-1, it's going to be very difficult to create marketing copy or videos that will do the job. Sales is one of the most important forms of feedback you can get, especially early on in a business. Make sure you have the sales conversations yourself, and ask deep questions about what your customers are experiencing and about what they want and don't want.

Marketing tests: Remember that everything is a test when you run a marketing campaign, and do your best to test out any marketing idea you have as quickly as possible, and as cheaply as possible. Spend $50 or $100 on a test, and get some results in the form of clicks, followers, subscribers, or buyers. This will teach you so much if you continue to run small tests, then refine them as you find winning combinations.

I think of success as being like a staircase, with the stairs in front of you being in the dark. You can't know exactly where the staircase leads, but you can be sure that there is a pathway upwards somewhere. When you step up to the next step, it lights up one more step in front of you, so you can look at it, and get your bearings. Then you must do the work to climb up to that next step, so you can have the next one light up.

Getting lots of feedback, and being open to the lessons that the feedback has for you is how you navigate from one step to the next. It's how you flip on the light at the next stage, so you can see where you're going. And even though you can't see the entire path forward, what you can see is what to do next. Feedback is your system for this type of navigation.

REMINDER: Download the "Opportunity Companion Guide" to Get Your Summaries, Checklists & Exercises

This book has an **Opportunity Companion Guide** that goes along with it, which you can download for free. It includes key chapter summaries, implementation checklists, and written exercises - plus extra chapters and other bonus material. Go here to get it now, so you can review the summaries and start implementing what you're learning:

OpportunityBonus.com

Opportunity Iteration, Scaling & Management

AS YOU DEVELOP YOUR product, or as you develop your marketing (or even as you develop yourself or your relationships), it's useful to keep in mind that we live in a world of iteration.

Software is typically released in versions, with small steps being light upgrades, and major steps involving new interfaces and core functionality. These are iterations.

Cars are often released in yearly upgraded models, and every several years there will be a major redesign on many levels. Each new model is an iteration of the previous model, building on top of what was learned in all previous iterations.

If you look at how life works, you see that living entities are born from a reproductive process involving parents of some kind, and that the children or offspring of lifeforms are latest versions or new models of their parents. You are the latest iteration of your line of the human lineage, after your parents, who were the previous latest models in your family.

If you zoom out and look at the evolutionary steps that are taken in the development of everything from printing presses to telephones to typewriters to computers to fish to birds to apes, you'll see an iterative process. Between each of the evolutionary steps was a huge amount of experimentation and iteration, keeping those adaptations and changes that conveyed advantage to the original design.

When you find or create an opportunity, it's important to remember that the first version of your way of taking advantage of the opportunity is just that: the first version. If you design a product because you see a need for it, remember that it is a starting point, and that you will build new versions of it over time as you get feedback and learn more about what your customers want and what they are willing and excited to pay for.

The quality movement emphasized the Japanese concept of "Kaizen" (the Japanese word for improvement). The mindset is to continually improve all aspects of your business, from your products to your people to your processes. This is a mindset that understands iteration.

Go For Version 3.0

If you are creating a product, service or even marketing, the key is to get into the world and being used as soon as possible - knowing that it will require development and iteration. Most new entrepreneurs make the mistake of trying to design something that's perfect before letting anyone see it and try it out. This is a mistake that costs an unimaginable amount of wasted time and money.

The first version of your product or service should be created as quickly as possible, and then tested out with real people. That's the rule of thumb. In Silicon Valley, they call it a "Minimum Viable Product." I call it "Version 1.0" of your product.

The mindset is to go for Version 3.0, and get there as fast as you can. The first version is going to be rough. It's going to include just the key elements, and deliver just the most important results. Once you release it, you'll start getting feedback from customers, from sales experiences, and from many other channels. This feedback will tell you where to go for version 2.0.

When you create version 2.0, you get a chance to create something much better than the first version. 2.0 is the first "real" version. You created your first version in order to get something into the hands of real people quickly, and validate that people would buy it from you. When you create version 2.0, you're making something more substantial, that's a model for a sustainable, long-term design.

After iterating once, and then getting more feedback from customers and from your market, and after validating that you really have something that customers need and want, it's time to go for version 3.0. Now you can make something great. You will have enough sales coming in to give you the confidence to go long, and you will be knowledgeable enough about the needs of your customers to design something uniquely valuable - something that you can base a business on.

About nine months after releasing my book Double Your Dating, I decided to do my first live seminar. We had 23 people who paid to attend. I borrowed a video camera, and had someone stand in the back and video record the entire 3-day event. It was just one camera, but it worked.

It was my first time teaching dating, and my format was simple: I would put up a slide that had about eight or ten tiny sentences printed on it, and I would read each of them from my computer screen. Then I would look at the audience and make comments, then put up another slide with tiny print on it, read it all, then make a few comments. Honestly, it was not very good. And the video was "just OK" as well. It was only one camera, and the lighting was not very good.

But it was version 1.0, and what was important was that we did it, and we got it out. Once I could see that people wanted to buy this product, then I went to work making it better.

I started teaching that same program in different cities. I taught that program four or five more times over the next couple of years, tuning it up, and eliminating some of the more boring aspects of it. I also created other live programs, and figured out how to make the stage and the lighting look better. This was me working on version 2.0. As I taught the material, and saw how much men were learning, it because more obvious that this program was a "hit."

Finally, after I had everything worked out, I did another completely new video recording of the event. I planned out every aspect of the program, and invited amazing live guest speakers. We had better lighting, and better cameras (two of them this time!). I created a new video and audio version of the program, that really looked great. I had proven to myself that people wanted to come to the event, and that they would pay for it by doing it once initially... then doing a series of live events in different cities that worked as well.

When I finally did version 3.0, I was making something for the long-term. And now over 10 years later, we still have people buy that program regularly.

As a side note, I want to mention that many of the programs I've released never got past version 1.0. I would make a new course, teach it for the first time, and then release it as a product… and have it succeed. I have gotten busy enough with various types of projects, my family, and whatever else in my life that I never had time to go back and make version 2.0 and version 3.0. If I would have been too much of a perfectionist, and not just made something "good enough" then I likely wouldn't have gotten anything done… ever.

Scaling & Management

Once you find an opportunity that passes through these previous levels, that has proven itself to have high long-term potential, then it's time to put effort into actually building a business around it. It's time to scale the opportunity up and turn it into an enterprise.

I have had the privilege of building several successful businesses now, and of advising and investing in many others. There is a pattern to success in business that almost no one knows about before experiencing it themselves. In fact, it's not only a pattern of success, but it's also a key reason for long-term failure in business.

The reason has to do with the skill of successfully managing the growth of the business itself. You can be in the right industry, and you can have a great product or service idea, and you can even have sales coming in and money in the bank. But if you don't learn the skill of managing a team of people and the different parts of a business, it can all collapse.

The .com boom in the late 1990s proved beyond a shadow of a doubt that it takes more than just money and a product idea to succeed in business. Many companies had great ideas for products, great teams, and lots of money in the bank, but they still failed - because they didn't know how to run a business.

In this section, I'm going to share a set of tools and tips that I've picked up along the way for building a successful and profitable business. Remember as you learn and implement these ideas that they are part of a larger skillset. They all fit together as part of a bigger puzzle.

When you learn to use them together, along with other skills that you'll learn along the way, you are becoming a real entrepreneur. Don't underestimate the power of these tools, models and systems. You need them if you're going to succeed in the long-term.

Follow Your Winners

If you put everything that we've learned so far together into one bigger picture, you'll start to realize that the story of an opportunity that turned into a bigger success is the story of the intersection of both skill and luck. It's the combination of finding the right opportunity and also nurturing it through a series of progressive growth stages, all the way to success.

Tony Hseih started a company in the 1990s called Link Exchange, that helped companies advertise their websites online. He eventually sold the company to Microsoft. He then took the capital he had raised from the sale, and started an investment fund and incubator called Venture Frogs, which invested in startup companies. One of the companies they invested in was a site that sold shoes online, that called itself Zappos. A couple of months later, he joined the company as CEO, having recognized it as being a particularly good opportunity.

As CEO, he grew the company to over a billion dollars in sales, and then sold it to Amazon.com. Rumors are that his Amazon stock has likely made him a billionaire.

If you would have called Tony up early in his career and asked him what he believed that his big success was going to be, it's pretty unlikely that he would have answered "online shoes." But by following a string of interesting opportunities, he was able to navigate his way to massive success.

Too often, entrepreneurs aren't watching and following their successes, instead choosing to try to make something work that just isn't working. I have watched many friends and students who get their mind set on one particular idea, then waste huge amounts of time and money trying to figure out how to get customers to buy from them… rather than scaling up the things that people want to buy from them.

Often, it's a small part of what you're doing that reveals a more narrow path to success. It can even be a small part of what the company you're working for is doing, by the way. I have heard so many interesting stories of people who worked for a company, and saw a big opportunity that their employer didn't want to pursue - that became a winning opportunity for them.

I once had a conversation with the founder of a company called Brightroll, which built a marketplace and platform for video ads on YouTube. He was originally working at YouTube, and saw this opportunity to build a the platform. But YouTube wasn't interested in doing it because they were busy working on their core system. So he (and I believe, a partner) went out on their own and built it, and then sold it several years later to Yahoo for $640 million. I have heard many similar stories over the years in Silicon Valley, and in other places as well.

It's often a small part of what you're doing that winds up being the doorway to a new product or service, or a new way of doing business that winds up being transformational. If you're not open to seeing and following a new thread of success, then you can't take advantage of it, and you can't benefit from it. Follow your successes, and keep your eye open for small aspects of your product or service that can wind up being big markets of their own. And make sure to stay in close contact with your customers along the way, as they will help you discover the narrow pathway to success.

The Sign to Watch For

When you discover or create an opportunity that looks right, sounds right, feels right, and makes sense, it creates a "click" inside. When you get on the path to developing your potential winner, you will typically run up against challenges.

When you have a winning opportunity, but it also becomes very hard, I believe that this is a "sign from the universe." Whenever I'm in this situation, I remind myself that the increasing difficulty is an indicator that this is a much bigger opportunity than I thought. If I can see the opportunity, and I believe that I've found something special, AND it's becoming very hard, this means that if I can figure it out I will have a big lead over others who will be trying to pursue the same opportunity.

When most people run into increasing resistance in life, they tend to give up. In sales, they say that you have to persist through multiple "objections" before someone will make a buying decision. Most people will not persist, and

Denis Waitley, in his spectacular audio program "The Psychology of Winning" says that winners develop the skill of **manufacturing their own optimism**. This is an important concept, and one that can lead you to many creative ways of keeping yourself inspired, energized, and believing in yourself and your opportunity.

There's a subtle difference between being persistent and attaching yourself to something that is a losing proposition in the long-term. I am not suggesting blind confidence, and I'm definitely not suggesting arrogance and hubris.

If you're pursuing your opportunity, and getting signals that your hypothesis is valid, AND things start getting much harder, remember that this is an indicator that you have a bigger opportunity than you originally thought. And if you can manufacture the optimism for yourself and others, so you stay in the game, and do whatever it takes to bring it to fruition, your rewards can be much bigger than you originally anticipated.

Stars Only

As you learn to launch products and build businesses, you will see a common denominator in both successes and failures. It has to do with the teams of people who you work with on your projects.

If you're working with a great team of people, not only are you more likely to be successful, but you're also more likely to learn a lot and have a lot more fun. Your collaboration partners and team members are like links in a chain. If you have a weak link, the entire chain is compromised.

When you work with superstars, everything works better. And as we move more into a business environment that is increasingly virtual, knowledge-based, and dynamic, the difference that working with super-stars makes is multiplied.

As you work with more design, engineering, marketing and creative professionals, you also start to see that in these more "mental" domains, the difference between someone who is "good" and someone who is "great" is exaggerated. A great software developer is not just a little better than a good one, it can be 10x. A great visual designer can be 10x as talented as a good one. A great recruiter in your business can recruit people who are in another dimension compared to someone who is just OK.

The world's authority on hiring superstar talent is Brad Smart, the author of the classic book Topgrading. I consider Topgrading to be a "must-read" book for all entrepreneurs, as he lays out a very detailed model and plan for recruiting and hiring what he calls "A Players."

One of the big insights that you have as you begin recruiting and hiring people is that if you just play the numbers a bit, you can find much stronger talent to work with you. If you interview 10 people, one of them on average is going to be an A Player. They will be much better than the others in the group, and it will often cost about the same amount to hire them.

I have interviewed and hired a lot of people over the years in my various roles and businesses, and it always shocks me just how much better you can do by putting in some time and effort to interview a variety of different people for a role.

It's usually a mistake to hire someone "just because they are there" - and waste the opportunity to find someone who is truly great. Instead, run ads and go on a recruiting campaign. Ask friends, write to your network, and reach out to people you've worked with before who might know someone that would be good for the role you need.

If you run ads, be very detailed about what you're looking for. Make it clear that you're looking for someone who is great at what they do, who is talented and qualified, and who wants to learn and grow in their role.

If you're a coach and looking to hire someone to design a website for you to attract more clients, say in your ad: "I am a coach, and I am looking for someone to design an awesome website for me. You would ideally have several years of experience designing websites, and have a portfolio that includes several coaches and consultants. I need a website that attracts clients and convinces them to contact me to become clients. If you respond to this ad, please send me examples of websites that you've designed, and tell me about the difference that the site made to the client's business."

Assume that you're going to find a superstar, and write your ad to that person directly. Remember, they're the only one that matters. Raise your standards, and speak to what you want!

As you get responses, look through them to see who read your entire ad, and who took the time to give you a thoughtful, intelligent, qualified response. Many people will just attach a resume or paste a canned response, or will write something that shows clearly that they're either not qualified or not serious.

This begins with a simple decision that you make internally, yourself. It's the decision to work with "Stars Only." This is about raising your standards before you even begin, so that your projects and businesses experience growing success in the long-run.

Other benefits of working with superstars:

- They raise the morale and esteem of the entire group
- They inspire others on the team (and you) to perform at a higher level
- They know other superstars and will refer them to work with you
- You'll learn a lot more from them
- They have lots of options, and can easily move on if the project fails

We have already learned that you essentially become the average of those that you surround yourself with. This mindset goes "doubly" for the people that you work closely with. You will be interacting, communicating, collaborating, solving problems, and being influenced by the people you work with.

If you want to become more of a superstar yourself, then take care to find and work with superstars in every place you can.

It doesn't matter what the people on your team are doing, either. A great attitude, collaborative nature, and high qualifications make such a huge difference. There are A Players for every role in business and life, and you can find them if you go looking intentionally.

REMINDER: Download the "Opportunity Companion Guide" to Get Your Summaries, Checklists & Exercises

This book has an **Opportunity Companion Guide** that goes along with it, which you can download for free. It includes key chapter summaries, implementation checklists, and written exercises - plus extra chapters and other bonus material. Go here to get it now, so you can review the summaries and start implementing what you're learning:

OpportunityBonus.com

Opportunity Innovation & Collaboration

Innovation

IN THE WORLD OF business, innovation has become the holy grail. If you can create new processes, products and services that customers want to pay for, you are performing magic.

People like Galileo with his new telescope were what we would call innovative. Gutenberg with the printing press, Henry Ford and the Model T, Steve Jobs with computers (Apple) and computer-animated movies (Pixar), and Elon Musk with Telsa and SpaceX are other iconic examples.

What sets these innovators apart from others is that they were able to take several component elements and combine them into something that was revolutionary.

One of my heroes is a French man named Augustin-Jean Fresnel. Fresnel was born in the late 1700s, in the time of Napoleon. He was fascinated with light, and spent much of his time researching and studying how it worked. Fresnel investigated diffraction and how beams of light interfere with each other, creating mysterious patterns. He invented a special type of optical lens now called a "Fresnel lens" - for lighthouses.

Lighthouses have been used for thousands of years to help ships avoid crashing into the coastline. They started out as fires built on hilltops, an eventually evolved into what amounted to giant candles that used reflector dishes or lenses to create and beam the light. The wonderful book "A Short Bright Flash" by Theresa Levitt tells the story of how Fresnel created an innovative solution.

In the early 1800s, sailors were complaining that French lighthouses were inferior to English versions. A French commission ran experiments to figure out what the best technology was at the time. Fresnel was the engineer on the project, and in tests he had to repeatedly climb to the top of the Arc de Triomphe in Paris to secure the equipment, discovering in the process how difficult it was to get the current reflector technology to make a bright beam of light.

Fresnel saw that most of the light coming from the lamp flame was being wasted by the technology being used. Half of the light disappeared because even with a perfect mirror, half is the light is of absorbed and only half is reflected. Not to mention many the other issues with making curved mirrors a couple of hundred years ago. He realized he if he could create a large glass lens, that he could collect and project a lot more of that light, and make the lighthouse far more powerful. But a huge glass lens that would collect and beam this much light would have to be huge, very thick, and impossibly heavy. Someone had already tried it, and the glass had to be made so thick that most of the light was absorbed before it went out the other side.

In a flash of brilliance, Fresnel saw the solution in his mind: Build a lens by arranging small prisms in an array that was shaped like a giant lens. If you've never seen a Fresnel lens in a lighthouse, it's worth taking a moment to look them up to get a sense of what a masterpiece these things are.

To build his new innovation, he had to commission special glass-makers to make his new "puzzle piece" prisms. Fresnel combined various types of knowledge and technology together with his new multi-prism lens design, putting it all together into one unit, designed for this unique and valuable purpose. If he could get it right, it would save many lives and a lot of money, and enable a new era of world trade.

In his first public demonstration, the new lens design created a light that was so much brighter than competing reflector technology that it was obvious that the new design had instantly made the old technology obsolete. When Fresnel built a lens for use in an actual lighthouse, it increased the distance that you could see the light from a something like a few miles to thirty-three miles away. And it used half of the fuel, as well.

Now that's an innovation!

The new lighthouse lens design spread around the world, and every port that installed one became a hub of trade, literally lighting the way to the global economy we enjoy today.

In his legendary book "The Innovator's Dilemma" Clayton Christensen theorizes that much innovation in business is what he calls "disruptive innovation." The innovation of the automobile was disruptive to the horse-drawn carriage industry. Digital cameras disrupted traditional film technology. Wikipedia disrupted the traditional encyclopedia model. Uber disrupted the taxicab model.

Fresnel was a disruptive innovator. The competition never saw it coming. A new design or concept that offers a 10x or 20x price/performance ratio is a total game-changer. Technology is now making this type of thing "the new normal." In the past, an innovation could last a long time by making small, incremental changes before being made obsolete by radical innovation. Now everything is up for grabs.

Something interesting about disruptive innovation is that it often comes from people who work for a bigger company, who see an opportunity that the bigger company doesn't want to pursue. Fresnel was part of a team that was installing reflector dishes to figure out which one was best for making lighthouses. He realized that he could create a better design himself, so he set out to do it.

In fact, the "dilemma" that innovators face is this: If you have something that's working, is it worth investing money to find a better way to do things, and in the process threaten or cannibalize your own proven system for making a living?

In their book "Positioning" Al Ries and Jack Trout point out that new product and service categories are almost always created by "outsiders" - and very rarely are they produced by established companies. IBM dominated the computer business, and they were perfectly positioned to win the software game. But they didn't. Bill Gates won with Microsoft. Microsoft was perfectly positioned to win the search engine game, but they didn't. Larry Page and Sergey Brin won with Google in the 2000s. Google was perfectly positioned to win the social networking game, but they didn't. Mark Zuckerberg won with Facebook.

You'll see this pattern across industries and through time, if you look for it. Banks and credit card companies should have won online payments, but a little startup called PayPal beat them (it certainly helped to have Peter Thiel and Elon Musk as founders!). New entrants beat out established players in emerging categories so consistently that it's worth closely considering what's going on.

I believe that this dynamic has a root cause that's relatively simple to explain. When the time for change is ripe, and new technology and knowledge is emerging that could be combined to produce an innovative solution, the right combination of new ideas, technology, people, and other raw material is only meeting inside of a very few minds. These are intelligent, curious minds that are personally fascinated with how these new things and ideas work, and with combining them to create innovative solutions (and often, to make money as well).

Big companies are busy growing their core ideas and taking care of their sacred cows, and they are strongly incentivized to believe in a model of reality that supports their current money-making activities. The game-changing idea that spawns the next industry is usually far enough from the way that they do things that they won't see it. It literally takes someone who is thinking much smaller, and often someone from the outside, to really understand the opportunity.

The story of Tim Berners-Lee, who combined things like domain names, hypertext, and a communication protocol to create the World Wide Web, is a great example of several new ideas and technologies merging together inside of one mind to create something revolutionary. Steve Jobs and Steve Wozniak built some of the first personal computers by putting together several existing pieces of technology in a new way, setting the stage for Apple, which became the most valuable public company in the world. Satoshi Nakamoto, the mysterious inventor of the blockchain and of Bitcoin, combined and wove together several elements of technology to create a masterpiece that allows you to own and trade unforgeable digital assets. Each of these inventions has made multiple people into billionaires, and it's fascinating to think that they and most other big innovations were created by individuals and small groups of people who were combining elements to solve new problems and create new forms of value.

Vertical Innovation

I would like to introduce a concept that I call "vertical innovation" - to draw a distinction that I find particularly useful when engaging in creative work, entrepreneurship, design and artistic endeavors. I borrow this term from developmental psychology, where they speak of vertical development, and from

We could just as easily call it "developmental innovation" but I prefer the term vertical innovation, so that's what I'll use here.

If you look at how reality seems to organize, you see this pattern of components on one level coming together in groups to create higher-order emergent properties. Remember the example of individual ants acting together in synchrony to create the emergent property or entity of the ant colony?

Consider subatomic particles coming together and uniting in the particular combination that forms a stable emergent property called an "atom" on a higher level or order. And how atoms come together, sharing electrons to form bonds as they create the foundation for emergent properties called molecules in a higher dimension.

It's this interesting ability to organize on your own level and "be yourself" while at the same time organizing in such a way that another entity forms beyond, on a higher order, that's so interesting.

Molecules come together with other elements and form emergent cells on a higher vertical level. Cells come together to form tissues on a higher order. Tissues come together to form organs on a higher order. And organs come together to form bodies.

Individual cells remain in "sovereign integrity" in the process of living in these larger entities of the tissues that emerge beyond them.

To imagine vertical orders of emergence, I like to visualize an atom with a proton and neutron at the center united in a nucleus, with an electron whirring around in an orbit like planets orbiting the sun. If you were standing on the electron and and you could see other atoms and the nucleus, they would look like tiny stars far away in the distance. From the level of the electron, everything is very tiny, and moving around very quickly. But from the perspective of the molecule that this atom is a part of, things are very different. At that scale, the atom is a unified "cloud" of an entity, united with others to form an even larger structure. At each order, a new type of structure or entity emerges, and each of these structures is only visible as a structure from the higher order, or higher vertical level.

You can also imagine a cell, composed of billions of molecules, all self-orchestrating and acting together in a great society. From the perspective of one molecule, reality might look like a great school of fish, with you being one of the fish swimming around with the others. But from the perspective of the cell, you are this entire planet of interesting living ecological dynamism emerging in a higher dimension, beyond the scale of comprension to the individual molecules that compose you.

This kind of thing is very weird to think about, and even weirder to try to talk about (especially when you start using terms like "entity" to discuss them, and suggesting that they exist in different dimensions of reality, which I tend to gravitate towards).

But "something is going on here"… and there appears to be a universal pattern or force that seems to invoke each self-quantized and self-organized level to join together with others, and form a stable foundation for something novel and dynamic to emerge around-beyond it.

Arthur Koestler coined the term "holon" to describe something that is both a whole and a part. It's a whole, individual, complete entity on one level while at the same time being a part or building block of something else on a higher level. He also created the term "holarchy" to describe networks of these holons, so that we could think about this model more dimensionally. I believe that the terms holon and holarchy are in a small group of the most valuable concepts that have been created by humans so far, as they give us a way to conceptualize this vertical, nested, emergent aspect of manifest reality.

Ken Wilber, who I learned about the holon model from, also makes a subtle and important point about the concept of transcendence. Most people use the term "transcend" to mean something like "go past" or "get beyond." But when they use it, they are implying that they have thrown off or discarded what came before. Someone who says "I have transcended my need for approval" or "I have transcended my compulsion to have sex" is typically trying to say that they no longer need approval, or that they no longer compulsively have sex. But Ken Wilber points out that to actually transcend something, you include it. Moving beyond doesn't mean rejecting or denying. It actually means accepting and embracing, in a higher order structure, identity or model.

When an atom transcends the subatomic particles that compose it, the atom doesn't reject them or deny that they exist anymore. It gathers them together weaves them into the fabric of itself, each a precious and absolutely necessary part of the atom's existence.

A body that transcends the organs that compose it does not try to escape from them, or deny them individual integrity. The body is itself the organs, plus something far more at a higher level... in a higher dimension of existence.

When I am creating something new in my life, whether it be a new course that I'm going to teach, a new design for a logo, a new product or service for my business, a new collaboration, a new social group or mastermind, I use the ideas of emergent properties, vertical orders, holons, and transcendence as my models.

To me, a real innovation is creating something on a higher order. It's producing an emergent property, that transcends and includes the best of what already exists now, in a higher dimensional design that produces a new type of value that hasn't been produced before. This is what I'm talking about when I say "vertical innovation."

This concept has been revolutionary for me in my life, as it really expands the the creative canvas in my imagination to include not only making something new - something that has never existed before - but to also do it in a way that honors and includes the best of what has come before.

I have designed this book to be a vertical innovation, and the information to produce an emergent property inside of your mind when it is read and understood. I have taken the best of what I have learned about entrepreneurship, mental models for success, emotional self-regulation, collaborative partnership, productivity, and much more, and organized it to transmit a central organizing concept called "Opportunity" to you. I'll use the term here in a capitalized form, to denote a more abstract and fundamental principle of life, growth, creativity, success, relationship, and evolution.

As I endeavor to transfer this dynamic and important concept over to your mind through the channel of the written word, I am imagining the spirit of Opportunity, made up of these many ideas that I've learned in my life, coming to you and blessing you with the hands to create, the heart to feel, and inner eyes to see Opportunity throughout your life. When I imagine Opportunity as a kind of fairy spirit, made of of dozens of light concepts, each a fractal emergent built from many smaller ideas and examples, the concept of Opportunity and also of vertical innovation makes more sense to me, and is more relatable.

I realize that this visualization borders on mystical fantasy. But somehow, imagining Opportunity as an emergent spirit that transcends and includes the unique combination of living concepts in this book makes it more real, and gives me something to strive for. It inspires me.

When I am working on a new design for something, or experimenting with combining elements from different domains to see what happens, I keep the idea of higher order emergent properties in the back of my mind. I'm always looking to produce something that is not only a novel combination of elements, but also that special extra something that is the mark of an emergent phenomena.

When approached the way I am imagining it, you are able to freely combine elements from many domains of life, knowing that the more diverse the combination of elements, the better and more robust the emergent innovation is likely to be.

Don't just use a new fabric in your clothing design, take some inspiration from Lady Gaga and use a disco ball as your starting material for your dress!

Infinite Pent Up Emergent Value

Once you understand emergence and creating value on a higher order or in a higher dimension, it opens up possibilities that didn't exist before you understood the model.

And once your mind acclimates to thinking in the vertical dimension, you eventually have a big realization: That there is going to be an infinite progression of vertical development and emergent innovation in the future. Combining elements on one level to create a higher order value is going to be a never-ending evolutionary process.

The way I see it, this higher-order value is essentially "pent up" and waiting to be produced, created, and released. There is an infinite supply of pent up emergent value. Because most people are thinking sequentially, and linearly, and not thinking vertically and in terms of emergence, they are missing the possibility of tapping into what I believe is the greatest domain of opportunity of all.

Value and opportunity is different for a cell than it is for an organ, and it's different for organs than it is for bodies. Opportunity and value are different on different levels, and when you start looking for how you can combine elements on this level to produce and create the next level, you can open doorways to places that will change your life.

Scenario Planning

"By imagining the handful of the most likely ways that a situation will turn out, you prepare your mind to spot the early signs that one of the futures is coming true."

I'm fascinated with people who call themselves "futurists" (and with those that are just great at seeing what's going to happen, whatever they call themselves). One of the brilliant ones is Peter Schwartz. He wrote a book titled The Art Of The Long View.

Inside, he lays out the methodology for a powerful method called "scenario planning" that Shell has used for decades to become very successful in the highly competitive energy market. The idea is to envision what the most likely outcomes will be in the future, and then think through what the signs will be that one of the scenarios is coming true. As you do this, you create a series of stories about how the future will unfold, and you'll then know what to watch for as "road signs" along the way.

Shell has used this approach to spot signals of oil crises, stock market crashes, and cultural transformations, and then used these signals to better position themselves for the future.

If you don't think through what the most likely different scenarios are for the future of your opportunity, then you are far more likely to fall prey to things like confirmation bias, sunk cost bias, and general attachment to things going the way you want them to.

On the other hand, if you think through the different types of scenarios that might play out, and then ask yourself what the signs will be that one of them is coming true,

I remember reading a story several years ago about a big computer manufacturer that had created several scenarios, and was using them to watch for signs that one of them was unfolding. At one point, a huge storm threatened a country that made many of their components, and they realized that if the storm hit this country and shut down the plants, that it would really hurt them. They took action, and bought up all of the inventory that was available on the market as insurance. Sure enough, the storm hit the country full-force, and shut down all of the plants. It was because they had been paying attention and thinking through the scenarios that could unfold, the signs that one of them was happening, and how to respond, that they survived (and out-performed their competitors, who were left without the parts to build computers).

If you don't actually think through the potential future scenarios, and then ask yourself or your group what the signs are that would indicate that one of them was coming true, then you won't spot the signals in the first place. This is the key. You will misinterpret one of the signals as being "no big deal" rather than recognizing it as the indicator that things have potentially changed course, and that you'll need to make new plans and take new actions.

Scenarios, in this sense, turn out to be stories about how the future will unfold. Most people are uncomfortable holding multiple conflicting stories or ideas in their minds, and so they skip doing exercises like this one. It's easier to just pick one story that you prefer, and stick with it until forced to change. But this exercise of thinking through diverse potential future scenarios, and then mapping out how they might unfold along with key signs and indicators to watch for, really prepares you for the future that I believe we're moving into.

And remember: The point isn't to predict the future here. It's to pre-imprint your mind to be ready for the road signs that indicate that one future is manifesting vs. another future. It's to pre-vision a set of indicators so that when one of them happens, you say "oh, yes… I've seen that before… I know what this might mean… let me consider this in a new way."

Opportunity Collaboration

"When you need to innovate, you need collaboration."
—Marissa Mayer

To take opportunity to the next level, let's look at what's possible when you team up and collaborate with others. In this section we're going to learn about the power of collaboration and partnership to create and take advantage of opportunities.

Consider the distinction between these four words and their definitions:

COMPETITION: Rivals competing for resources, status, or prize. Characterized by the perception of there being winners and losers. Can be highly motivating, but also perceived as zero-sum.

COOPERATION: Working together toward a common value or purpose. Characterized by a spirit of common interest or struggle. "We're all in this together."

COLLUSION: Working together for an illicit or immoral purpose. Typically used to describe illegal cooperation. Characterized by secrecy and the danger of being caught.

COLLABORATION: Combining and synchronizing diverse skills to produce a multiplication of value. Characterized by the production of a higher order or emergent level of benefit.

Each life level and form specializes in a particular way of making a living. Together these forms work to create emergent, higher-order entities and higher-order forms of value.

You may have heard of Adam Smith's pin factory. If you have one person working in a pin factory and they have to do all of the different jobs - make the wire and cut it, and sharpen the tips, and make the pinheads, and solder them together, they can only make a little handful of pins in a day. But if you take a group of ten people, and they all specialize, and each of them does one job, and they set it up in a factory, they can make 48,000 pins.

Adam Smith uses this example to describe what he calls "division of labor." It's a powerful example of what's possible when we specialize, and when we work together toward a common outcome.

But there's something else going on here that deserves closer attention. It's not just the division of labor, it's the specialization, the coordination, the synchronization, the orchestration of the people involved. The term "division of labor" sacrifices the magic of what's happening, in my opinion. There's actually a miracle happening here.

M.C. Escher created a famous series of fine art pieces using a technique known as "tessellation." This is the process of arranging shapes so that they repeat in a pattern. Escher would often tessellate animal shapes, an example being this piece that combines fish and birds:

TESSELLATION IS "MATHEMATICAL ART" as it requires exacting precision. If you look at the center of this image, you will see the abstract bird and fish shape that fit together perfectly in a repeating pattern.

Tessellations are my favorite metaphor to use when thinking about and describing collaboration and collaborative partnership. In order to create a tessellation, you must fine-tune and sculpt your starting shapes in order to fit them together into a pattern that "works" as a unified composition. It's the diversity of the images plus the fitting together of the different shapes that creates the surprise and the magic.

Likewise, in order to successfully collaborate, two or more diverse people must learn about themselves and about each other, and then work to both divide the tasks that need to be accomplished, and also synchronize their efforts by sculpting themselves to fit better with the other or others involved. There's an artistic dimension to collaboration.

Steve Jobs described the team that built the first Macintosh computer as being composed of artists, musicians, business people and scientists, all working together and fitting a thousand different elements together in order to create the final beautiful product. One of Steve's favorite metaphors for collaboration was putting plain rocks together into a rock tumbler with soap and grit, and then letting them crash into each other and polish each other in the process.

My first job was working for a coppersmith in a metal shop, making copper kitchenware and artistic decorations. We used tumblers to clean and polish the copper, and these devices do have a type of magic. You put in the dirty, unpolished material and you come back a few hours later and take out shiny, new-looking surfaces.

When you work together in collaborative relationship with a person who has different skills, and a different way of seeing reality, you activate a sort of "relational binocular vision." You can see not only the two perspectives or the two views, but you get a third type of vision, almost like a "relationship depth perception" that either view alone doesn't possess.

When you have a collaboration with different people who have different skills, you get the same kind of thing. You get this third power that's beyond the power of the individuals. When you have two different people that see the world in different ways, the combination can do something that no one person can do. That's the essence of collaboration.

The more diverse your competencies, the more powerful the collaboration. This is very counterintuitive. It's more challenging to synchronize different worldviews, different skills, and different values, but it's worth it. You get a sort of "hybrid vigor" of the collaboration. In biology, hybrid vigor is when you take two subspecies or two very different strains that can still reproduce together, and then you marry those two together. You get an offspring that has more vigor, that has higher fitness than either of the parents did.

It's the same thing with collaboration. If you have very diverse competencies, you can get a higher form of value. For example, let's say that you're starting a business you want to start the business with a partner. If you are a great designer, and your partner is a great software developer, that's an extremely powerful collaboration.

Or if one of you is great at people skills, having social relationships with people, and one of you is great at numbers, maybe not so good with people but good with numbers, that's going to be a more powerful collaboration. If one of you is good with the big picture, more strategic, and one of you is better with the details, like managing the checklist, that's going to be a more powerful collaboration. It's all about diverse competencies.

This pattern extends to the next level, and also applies to collaborative groups. As you develop the ability to collaborate, try using this skill to coordinate and tessellate entire groups. Lead two diverse groups to take advantage of a shared opportunity. The emergent creative power of diverse groups is awesome and it's worth the effort to create. If you grow an organization, you will find that you need to get different types of groups of people that have different ways of viewing the world and different values sets to work together. This is one way to tessellate groups for collaborative synergy.

Just like there are classic personality differences... like the conflicts that arise between an extroverted person and an introverted person... or between someone that's more rational and someone that's more emotional... these same kinds of things emerge when you're dealing people that are from different groups within organizations. Some of the classic conflicts that show up are the conflict between the sales team and between the product team, because the sales team goes out and they promise the world. They say to clients: "Yes, we can make you anything you want" in order to make the sale. They get the deal and they bring it home, and then the product team says, "We're not going to build that, it will mess everything up." Then the sales team says: "But we brought in the money" and so on. These classic conflicts happen throughout organizations. When you can learn how to resolve these dilemmas and help integrate and align them, you can get a very powerful organization.

One of the great things about collaborating with others is it brings a natural accountability. When you have a partner who is also invested in an outcome, you have someone to bounce ideas off of, you have someone to brainstorm with, and you have someone to act as a sounding board. You have someone that can see your blind spots, as well. When you need to supercharge your power to take advantage of a big opportunity, many or even most times it's better to do it in a collaborative partnership. In Silicon Valley, many Venture Capitalists believe that the optimal number of founders for a startup is two.

The key that I want you to take away from this section is that there is a different level of opportunity available when you are collaborating. It's a higher possibility, a higher form of value that is available. Two hydrogen atoms and one oxygen atoms can serve valuable functions alone, but when they find each other, tessellate, coordinate, and combine efforts, they can create something much more profound: Water.

Keep in mind the higher opportunity that collaboration represents. It's often more challenging, but it's worth it!

REMINDER: Download the "Opportunity Companion Guide" to Get Your Summaries, Checklists & Exercises

This book has an **Opportunity Companion Guide** that goes along with it, which you can download for free. It includes key chapter summaries, implementation checklists, and written exercises - plus extra chapters and other bonus material. Go here to get it now, so you can review the summaries and start implementing what you're learning:

OpportunityBonus.com

My Favorite Opportunity in Business

EARLIER IN THIS BOOK, I introduced the concept of learning knowledge and skills that are "future-proof." The idea is to learn things that will become more valuable over time, and not less valuable. In this section, I would like to share my favorite business models, and my favorite future-proof skills to learn in business.

In the first world, we have recently emerged from a cultural context where individuals typically had a business career focused around one job or role, or one trade, that we did for decades, and then retired with either a pension or a social security check.

We're moving in to a future where we will have likely dozens of different roles, positions, jobs, businesses, projects… spanning several careers in different domains and industries. And the social support system that we have counted on to take care of us later in life is definitely in question.

I've read estimates that in a typical career one can expect to have a dozen jobs in multiple different industries. And this is accelerating. Think about what you were doing for work 5 years ago. Is it the same as what you're doing now? What I am doing now is very different from what I was doing five years ago. I can't even imagine what I'll be doing in another five years as my work. I have some rough outlines, but who knows?

The things I can predict, the hard trends, about work in my future are:

- It will involve learning new skills and ideas
- It will involve creating valuable products and services
- It will involve sales and marketing to get customers
- It will involve knowledge and education

Whatever you're doing, I assume that your future will be similar in this way. Whether you're working in a job, or building your own business, or investing, your work will involve these elements.

With that in mind, it's important to be having experiences that help you learn the key skills associated with each of these areas, so that you can quickly adapt to your new roles and environments, learn and understand how value is produced for others in your new role, and that you're able to financially and personally benefit from what you're doing.

The following business skills and models are the ones that I feel are most important to learn for success in the future business environment that's coming.

A Few Important "Information Economy" Frames

We are transitioning from a work environment of physical productivity to a work environment of mental productivity. Peter Drucker coined the terms "knowledge work" and "knowledge worker" to describe people that primarily work with their minds rather than their hands. And now, most of the people who work in first world countries are knowledge workers, and are paid primarily for what they do in their minds - not with their hands.

Knowledge work involves searching for knowledge, analyzing information, making predictions, making decisions, mentally designing, communicating, collaborating, and persuading others to act on your ideas and conclusions. These are skills that require a different type of educational experience than our current education system provides.

Knowledge work is much harder to measure and evaluate than physical work. If you are doing manual labor, I can watch what you're doing and see if you're producing the output that is required. If you're doing mental work, it's much more challenging to measure productivity.

We are entering a more entrepreneurial phase of our business evolution in general. This means that not only are we working more primarily with knowledge and ideas, but we're also increasingly going to be doing it in the context of our own businesses.

These will range from research, coaching, and consulting businesses, to the production of educational courses and knowledge products, to the creation of new business organizations to educate people in large numbers, and much more - not to mention the business models that fuse knowledge work and technology, like software.

And finally, a key point that I am making in this book is that you can learn to improve your knowledge work skills. There are methods and models for becoming better at learning, thinking, decisions, design, communication, collaboration, and more. This book is mostly devoted to teaching new models for learning, thinking, and creative imagination, in order to help you adapt to and be attractive in the coming environment.

One way to take yourself up to the next level relative to this knowledge work game is to start and build an "information business." We could define an information business as any business model that offers as its main "product" information, knowledge, or learning. Examples include:

- Writing a book
- Doing seminars or webinars
- Coaching and consulting
- Creating an online course
- Producing a digital product
- Doing a podcast
- Making a news site or service
- Writing a blog
- Building a research business

What makes these models unique and special is that the core of their product or service offering is mostly about information and knowledge. They don't focus on making physical products like shoes or cars, they don't provide labor for the production of physical products. They work more or less in the domain of "pure knowledge."

I began my serious business career by working as a real estate agent. My product was the homes that I was selling. Later, I went to work for a company that produced real estate seminars and training courses. At that company, our product was the knowledge of how to get clients and sell more real estate. Later, I started my own independent "one man" consulting and coaching business, teaching real estate professionals how to get more clients.

This is a key distinction when learning about knowledge work and knowledge products and services. Packaging up information and knowledge about how to do something is very different from doing the thing.

Because the right piece of knowledge can dramatically improve your ability to do a particular thing or get a particular result in life, some knowledge can be very valuable. I know people that sell online training courses for thousands of dollars, and some that have digital courses and online programs that are tens of thousands of dollars or more. These courses and programs offer knowledge that is extremely valuable, and so justify the high investment prices.

My Journey With Knowledge Products

On April 18th, 2001 my life changed with the self-publication of my first book. We had just emerged from the tech-driven stock market crash in 2000. When I told people that I was starting an online business, they looked at me as if to say "I'm sorry."

I had spent the previous few years trying to figure out the dating game, and once I did, I realized that this was a perfect opportunity to create an "information business" teaching other men the knowledge of how to get dates. I told you part of this story earlier, but I want to share a few more details with you here, so you can see how important this new domain of opportunity is.

When I started this company, I had to learn how to do all of the aspects of the business myself. I was literally launching it from my bedroom. Because the business sold information, in the form of an eBook, it was a highly educational experience.

When I completed my book, then put it online for sale and had my first sales, the lightbulb really went on in my head. People around the world were going online, looking for advice on dating, finding my website, and then paying me for a digital copy of my book. They were trading digital money for digital information, and it was all happening instantly.

Information and knowledge businesses were already fascinating, but this took things to another level. Instead of having to do a live seminar, or send out a package in the mail with video and audio recordings or big workbooks, this was all happening completely in the digital domain. I could tell that this was going to change everything.

A few months later, as I was experimenting and learning more about online marketing, I decided to do a price test, and see if another price would work better for my book. I started out selling my book for $29.95, and I decided one day to test selling the book for ten dollars more, for $39.95.

I woke up that morning, changed the price, and then drove a couple of hours to spend the day with two friends of mine who were visiting. I was living in Los Angeles at the time, and they were in San Diego for a conference, so I drove down and hung out with them for the afternoon.

Later in the day, I asked one of them if I could borrow his computer to check my sales stats. When I looked, I couldn't believe my eyes. I had a record day, selling ten copies of my book that day. Because I had raised my price by ten dollars, I had made about $400 in total sales. I quickly did the math in my head, and realized that if I kept up this sales pace, I would make $12,000 in sales in a month. A feeling came over me that I'll never forget. "I'm free" I thought to myself.

At this point, I hired my first virtual assistant, for $6 per hour. She came to work with me 20 hours per week, doing things like customer service, handling download problems, and managing refund requests.

It was incredible to be able to have someone working with me on my team, who was a couple of thousand miles away, and instantly have 20 hours of my time freed up to work on other things!

As I hired people to build my business, everyone worked from home. We never had an office. This has proven to be a great model for me and my team, and for all of our lives.

From that point, I went on to do my first live seminar. I had 23 people pay to attend, and with my team and guest teachers and friends, there were maybe 40 or 50 people in the room total. I borrowed a video camera, and had someone stand in the back of the room to video tape it.

From the recordings, I created my first audio course, which I sold for about $200. The day I released this audio course, my business doubled. After that I started interviewing dating experts, and selling a monthly subscription to the audio recordings for $20 per month. Soon I had hundreds of people signed up as subscribers.

In my first year, I did $133,000 in sales. Then things really took off. I did about $500,000 my second year, then $1.5 million the next year, then $5 million the next year.

As I built my company those first few years, friends became very interested in what I was doing. Many of them asked me to show them how I was building this business, and working from home. I showed one friend the model, and he partnered with his wife to build a company selling ebooks on how to plan your own wedding. He quickly got that business up to tens of thousands of dollars per month in sales, then someone bought the company from him for hundreds of thousands of dollars. Another friend used the model to launch a business teaching people how to play poker. He sold that business, and it made him a millionaire in his early 20s. One of the guys on our team wrote a book, and put it online, and then he partnered with our company to promote it. We grew that business to many millions of dollars in sales, and it still makes sales every day, many years later.

As more and more people came to ask me about how I was building this business, I realized I might be able to start teaching business in the same way that I was teaching dating.

In 2007, I offered a live 5-day workshop called "Altitude." I marketed it to entrepreneurs, and offered to teach them how I grew my virtual business to millions in sales. We had about 100 people fly in from 26 different countries, and invest $10,000 apiece to attend.

I used my information product model, video recorded the course, then produced a video version, which I did a product launch for online. We did $1.7 million in sales in four days and four hours. We had to shut down early, because I completely sold out. That was a crazy few days.

I have since gone on to create dozens of courses on all aspects of online business and entrepreneurship, offering programs priced between a few dollars up to $30,000 for my highest-end mastermind.

Today, the entire information industry is a multi-trillion dollar affair. If you think about it, companies like Google are actually selling… information. We humans are waking up to the fact that information can be extremely valuable, especially when it's information that can help us get more of something we want, or avoid something we don't want.

My friend Alex Mandossian says something profound: **"Every business is in the information business."**

My companies have sold our information and knowledge products to over a million people now online. I have never met most of those people in person, or talked to them in a live conversation. The majority of them visited one of my websites, decided to purchase one of my books or courses, and then went through the course online or on their computer. We've done well over $100 million in sales of information and knowledge products in total.

What was particularly interesting was that I was getting paid to figure out how to make my business successful and my life work, and then teaching others what I was doing. This is how I approach life in general now. When I find an area of life that I'd like to learn about, I assume that someday others will be interested in learning whatever it is that I can figure out.

Right now, for example, I have a daughter who is almost five years old. I have been learning about parenting for the past five years, reading books and getting to know people who have knowledge and experience in this area. I have a couple of documents where I keep notes about what I'm learning, and so far I have probably 100+ pages of notes, links, quotes and references about what I'm learning.

Every once in awhile, I have a big breakthrough in understanding some key domain of parenthood. When I have one of these insights, I make sure to write down the insight, how I learned the elements that led up to the insight, the experience or situation that triggered the insight, etc.

I have very little experience with children before my daughter. I didn't take courses on early childhood development in school. I don't have nieces and nephews that I grew up spending time with. And I am not a "natural" with children - I can tell you that for sure! But I'm a good student, and I want to learn. I want to be the best parent I can be, and I'm learning a little at a time. When I learn a tip from someone else, or read a great book about parenting, it all goes into my notes. Someday, I will likely take all of this knowledge and teach a course on parenting and teaching children.

Because this is a domain that is not a "natural" for me to learn about, it might be several years of continuing this process before I'll feel like I have enough material and enough confidence to start sharing it with others. But I believe at some point, what I've learned will become extremely valuable. I have had a few insights over the past few years about how children experience the world and how they develop, and about family dynamics, that I think are going to help a lot of people.

By the way, I mentioned the idea of the "critical counterintuitive" earlier. When I am learning about a particular domain of life, this is what I'm always watching for. It's those lessons that really hit my by surprise, where I must do something that is radically different from what I would have guessed would work... that I know will be valuable later to others. I pay particular attention to those insights.

Because this approach is now wired into my thought process at a belief level, and a habitual level, I approach every experience in life as an opportunity to learn, an opportunity to have insights and get valuable lessons that will someday be used to teach others.

Many of the insights that I have never make it into my courses or products (or at least, they haven't yet). But they are all useful and valuable to me. My experiences become stories for when I'm coaching someone individually, or if I'm helping a friend to move past a block in their lives.

Some Knowledge is Worth a Lot More to Others

The value of knowledge varies wildly. What is it worth to know yesterday's winning lottery numbers? What is it worth to know tomorrow's winning lottery numbers? These two pieces of information are clearly very similar, yet they are worth vastly different amounts.

A domain that I have been studying for several years is futurism. There are brilliant futurists who have been working on predictive and creative models of the future for decades, and you can learn these models and approaches in a few hours by reading their books or watching their videos. Some of my favorites include Ray Kurzweil, Daniel Burrus, Joel Barker, Peter Schwartz, Peter Diamandis, John Naisbitt, and Alvin Toffler. Their models and mindsets are priceless when it comes to learning how to see how the future will unfold.

In an ideal world, you would imagine your future, and visualize the life that you'd like to be living, and then go and find opportunities that give you experience learning skills and models, and building relationships that get you to that future.

You would only have experiences that you learn from… that get you one step closer to the future you want to be living. This is the "return on experience" model that we learned earlier.

So the ideal experiential learning process or doesn't make sense:

- Teaches you something that you'll use to create the future you want to live in.
- Becomes more valuable over time, and at each level of your personal and professional development.
- Combines with other skills and models to have a multiplying power.
- Prepares you for the next coming level of opportunity, so you recognize it and have what you need to get a foothold and a great start.

I am always on the lookout for these types of models, skills, experiences… because they are "future-proof."

What's the most interesting, educational, and future-proof set of skills I know of? It's these "knowledge work" skills that I'm discussing with you here. It's going to the point of creating information and knowledge **products**.

Here's a roadmap to follow if you're ready to build a knowledge-based business...

Begin With Coaching

Coaching is a universal "swiss army knife" skill that is becoming core to almost every type of relationship and situation that we have in our lives. From friendship to business collaboration... from management to leadership... from romantic relationship to business partnership... the skill of coaching helps you create more success and growth.

When people ask me which type of business I think they should start, I very often answer: "Coaching!"

I define coaching as supporting another person through a transition in their lives. When you understand how to ask the right questions to help a person get clarity and make decisions, this is incredibly valuable.

All of us are going through more transitions in more parts of our lives, and we need the support of others who understand how to get from one place to another in business, in health, and in relationships. This need is compounded by the fact that so many people are spending their time online and on social media, rather than in actual social situations with friends. We're all needing more support, but experiencing less. Coaches are stepping in to fill this gap.

Coaching is also a wonderful skill to learn because it helps you to learn about many areas of business, as well. To launch and build a coaching business you learn about online advertising, social media, and professional selling. You learn how to ask the types of questions that help others identify their blocks, and to identify what they want in life.

A survey that was done by the International Coach Federation a few years ago showed that the average professional coach was earning $214 per coaching session, which is also an excellent rate for a business that you can run from anywhere, using only a computer. I went through a phase in my life in my later 20s where I found myself unemployed, and needing to create income for myself. I started a "1-man coaching and consulting business" and started charging $200-$300 per hour right out of the gate, which allowed me to get back on my feet quickly.

Coaching teaches you so many valuable skills that I think it should be mandatory training for everyone as we're growing up. If you're interested in learning more about coaching, visit my website and watch my videos about our "Virtual Coach" course.

Online Courses

The explosion of interest in learning has created a situation where people around the world are investing in and consuming knowledge at an increasing rate. I have been creating online courses and "digital products" for many years now, and this is my personal favorite business model.

Each of us knows how to do something that would be very valuable for others to learn how to do, and often all that stands in the way is taking that knowledge and recording it in an audio or video course.

I like to teach live seminars (and live webinars), and then record them, and turn the recordings into online courses that I sell on my site. This has been my primary business model for many years. I create new courses and programs each year on various topics, and then market them to people who want to learn about that area of life or business.

I have created courses on everything from dating and relationships to productivity… from entrepreneurship and marketing to creativity… from leadership and personality types to mental models. In fact, whenever I learn about a new area or domain of life or business, I keep in mind that some day I'll probably create a course about it. This encourages me to learn at a deeper level, take better notes, and practice teaching what I learn to others to prepare myself for creating a bigger course later.

If you are interested in learning how to create an online course that you can sell for high prices online, visit my website and watch my video about my course. It will give you a lot more information on how to do it, and if you'd like, you can join me for a 90-day immersion course that will walk you step-by-step through the process.

Other Information Business Models

Along with coaching and digital products or online courses, you can also produce knowledge products in the following formats:

- Masterminds
- Membership sites
- Webinars
- Group coaching
- eBooks
- Podcasts
- Interview series
- Social media

The key is identifying a niche where people are looking for solutions, and then to create high-value information that they want to buy to get the outcome they want.

I believe that everyone should learn the skills required to build an online information or knowledge product business. What you learn in the process is priceless. This business model teaches you so many valuable life and business skills, it will surprise you.

To succeed at building a knowledge-based business, you must learn very important long-term skills and go through a series of important insights. You have to learn how to really understand people and their needs, create products and services that they want to buy, then market and sell what you've created in a high-integrity way… you must learn how copywriting and marketing funnels work, and how to manage a growing business. It's the ultimate "work study" job.

Even if the business model you try doesn't work out, you'll walk away with real-world experience and skills in areas that will become more valuable to you over your life and career. Even if you don't find success, or it's not what you wind up doing long-term, this adventure is still priceless. The models will stay with you forever, and again, they become more and more valuable over time.

As you transition to other types of roles, or start other types of businesses, and move into investing, you take all of this with you... and you'll be a much more powerful communicator, marketer, teacher, and explainer.

REMINDER: Download the "Opportunity Companion Guide" to Get Your Summaries, Checklists & Exercises

This book has an **Opportunity Companion Guide** that goes along with it, which you can download for free. It includes key chapter summaries, implementation checklists, and written exercises - plus extra chapters and other bonus material. Go here to get it now, so you can review the summaries and start implementing what you're learning:

OpportunityBonus.com

The Opportunity to Create a Fulfilling Life

The Art of the Passion Project

I BELIEVE THAT EACH of us should continually start new projects in diverse areas of our lives in order to grow holistically. I recommend starting "passion projects" yearly or so to keep yourself evolving.

A passion project is a new project that you start around a topic that you are passionate about. It is distinct from a general project by the quality of it being initiated around a personal interest **purely from inspiration**. You begin a passion project to pursue something for its own sake. After you start the project and it gets traction, then you concern yourself with whether it will be a business, a hobby, or a philanthropic initiative. Launching new passion projects is about following your curiosity, your inspiration, and your creative spirit.

A passion project is an investment in yourself, but it's also an investment in learning. As it grows, it becomes an investment in collaboration, an investment in community, and an investment in your future success. By experimenting with new projects across diverse domains of life, you will discover not only opportunities for personal growth, but also big long-term opportunities for business and financial success.

Each new project gives you the chance to experiment and build something new. It gives you the chance to learn about new people, new ideas, new tools, and new methods. It also gives you a fresh start, a blank canvas to practice manifesting in the Creativerse. Passion projects draw it all together and give you a way to investigate reality, starting with what sparks your curiosity.

When you begin a passion project, you don't know where it will go, or what it might become in the long run. The key is to launch a passion project around something that you're interested in, without knowing where it might go.

Where do you find topics for passion projects? Start by noticing what is newly interesting in your life. Ask yourself: "What is something that has caught my attention, that I've been learning about lately, that I would love to get more deeply involved with?"

Maybe you've been reading about a new subject or watching videos, or perhaps a topic keeps coming up in conversation. Maybe it's a new emerging technology, or a trend that you believe has huge potential.

In my life, I've started passion projects around topics as diverse as building my own guitar, learning how to get a date, and curating an art gallery at Burning Man…not to mention electronic music, personal productivity, direct response marketing, visual design, startup investing, parenting, and many more.

Each of these were initiated because it was something I wanted to learn about and do myself, based on a personal inspiration and curiosity. Each turned out to be a challenge on many levels, but each of these domains also became an important part of my learning journey in life.

When you begin a passion project, do it because you are truly and deeply interested in a topic, and because you want to learn more about it. Make sure that you're not only "doing it for the money" or because other people are doing it. Don't just follow a trend, or get involved in someone else's passion project because you think that people will like you more if you're associated with the project.

The main reason why you want to keep your passion projects "pure" from the beginning is that you're looking for subjects that could be interesting to you for years or decades, and that you believe will help you refine and develop your own personal gifts and unique genius. When you begin with this as the premise, it plants the seeds of long-term sustainability. If one of your passion projects takes root, and blossoms into something that gets traction and grows rapidly, you will find the challenge of supporting it and growing with it to be interesting. If you start something that you're not passionate about, that doesn't bring you a lot of HAPS, then when it takes off and grows it's likely to be a drag, and you won't feel inspired to stay with it and help it to become successful.

When you initiate a project from a place of personal passion, you instill it with a special type of inspirational spark that makes it far more sustainable. When a project gets traction, it begins to face challenges on many dimensions. People challenges, technical challenges, legal challenges, management challenges, financial challenges, political challenges, and more. If you're not passionate about the project, my experience is that you're likely to walk away at some point, because it just isn't worth it to continue. But when it's something that you are uniquely passionate about, that you are interested in personally learning about in order to develop as a human being, things are different. Like a soulmate, or a child, a passion project contains a special magical tenacity or audacity that will inspire you to stay loyal to for the long-term.

When you consistently work on new passion projects, you build a life that is interesting, fun, and challenging. This is the path to a successful life. It will bring you far more joy than working on a project just for money, fame, or power.

Here's how to approach a passion project: Start out by committing to a 30-day test project. Maybe it's just an initial commitment to research and learn for that 30 days. You could read books, watch videos, and join an online group or a local meetup. At this stage, you might just personally study, or you might find other people who are interested in the topic, and get a small group discussion together. Just go online or to your social group and find a few other people to get together and talk about the topic, whatever it is. Organize a hangout to share information and ideas. Do it quickly, and casually, to see if others are interested, and to ride the wave of inspiration.

If your first month goes well, and your little group has chemistry together, maybe launch a 90-day "incubator project." This might be a simple 3-month project to get "proof of concept" of some kind. Maybe you decide to teach a course on your new topic (either yourself, or with others), or write something. Or maybe you'd like to make a prototype for a piece of software. Perhaps you'd like to explore doing this thing as a volunteer project. Over that 90 days, see if you can come do a simple project to get your idea or project out there in the world and see if other people resonate with it.

If you get through your first 90-day project, and you feel like you have traction and momentum, then maybe commit to continuing for a full year. This is the point at which you start thinking more seriously about setting goals, organizing a group, and committing to building something that will make an impact. If you work on a project for a year, and build a successful product or work group, this is the point where you can start considering what this project will be "when it grows up." At this point, you can see more clearly whether it should be a business, a hobby, a philanthropy, or something else. And at that point you can choose the path that you're going to take to scale up.

Only some of these passion projects will work. One in three or so will get enough traction to become a "real thing." This is normal, and it' actually great because you'll enjoy all of them. Even if a particular project doesn't go anywhere, you still get to learn and explore a topic you're passionate about. And some will turn into great opportunities in business and life.

And the best part is, what you'll need to learn in order to make your passion project work is what you need to learn to become your highest self. As you start working on a new project, you'll see that there are things that you need to do that require you to learn new skills because this is a new project and a new domain. You may have to learn about new tools, or you about group dynamics, or new ways to collaborate

By learning those skills about around a topic that you're interested in, you also develop more holistically. Passion projects as your own personal self-development dojos, your own practice studio with mirrors for reflection and development. Some things come will naturally to you, but it's those new things that you must learn about that put you at the edge of your comfort zone. That is where the bigger self-growth opportunities are.

If a passion project moves beyond this learning dojo stage, if it gets traction, it will probably go in one of a few directions – it will either become something for profit, a philanthropic project, or a hobby. I think that you should have at least one business project, one contribution project, and one hobby going in life.

When you start a passion project as a hobby and you do it because you want to see if you can make something work, you don't need to commit to doing it for business or philanthropy. You're just doing the project to see if you can get traction. You're just doing it because you want to learn more about the topic and interact with other people. Then later, once you start to find your emergent strategy, that's when you can direct it more towards profit or more towards philanthropy. You don't need to know at the beginning.

That's the theory of passion projects. So what does a passion project look like in practice? Here's a famous example: As I mentioned earlier, Steve Jobs and Steve Wozniak used to go to this computer club called Homebrew, which was a bunch of computer geeks who liked to hang out and share ideas. They were putting together their own computers and experimenting with software just for the fun of it. They were working on passion projects - things they were really interested in. The business, Apple, emerged out of that. This isn't an unusual company backstory. Often times you find that a subculture where people are all really interested in a topic, that then becomes a place where great business and philanthropic ideas come from.

Let me also give you an example from my own life. I'm personally very interested in mental models. I mentioned that Charlie Munger (Warren Buffett's business partner and one of the most successful investors in the world) talks about how you need a set of diverse mental models to use to analyze different situations. He takes this from an investment perspective, but mental models are really interesting to me in all areas of life and I collect them. And because I'm really interested in mental models, I've thought for a long time that it would be cool to make a big collection of mental models and put it online so that young people growing up could get access to them. I've always had this little "secret idea" but never acted on it.

So last year I got a mastermind together and I invited about 15 people that I know, who are all interested in mental models, to come hang out for a weekend and share our favorite mental models with each other. Several months ago we all got together and talked about what a mental model is and how to develop them. Now we've got this little study group. It's just "mental model geeks" who are really interested in trading & exploring the structure of mental models. We're doing some interesting work and we're making progress towards this vision I have. A business project has emerged from these meetings, and I believe that it will lead to many more positive things as well.

I think that everyone should start a new passion project at least once a year. Maybe make it your New Year's resolution each year. Passion projects make great resolutions because, when you come into a new year, you're looking for something new, something different, something exciting. Passion projects offer that. When you create that little social group, if an idea sparks, if it catches fire, that can be one of the best ways to uncover opportunities out there.

So get started now. Take some to consider what you could do for a passion project right now. Answer these questions:

- What have I become interested in lately that I would like to learn more about?
- What could I start or build over the next month to see if I could get a "proof of concept"?
- How could I organize a small group of people who are also interested in this topic to get together and share ideas?
- How could I get this group together quickly, like tomorrow... or next week?

Even if you meet on a call or an online hangout, get together and meet up with a group of others who are also passionate about your topic!

When you get your group together, ask the following: What's the first thing that you could create together as a collaborative effort? Could you design something together? Could you 3D print something? Could you produce a white paper? Could you teach something together? Could you produce a product? Could you create a model and share it with others?

Follow your curiosity and your inspiration, and you'll discover opportunities that bring you joy, success, and growth in your life.

Go on a Personal Vision Quest

What is your greatest opportunity in your life right now? It's an important question. It's so important that it can be overwhelming. But I think that we can all find, what I call, "our highest opportunity for personal evolution." Each of us has one at any given moment. Your highest opportunity for personal evolution is the hidden opportunity that would allow you to grow and develop the most.

What action would call out the greatest version of yourself? What project could you go to work on that would produce the most self-actualization? What relationship would pull you up the fastest? What is that big opportunity that would inspire the most personal evolution?

The answer to these questions is waiting. It might take a bit of work to answer them, but as you might imagine, it's worth it. At any point in time in your life in your life there is one thing would bring you the most growth. This isn't just something to make some money or have some pleasure. It's your highest opportunity for personal evolution.

Highest Opportunity Personal Evolution: the first letters are H-O-P-E. Your highest opportunity for personal evolution is your highest HOPE.

It's not the type of hope that you wish for, but an opportunity you're actively looking for. We all need to have this type of HOPE, because if we're on the lookout for our highest opportunity for personal evolution, it will pull us up to the next level and make us become all that we can become.

What is your HOPE? What is your highest opportunity for personal evolution right now?

I'd invite you to imagine a space in your mind that represents the next level of your growth. It's what you and your life will look like at the next level. Next, imagine an opportunity that you could take advantage of right now that would that would force you to grow into that space... and inspire you to show up as your highest self.

It might be that passion project we talked about in the last section. It might be a new relationship. It might be a new mastermind or a new social influence. It might be reclaiming some of the energy that is being wasted on harmful compulsion. But right now, what is your greatest opportunity for personal evolution?

To best find the answer, I'd like to ask you to take a weekend and go on a personal vision quest. I also call this a "personal strategic planning summit." Big companies do strategic planning summits to map out the future of the business, to set a course for the future. They're usually done off site. They take the executive team and they all go somewhere, usually into the woods or to a remote location where they are completely away from their normal work environment. They talk through what they've learned recently, discuss their potential projects, and collaborate on their vision for the business. They talk about their values and they work out their identity.

Following this example, I recommend that you plan two days in the near future to create a personal strategic planning summit for your life... and to go on your personal vision quest.

This is something that you should do alone for your own life. You could also do this with your romantic partner for your relationship. You could do it together for your family, but you should definitely do one for your own life alone - even if you're in a relationship - because I think we need to do this for ourselves personally before we do it well for our partnership or family.

For your personal strategic planning summit, you're going to go offsite for two days. Ideally, go away some distance. Go to a place that inspires you and where you can completely unplug. No work, no social media, no surfing the internet. None of the normal stuff. You've got to totally disconnect.

Dedicate day one to deep rejuvenation. Deep rejuvenation involves a peak relaxation experience, so do the things that put you into that state. Maybe it's going for a big hike. Maybe it's getting a massage, or sitting on the beach and reading one of your favorite novels. Whatever it is that you love to do in order to relax and rejuvenate, plan to do that all day your first day.

Ideally, you would go somewhere in nature, and some of this day would be spent walking or exercising, getting your heart rate up and doing something that involves movement in the real, physical world. Ideally, another part of that day would be spent doing something that's very chill and relaxed, eating the kinds of foods that make you feel really good and totally unplugging from your normal life. Also, make sure you get a good, full night of deep sleep.

Spending time to reach peak experience is key, because if we're not in our peak state, then we don't have our highest vantage point available to us. In your life you've probably noticed that if you're triggered or if you're upset, if you're fearful or angry, your executive center shuts down and you just go into protective thinking. You get defensive, or you become aggressive. You try to not lose in life (we talked about this earlier when we discussed fear). But the opposite is also true. If you become more happy, more optimistic, all of a sudden new possibilities open up. You can start thinking long term instead of just thinking about right survival now.

And this is doubly true if you put yourself into a peak state - because when you're in a peak physical, emotional, and intellectual state, the highest levels of strategic insight come to you. You can start seeing not just months and years ahead, but you can start seeing in the context of your whole life. You can start asking, "What do I want my life to mean? When I'm at the end of my life and I'm looking back, who do I want to have been? What do I want to have accomplished?" This kind of perspective is only available from a peak state. That's why, on day one, we want to do deep rejuvenation... so that on our second day, we can see more clearly.

Day two is the strategic planning day. Now that you've put yourself into a peak state, you're going to create a vision for your life from that perspective.

Ask yourself: What do I want for my life? What's next for me? What is my next passion project? Who do I need to add to my life as a social influence? What new practices do I need to integrate to achieve peak physical, emotional, and mental health?

Go through the exercises that I've given you in this book to identify opportunity, to reclaim some of the energy that you're wasting, and to think about the intersections in your life and how can you can weave together all of your resources and emerging opportunities. This is how you can discover your highest opportunity for personal evolution. It will likely come to you in a flash, while you're contemplating your life.

When you intentionally plan a vision question or strategic planning summit like this, it pulls your consciousness up to the next level, and gives you access to your higher self.

I highly encourage you to plan and schedule your vision quest. Make a commitment right now to do it. Put it on the calendar and then use this process to discover your greatest opportunity!

The Transformational Dilemma

At each stage of your personal evolution, you will arrive at a place on your path where you have reached the end of one phase, and are on the threshold of the next. You will know that you are in this place because something has happened that has caused you to realize that you can't go on thinking and living the same way anymore. You can see the next level, and what you will need to do in order to get there. But you also don't want to leave the comfort zone of your current reality.

My mentor Wyatt Woodsmall and I call this the "transformational dilemma." It's the point in development where you can see where you need to go next, but a part of you also doesn't want to go, and you become stuck. It feels like an intractable double-bind.

> **"The Chinese use two brush strokes to write the word 'crisis.' One brush stroke stands for danger, the other, for opportunity. In a crisis, be aware of the danger, but recognize the opportunity."**
> **—John F. Kennedy**

In systems theory, they point to a pattern in systems where they reach a point of maximum chaos, polarization, and intensity... right before they experience a phase-shift to a higher-level order. The transformational dilemma is the point in life right before you awaken to a higher perspective. It's the moment before you achieve "simplicity on the far side of complexity." It's the feeling before you break through what Dan Sullivan calls the "ceiling of complexity."

When you are in the throes of a transformational dilemma, you have a stark realization that what you're doing in your life isn't working. And you also realize that this has to do with the way that you see reality itself. It's about your paradigm.

You came to believe that the world was one way, and that belief is now undermining your success. You are now looking out through a crack in your paradigm. As Leonard Cohen says, the crack is how the light gets in.

With light painfully streaming through, you are faced with the dilemma of staying where you are and not being able to live in integrity… or leaping off the cliff, hoping to sprout the wings to fly to the next level.

Steve Jobs tells the story about how Apple had released the Lisa Computer, but had it flop in the marketplace. They needed to do something in order to save the company. Steve assembled a team of creative geniuses, and set out to reinvent the computer. As he said they were "on a mission from god." This led them to invent the Mac computer, and the rest is history.

When I met Annie, my wife, I was in a place in my life where I had recently accepted the fact that I was going to remain single for life. Relationships for me had never worked out long-term, and I decided I was going to need to create a life where I was happy as a single person. As we started dating, I saw her as another person to see casually, and to add to my circle.

One night, she and I stayed up late sharing ideas. At one point while she was talking, I had the powerful revelation that she was supposed to be my life partner. I remember feeling that my heart had a place inside that had never been awakened before, and somehow she was made to fit into that space.

But then a terrible fear came over me, one I felt down in my stomach… all the way to my soul. I realized that if I were to fall in love with Annie, this might mean we'd have a child together. This caused a kind of existential terror that I had never felt. Once a child is born, there's no going back!

That night, on January 23rd, 2010, was a turning point for me. I felt it happening on multiple levels, and in many dimensions. I knew that if I went for it, that I was embracing a completely unknown future. I would have to leave behind the single, free life I was living… and create something new. I was in the biggest transformational dilemma of my life.

Fortunately, I went for it. We now have a daughter, and she has become such a miraculous gift in our lives. Being in this relationship, and in love, is the hardest thing I've ever done. I can't even think of a close second. However, it's very clear to me, this is what I am supposed to be doing.

In dark moments, I've felt like leaving. Sometimes I wonder why I ever did it in the first place. This is all part of the journey. But through all the intensity of being in love and becoming a father, I'm absolutely sure I made the right choice. My wife and my daughter have been my greatest opportunities for learning, growth, happiness and fulfilling success.

As they say, necessity is the mother of invention. But there is also a father, and that is your creative vision. When you reach a transformational dilemma in your life, remember that this is exactly where you are supposed to be. It is the indicator that the next phase of your growth, development, and evolution is in front of you. It's the signal that you are about to go to the next level.

Allow the waves of fear to wash over you, and stay in touch with your body. Between the pangs of terror, notice the excitement and world of possibility that is opening up at the next level. A higher part of you is about to be born. Release attachment to the old version of you, and with those open arms, embrace the opportunity to "die into" the next version of yourself.

Design an Evolving Life

Once you understand that you will continue to grow and develop into new, higher, emergent levels of your potential, things start making more sense. You realize that this is the natural direction of evolution, and you begin to dance with the process more.

I read that Ken Wilber sometimes refers to different stages of his life as "Wilber 1" and "Wilber 2" and "Wilber 3" to refer to the previous paradigms and reality versions that he lived in. This might seem strange to some people, but it makes perfect sense once you move through a couple of key identity and life transformations.

The next step, once you have embraced this process, is to start designing your life so that it actually invites transformation and evolution. You move into new interests and new domains of learning expecting that there will be a time when you use what you have learned in combination with other knowledge, and as part of a higher version of yourself. This causes you to structure your learning experiences, environment, and relationships expressly for personal evolution.

The most important change that you can make as you begin creating a life that is designed for transformational development is in the way you attract people into your life, and participate in social groups.

Your social influences tend to become your destiny, so it's vital that you intentionally surround yourself with role models for your future self. In this paradigm, you are specifically looking for people who understand evolutionary development, and who are passionate about personal and relationship transformation. These people are rare, with one reason being that it takes courage and bravery to be a self-developer and self-transformer.

You're looking for those who have a "growth mindset" - meaning that they believe you can change yourself and your environment. These people believe that they can increase their knowledge, intelligence, and help shape their own destiny.

Fortunately, there are increasing communities and teachers who are evolutionary in their thinking and teaching. You can find workshops, retreats, masterminds, and learning programs in many different domains that have this paradigm infused in them. The more you build your social circle based around this key idea of designing an evolving life by surrounding yourself with people who are building evolving lives, the more you make personal evolution inevitable.

The Weighing of the Heart

In Egyptian spirituality, when a person died, they went through a process called the "weighing of the heart." They went before Osiris, the god of transition to the afterlife. Osiris would put their soul's heart on one side of a special scale, on the other he would place the feather of Ma'at. Ma'at was the goddess of truth and justice, and she wore a special ostrich feather in her hair, which was the symbol of truth.

If the heart weighed more than the ostrich feather, then it would be devoured by a terrible goddess named Ammit, who was part lion, part crocodile, and part hippopotamus (a combination of three animals that ate humans in those times). Once eaten by Ammit, the soul would cease to exist.

If the heart was lighter than the ostrich feather, then the soul would be allowed to travel to Aaru, the field of reeds, where they would exist forever in an idealized version of the life that they had lived while mortal.

The message was clear: If you live in a way that makes your heart feel heavy, or that weighs on your conscience, then you are not living your highest potential. This was a mythological encouragement to live an ethical life of goodness, integrity, and virtue. When I read this spiritual allegory, it touched me deeply. I instantly realized that optimizing for my heart's lightness with my actions the way to navigate through life.

Imagine the spiritual aspect of yourself, or your soul. Imagine that it has a heart, which is your soul's seat of intellect and feeling. Now imagine that this heart has a particular type of sensitivity, which allows you to intuit in advance whether or not a particular opportunity will create more fulfillment and joy in your life. When an opportunity is right for your life in a holistic sense, it always makes your heart feel lighter. It has a quality of inspiration.

This special soul-heart also informs you and gives you insight about places in your life and relationships where you have clean-up or repair work to do. It acts as an emotional indicator of unhealed past wounds, and of opportunities to hear your conscience and have it guide you.

We don't need to wait until after death to feel the weight of our heart. If something makes you feel heavy, then it's likely that it isn't right and trespasses on your own values.

Our bodies, emotions and minds are built for a time when opportunity was far more scarce. Now, we have the option to find and create opportunity as much as we want in life. Follow those opportunities that lead down the path of a buoyant heart, of a lighter soul.

Each of us received the greatest opportunity of all from our parents and from our planet: To be alive.

Let's pass on the gift of life and evolution. Let's work together to reduce suffering. Let's join together and contribute to the actualization of fellow beings. This may be our greatest collective opportunity.